USE
THE
HEAD

A New
Approach to Golf Instruction
by MEL FLANAGAN

A MEL FLANAGAN PUBLICATION

ISBN O 9512919 0 4

First Edition, October 1986
Second Edition, July 1987
Third Edition, September 1988
Fourth Edition, April 1989
German language edition, October 1987

Published by Mel Flanagan Publications, 19 The Park, Kingswood Heights, Dublin 4
Cover by Pete Sluis.
Drawings by Charles MacNeill and Pete Sluis.
Pictures by Eddie de Barra.
POrinted by the Leinster Leader Ltd., Naas, Co. Kildare.
© Copyright.

Preface

To succeed at golf, consistent practise of the mental and physical sides of the game are essential. There are no short cuts. And, as with all sports, planning must be done in an effective manner. The mental side begins with motivation, attention, and concentration, anxieties and ends with preparation to understand and to improve your game. The physical approach opens with the swing. (The book that brings us together requires that the reader use some brains.) To help, I have enlisted the backing of artist friends Peter Sluis, Charles MacNeill and photographer Eddie de Barra to assemble a comprehensive visual presentation. The result, I hope, will give you a deeper insight of a great game and help you achieve match-winning scores on the course.

I want you to develop your own style, your own swing. You must also understand, however, that you cannot expect to learn the game overnight. Look on it in the same way as one would learning to play the piano. Could you learn to play it in one night? Of course not! You must allow yourself time to improve and make time to practise without actually playing. You can practise as you are reading. Have a club beside you, preferably a number eight iron, and work with it as you see the concept that appeals to you straight away. In this way you will allow your muscles and brain learn together. It is also very true to say to you that you should never try out a shot on the golf course unless you are happy with it on the practise ground.

In the game of golf there are only nine bad shots, just two moves in the golf swing and two parts to the golf club. Every shot you strike has three basic characteristics. Six out of a possible nine bad shots are struck from the outside-in. The first move in the golf swing is to create power and the second is to use that power and release it properly. The only difference between the great player and the "trier" is simply in the "trier's" swing the power he/she creates stays with him/her above the grip end throughout the entire swing. The great player is able to combustionise the power to deflect it away from his/her upper body down the shaft to the clubhead end. The first move is coiling the muscles against the right knee resistance to create the power high in the body (back swing). The second is to deflect it low where the ball is. You must learn then to **resist high and strike low**, to release the clubhead end against the resistance of your left hand arm shoulder (top end). The resistance is low on back swing and high on forward swing. To explain it further the golf club is like a machine. It has a certain

3

way of working. Few master it. The grip end is the **holding** end, the clubhead end is the **working** end. Quite a majority of golfers try to work the holding end. You must learn to **hold** the **top** of the club back while you **hit** with the **bottom** end.

Finally, to practise intelligently, to use **real evidence**, the divot, and most of all to be able to read ball flight. You can never see your swing (unless on video – recommended), you will **never** be able to witness impact. What you can see and you should begin to observe, is the flight of the ball. When you strike a bad shot never ever say what have I done wrong in my swing. Rather what does the flying ball tell me? To quote Lang Willie, the famous St. Andrews caddie, "Ye see, professor, so long as ye are learnin' the lads at college Latin and Greek it is easy work. But when ye come tae play golf ye must **use the head.**" You do not have to keep all the theory in your head as you set-up to the shot, all you have to do is simply base your next swing on the flight of the last shot you hit.

Best wishes,

Mel Flanagan

September 1988

To my wife Imelda

4

Contents

CHAPTER 1

Some of golf mysteries solved

Spin the ball correctly – cultivate left-spin

One of the factors you must consider is the fact you have not only to strike the ball correctly **but also to spin it**. What it really means is that you may strike a ball in a specific direction but it may not have the decency to stay there.

There are a lot of threes in golf. The ball may spin leftwards rightwards or backwards.

The top class player encourages left spin the poorer player (in every sense) suffers from right spin!

What's so good about left spin and so bad about right spin?

Right handed golfers can only inflict right spin by swinging the club across the ball from right to left – a glancing blow with an open face (pointing right).

If you swing from the **outside across**, the clubhead will always come in at a very steep angle – the power is directed downwards and is leftwards. The angle is **acute** and the blow is **glancing**. Shots are high, weak and right of target.

In order to create left spin the clubhead must be dragged in from a **very low angle behind the ball** and across it from the inside (with the actual face square to the target) maximum distance shot.

You may say, well this is all very strange. It is not really. Take any other ball game e.g. Rugby.

"Converting a try"

The rugby player places the ball on the ground and he does not walk straight back behind the ball and toe it forward. No – he moves around **at an angle inside and runs from inside the ball and swings his right foot (using his instep) from inside to outside the ball**. Whenever a ball is on the ground and you want to drive it the maximum distance forward that's the only way possible. Imagine a rugby player cutting across (from the outside) the ball putting right spin on it!

Consider not only **striking** the ball but also **spinning** it correctly – slightly left as you strike. When driving at address close your shoulders (aim them right of target) and your hips. However, aim the clubhead square towards the target. You have set up the angles – clubhead will be slightly closed to your swing-line at impact. Arms travelling out, clubhead pointing towards target.

Visualise a hook shot. Now you can play! (*See page 274, the draw shot*).

T–E–M–P–O

Big muscles v. small muscles

The vast majority of practisers who come to the range are **Bashers** of the ball. Their swngs are out of tempo. It is invariably too fast, too much effort, a physical swing. Tempo is very important. It is also possible to swing too slow – to have a very slow backswing and a rapid forward swing. In the main however a **fast tempo**, a **hurried physical swing** is the most common fault.

A poor golfer **hits,** the better player **swings**. A bad golfer grips the club very **tightly**, the better player **lightens** his/her grip.

How is it possible to swing in tempo?

Practise with a short distance club (a number eight iron). **Practise your driving swing with a number 8 iron**. Hit the ball **soft**. Adopt the motto **you do not hit the ball – you just swing the club and the ball happens to come in the way of the swing**. Use your **practise swing** to **hit** the ball. Take the ball out of the swing take the **lash** out of it.

Why is there a terrible tendency to swing out of tempo? Because we associate distance with effort. When we are on a tee we look down the fairway we see the green. It seems a long way off. **So we gather ourselves up for a big effort** to drive the ball as far as we can.

In your body you have big muscles and small muscles. The bigger are your arms, shoulders, and leg muscles, the smaller are your hands, wrists and forearms. The **smaller muscles** (in golf) are unfortunately easier to move – much more flexible, and as such **difficult to control**. They are liable to "run away" in the swing and use the left elbow joint as a breakpoint early in the backswing. As a result of this the bigger muscles come into the hitting area causing a "body shot" lacking distance.

The great players reverses all this, **using their bigger upper muscles to start their backswing** – a one piece takeaway – (*See page 60*) initiate their forward swing from their lower body muscles (legs) and their arms and ultimately use their smaller muscles to release the clubhead. They release the clubhead with their hands and wrists. The "novicy type" player grips the club very tight, **snatches** it away with his/her hands (smaller muscles) and lounges his body (bigger muscles) into the shot. **In a nutshell the novice uses small muscles at takeaway and big muscles at impact**. The great players use the bigger muscles at takeaway (to create power) and to control their swings and **use the flexibility of their smaller muscles to release the clubhead at**

7

impact. This is why they give the impression of swinging slowly because they are using bigger muscles, yet they drive the ball enormous distances by releasing the clubhead off the solid base with their hands and wrists. I call this the **slow fast swing**. (Bigger muscles always move much slower than the samller ones.)

Here's a practise routine. Use a number 8 iron. Decide that you are not **obsessed** with **distance** – to concentrate on **T–E–M–P–O**. Grip the club lightly. (Sam Snead once remarked "Feel your writsts are oily".) Put a **30 m.p.h. gauge** on the top of the club. At the start of your downswing delete the word **hit** from your mind and replace it with **swing. Sweep** from the inside out **through** the ball and allow the clubhead to release itself. Finally **take out your driver** grip it **lightly and use exactly the same tempo – an 8 iron tempo**. At practise you are not there to hit shots rather to learn the swing. The cultivate the tempo of the great players you continually admire on television at the various televised tournaments (e.g. Nick Faldo) to **learn** to release the **clubhead off a slow tempo**.

Here is the exact swing sequence used by the top players re-Big muscles and Small muscles.

1. (Big) Arms – one piece takwaway..
2. (Small) Wrists hinging towards end of backswing.
3. (Big) Legs start downswing.
4. (Big) Arms move as a unit forward.
5. (Small) Wrists release clubhead.
6. (Big) Arms and legs continue follow through to end with **left elbow joint remaining straight long after impact**.
7. (Small) Wrists and arms fold at end of swing.

In general the state of your game depends **upon the balance between your bigger muscles and smaller ones**. If you have a very wristy action you will drive the ball long distances, but have little control over the direction. If you have a locked arm swing you may have control but lack clubhead speed and therefore distance. But if you are able to marry the two Arms and Legs controlling your swing yet releasing with your wrists you have the perfect balance. As Arms provide necessary width and prevent letter "V" swing **(steep)** ensure a square hit from a **shallow angle** towards **the back** of the ball, yet wrists release enable you to have clubhead speed and therefore distance.

Arms and legs controlling the swing towards the target. Wrists and hand speed creating clubhead speed therefore distance. You could call it a **swinging wrist cock**. Adopt this motto – **I am going to swing slow but let the clubhead go at impact. A slow swing with a fast clubhead**.

Happy muscles! **(See lesson "The Ultimate Shot", p. 294).**

B.A.L.L.S.

When you are practising you are either having fun or trying to learn. If it is fun you are after, bash away with the driver. If on the other hand you want to learn a technique and improve, use the training club – 7 iron, and tee the ball up. Another thing – you should not hit every shot full out. (I often feel golfers somehow think they are not actually practising when they are hitting "soft" shot, half shots, etc. I always encourage golfers to do so at my golf range but I feel they nearly look for their money back because they weren't "bashing" the ball.) The one major factor in striking a ball forward is that the clubhead must approach from **behind** and never **above**. In other words the letter "V" swing must be avoided at all costs as it has a very narrow base. Practice the **"middle"** part of your swing – **"tapping"** the ball using **a wide shallow approach.**

Here is another way to vary your practice, and to help you understand certain things that are difficult to explain – for example what it means to **strike from the outside!**

Use two balls – the striking ball and place another just outside it *(See diagram a)*. Practise hitting shots taking the inside one only. Go on, – and have the patience to carry this out. Remember if you strike a dozen balls with thought it is better than 100 without (replace the outside ball every time). Try another.

Are you cutting in on the ball? Are your divots going left-wards? Place a second ball ahead of the striking ball at a slight angle. Strike the real ball (**See diagram b**). If you swing in you will hit the inside one.

Finally, learn the true swing path from the inside out. It is very difficult to believe that by swinging out towards the right the ball won't go there!

Practise this way

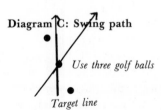

Diagram C: Swing path

Use three golf balls

Target line

Suddenly you will realise that you cannot come straight in from directly behind the ball. The gap you have created is out through the two, very much towards the right. If your swing plane is outside you will catch the outside ball. If you cut in you will catch the inside one. If you succeed in missing the two outside balls you will hit a good shot and more important learn something about striking a ball from the **inside out**. It may take more time than you like but it won't be wasted time.

9

Diagram A

Diagram B: If you strike the inside Ball you are cutting across the ball.

Diagram C: The "gap" you see is very much out to the right of the target.

Diagram D: Striking from the "inside" out to the right of the target".

Target Line

Swing Line

Opposing forces
the secret of power

Push your left hand back at impact

To create power you need **opposing forces**. A spring is coiled by pressing it against a wall. If the wall happens to move back there won't be any coiling action – no collison.

Let us now look at how this works in the good swing.

You create power on your backswing by turning your shoulders against the resistance of your knees. Knees resisting upper body turn creates power. **One part of your body working against the other.**

Here another clubhead speed is created by turning your wrists against your forearms at the top of the backswing, i.e. the wrist cock. By setting or hinging your wrists they will automatically unhinge as you strike.

Finally, at impact opposing forces play a crucial role – **Reverse weight shift AT IMPACT**. Your left hand must **oppose** the club coming forward at the upper end so that your right hand and arm **drive** the clubhead end forward out through the ball. What normally happens is golfers try to **push** the two hands forward therefore clubhead speed is allied to arm speed – a push shot. It is only by stoping your left hand (and so the shaft) at impact will you allow the other end up(of the clubhead) and through for the strike.

Think of a circus where the ringmaster is winding a whip around and around in a circle. (Holding the whip by his right hand.)

When he wants to crack it he uses opposing forces, by suddenly pushing his right hand back directly in the opposite direction to which he was winding it. This creates a collison of forces with the final result of the whip crack at the end.

Golf energy, distance without effort uses opposing forces throughout the swing. A fast swing has nothing to do with a fast clubhead (*See Lesson*). Your must create opposing forces in order to release the power.

The power gauge

If there happened to be a power gauge on the Driver as the strike was made **certain variations would be noticed**.

The high handicapper tends to **grip** the club **tightly** and have a very **high power rating** in the top of the club (the grip) as he/she strikes.

The middle handicapper on the other hand tends to register his/her swing power slightly lower below the grip at impact.

The top class player through experience knows well the **"folly"** of

11

'**high handled power**' and registers his/her swing power near the head of the club at impact.

Let me put it this way. Unless your swing power **manifests** itself around **the head of the club** at **impact, it's wasted**. The secret to the game is that you have to try not to **HIT** the ball – yourself – not to become **personally** involved – and allow the clubhead to strike it for you. The more experienced you become the lighter will you grip and better you will be able to deflect your swing power away from yourself and out to the ball. What you need is **ghostly power** around the ball area at impact.

Plane and power kick

Your overall aim should be to swing on plane towards **the back of the ball** and register your **swing power at the bottom of the club.** At impact use your left hand as a block to push the handle back and your right hand to push against the left and so push the clubhead forward, and through the ball. You must be able to use the head. To sum up – **"feel that you are letting the clubhead go past your hands through impact"**. (*See lesson "Parole the clubhead", page 113*).

WRONG

PAROLE THE CLUBHEAD

Swing power escaped – thus weak-clubhead-power. Power here is at wrong end of shaft – grip end – as left arm has collapsed. There is no solid base for the lower end of club to be released.

CORRECT
Resist at handle end, strike at head end. the ball . . .

Power stored and used at clubhead

Note: The one reason why the vast majority of golfers never improve is because the energy they create in their swings is allowed escape by the collapse of the left side through impact.

Note: Left hand pressing back against the emerging force of the upper body and so blocks upper body force, levers it down the shaft and creates power at clubhead end where it is very useful.

This illustration shows clearly the player deflecting the power of his swing away from his shoulders down the shaft by blocking the forward thrust of his swing with his left arm and hand and so causing the shaft to bend on the ball.

You should try to bend the lower end of the shaft on the ball.

Another one of golf's mysteries solved. What is the difference between a fast clubhead and a fast swing?

There are many misconceptions in golf – for example the idea that the club should be swung straight back and straight through – this usually results in a vertical swing plane. (Which of course is wrong.) Another common misconception is swinging to the left in an effort to prevent a slice right as it will always exaserbate the problem. But the most common misconception is the players **idea if you swing hard it will give you more distance.** In other words that a **fast swing** will result in a **fast clubhead.** In an effort to do this the golfer tends to grip the club very tight and put a lot of force into the upper end of the club. (*See diagram*).

Force in handle of club. Body too fast for the clubhead.

Thus the **clubhead becomes locked into the arms and body swing. Clubhead speed is totally dependant on arm speed.** The better players are not happy with this. They grip the club much **lighter** and use the ''power-kick'' – the slow fast swing. The actual forward movement of the hands is stopped as the clubhead is suddenly ''power kicked'' past the hands through the hitting area.

This demands two opposite movement – holding the top-half **back** while at the same time working the other end **forward**.

A slow upper body movement always allows for a fast low swing. A fast moving upper body swing will not allow the lower part (the clubhead) to take over. To put it bluntly **anybody can put force into the top of the club but it takes a golfer to apply it to the clubhead** – to have the patience not to hit the ball to hold the body back high while releasing the clubhead low.

13

If you study an impact action picture of any top player you will notice he/she is always grimmacing at impact. This is not because they are trying to put an extra effort into the shot (to speed up the swing). **It is because they are trying not to hit the ball.** To conserve their swing energy so that they will be able to release it near the ball on the ground. **They are trying to hold their upper body back while at the very same time move the lower half of their body and the clubhead forward.** One part (that is of no use) is held back while the useful (the clubhead) part is whiplashed forward.

It takes many years to perfect this but why not try it.

Visualise this as important.

Push your left hand back against your swing at impact.

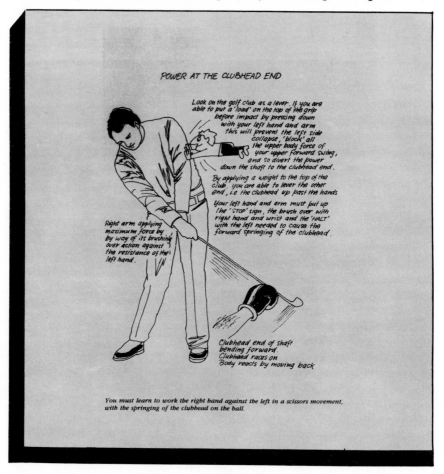

POWER AT THE CLUBHEAD END

Look on the golf club as a lever. If you are able to put a 'load' on the top of the grip before impact by pressing down with your left hand and arm this will prevent the left side collapse, 'block' all the upper body force of your upper forward swing, and so divert the power down the shaft to the clubhead end.

By applying a weight to the top of the club, you are able to lever the other end, i.e. the clubhead up past the hands

Your left hand and arm must put up the 'STOP' sign, the brush over with right hand and wrist and the 'HALT' with the left needed to cause the forward springing of the clubhead.

Right arm applying maximum force by by way of its brushing over action against the resistance of the left hand.

Clubhead end of shaft bending forward.
Clubhead races on
Body reacts by moving back

You must learn to work the right hand against the left in a scissors movement, with the springing of the clubhead on the ball.

Golf psychology

Why should you be mean to yourself?
Play within your present ability

I have a very good friend, a golfing fanatic, who was involved in one of my night schools. His wife, who had been listening to him for many years coming in from his golf, decided to take up the game. At the outdoor session he had a very good practise swing, but it tended to disintegrate under pressure. He would continually carry on a conversation berating himself about his swing. I was observing this when his wife turned to him and said: "I don't mind you talking to yourself but you are saying all the wrong things. You are always running down both your game and your ability to improve it." She was right.

If you don't feel good about yourself, how do you expect other people to do so. **If you don't feel your game is going to improve, how do you expect it will improve, or how do you hope to stand up under pressure. You should encourage positive thoughts about your game.** Continually imagine yourself improving. This does not mean that you get into an anxious state and start over-concentrating and build up tension internally. Your goal is relaxed imagery.

It is now well established that there is a direct relationship between your nervous system and your brain. The brain cannot distinguish between a real and an imaginary experience. Therefore it is essential to combine mental imagery with physical practise. Your thoughts influence your emotions and your emotions affect your behaviour. **What you say to yourself greatly influences your play.**

So, rid the mind of bad thoughts, bad images and try to figure out what is the most realistic way to deal with the situation. Then make your decision and stick with it. In the final analysis what it will help you to do is get a clear mental picture of the shot you are going to play. You will get rid of the fog hampering your vision and have the confidence to play it! Use the club you are most confident with and play the shot to the target. You have to remember the moment a belief enters your mind it becomes subjectively true. You must believe your body will do what you want of it.

Seve Ballesteros was very worried about the conditions at one British Open until he realised that it would be much harder for the other players to master them. In fact he felt he had an advantage rather than a disadvantage.

Visualisation

Plan for success rather than failure. Present your brain with positive images and with success-orientated images. Let me be a little more specific. Do you see practise as a waste of time? Would you consider that you might be practising mistakes or that you cannot improve? **Is it your attitude that you have a lot of natural ability and that you will certainly improve through intelligent practice** or do you think that you have not got time to practice or that you are too busy? Do you look on it that you are an organised person and **that you will make time?** Do you think that you might be too old to play to a high standard, or that **people would admire someone of your age improving or reaching such a high standard?** Do you think that you can only get better if you have a natural ability to improve, or do you look on the great players of the world and consider that once they were very much like you?

Search your mind for tendencies which are helping or hurting. If they are negative face them. Go about it in a practical way. Think of the good salesman who is trying to sell you something. He will start by asking you questions to which you can only answer yes – on his way to what he hopes will be the big yes.

It is the same in practising golf. **Sell yourself to yourself.** Do it by setting up **small sequential short-range goals that are attainable.** That will encourage you and that will lead to a long-term overall goal. For example, set up your short game. Improve your shots from 40 yards out to the flag and better your chipping around the fringe of the green. Then take your putting in hand.

Give yourself a target and gradually start to make the targets more difficult and develop yourself on that road. Your overall game will improve. If you see it as one big effort it will never occur. You have got to see the steps along the way and when you go out to practice it is best to take the clubs you are more comfortable with. In this way you will work the good stuff into your game.

The great teachers all began working with number seven or eight irons. Remember – success with small sequential shots will lead you to a long-term overall goal. A number of small yeses can lead to a great victory for you. **On the golf course** it is important to control your imagery and build confidence by avoiding negative or anxiety-building thoughts during the round. If you find you cannot and fall into the negative trap, take a deep breath until you have regained control.

16

If you study an impact action picture of any top player you will notice he/she is always grimmacing at impact. This is not because they are trying to put an extra effort into the shot (to speed up the swing). It **is because they are trying not to hit the ball.** To conserve their swing energy so that they will be able to release it near the ball on the ground. **They are trying to hold their upper body back while at the very same time move the lower half of their body and the clubhead forward.** One part (that is of no use) is held back while the useful (the clubhead) part is whiplashed forward.

It takes many years to perfect this but why not try it.

Visualise this as important.

Push your left hand back against your swing at impact.

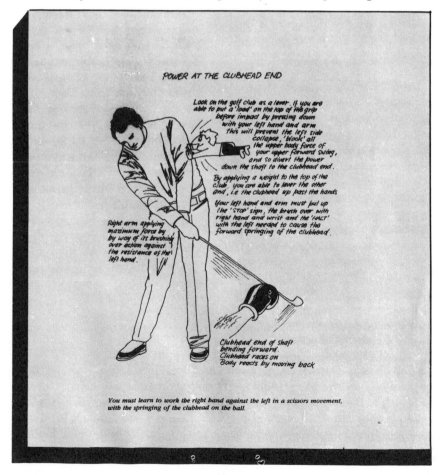

POWER AT THE CLUBHEAD END

Look on the golf club as a lever. If you are able to put a 'load' on the top of the grip before impact by pressing down with your left hand and arm this will prevent the left side collapse, 'block' all the upper body force of your upper forward swing, and so divert the power down the shaft to the clubhead end.

By applying a weight to the top of the club you are able to lever the other end, i.e the clubhead up past the hands

Your left hand and arm must put up the 'STOP' sign, the brush over with right hand and wrist and the 'HALT' with the left needed to cause the forward springing of the clubhead.

Right arm applying maximum force by by way of its brushing over action against the resistance of the left hand.

Clubhead end of shaft bending forward. Clubhead races on Body reacts by moving back

You must learn to work the right hand against the left in a scissors movement, with the springing of the clubhead on the ball.

You should ignore the shaft think clubhead and let it go when striking the ball.

You should ignore the shaft think clubhead and let it go when striking the ball.

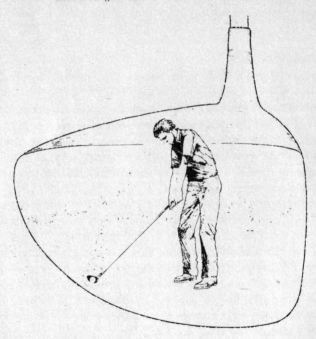

Diagram 10
Is your clubhead laughing at you?

SPECIAL LESSON 1

WAITING FOR THE HEAD

The majority of amateur golfers do not wait for the clubhead.

Why is it that the high amateur rarely waits for the clubhead to come through? Simply because we tend to associate force with distance. When we have a driver in our hands and look for 240 yards, we mistakenly think force is needed. The facts are, however, the more force applied, the greater is the tendency for the body to move forward into the shot and to leave the clubhead out of it. Ask yourself have you ever tried to hit an easy drive and the ball flew miles! Why? Because for once you personally kept out of things and gave the outer extremity a chance. The slower your top half moves, the more you resist with your left side at impact, the greater is the chance of the clubhead actually catching up, and passing out your hands through impact. Hold your hands back and let the clubhead pass them out.

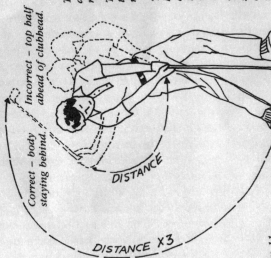

Correct – body staying behind.

Incorrect – top half ahead of clubhead.

DISTANCE

DISTANCE X3

Diagram 11
Waiting for the head.

The clubhead is approx. 3 feet away from your hands and two-months from your brain!

The Head: *The head must travel three times as far as hands to reach the ball.*

The Hands: *The majority of high handicappers' hands arrive at the ball before the head, when the head is late, i.e. open, shots will lack distance and often end up right of target.*

The Ball: *The sole aim for your swing should be to deliver the club head to the ball – metal to rubber ignoring the shaft.*

CHAPTER 3

Learning to learn

Avoid practising mistakes

Mastering golf offers a difficult challenge. Having to set up when you are in the static position is not too difficult. Swinging without a ball doesn't offer a great challenge. Hitting the ball when you have a bucket full of them to practise is not so bad since if you miss one shot you have many other chances to make amends. On the golf course, however, unlike tennis, not only is it a case that you have to get over the inertia of the ball but that you have only one chance to do it. If you happen to mishit the tendency is to try to makè a super human effort on the second attempt in order to amend the wrong. All this illustrates the need to know the basics, learn the drills, go through the rituals, develop a routine for yourself for your ultimate challenge which is playing a round of golf with one chance and many "shuddas".

The first essence is one of understanding – that is **understanding** all there is to know about the **implements** you will be using – the club and angles of faces, open clubface = slice, closed clubface = hook . . .

The second relates to the job you are going to have to do. Like any job preparation is very important. Somehow when it comes to golf people seem to think the normal rules don't apply, that they are some kind of a genius whom God has picked out and said you are going to play like Severiano Ballesteros without even trying. Some people regard it as a hobby and want to play but don't really want to learn, or they just plain do not like to be corrected.

Compare hitting a ball with a normal job. It is like me saying to you **"I am going to give you a job to do. You will only be allowed two seconds (swing time) to do it and you cannot see what you will be doing."** You would immediately realise that no matter what the job was you would have to be organised for it. If it was a job in ordinary everyday life – the secret of its success lies in the homework, the briefings, the background information, or the ingredients. If something goes wrong with one of these jobs you may have time to correct and try a different angle. But in a golf swing that takes 2 seconds, if something goes wrong you have no time to correct it. This is why you have to make sure of your preparations.

Like learning how to drive a car, fly a plane, or even in the same way as astronauts are trained to fly into outer space you have to

20

simulate the real situation by practising dry runs first and perfecting the preparation. Perfect your technique in an artificial situation before entering the real world of hitting a ball.

Unfortunately most golfers do not have the patience to do this and **end up practising with little or no knowledge of the clubs they are using, with a bad set-up, an ugly swing and no instruction. They are invariably practising mistakes.**

You learn to organise yourself first and then get a decent shape of your swing before you bring it out into the real world to the ball.

How you go about it

Preparation entails knowing what causes the different strokes e.g. slice = out to in swing with clubface open to swing direction etc. Also **an awareness that the way you organise yourself determines the way you swing and the shot you hit** (if you want to change the shot, change the way you stand to it).

First you must learn in a simulated situation how to stand to the ball in order to accommodate the wooden and low iron clubs in such a way that will produce a shallow attack on the ball. In order to do this you have to organise your weaker left side in a strong position in order to give you width on your back swing.

Aim. It is the most important aspect of the game having learned how to set-up. As the swing takes two seconds if you aim the clubhead at target then it has a good chance of it coming back to the same position when you are striking the ball. (It will be difficult for you not to do so.) It also means that if you do not aim correctly you will try to correct a bad aim in your swing and end up with two faults: (1) bad aim; (2) bad swing. These will be avoided if you aim the clubhead at the target and a whole chain reaction follows where everything is synchronised on the target and you have the freedom to swing where you are aiming.

The first part of the chain reaction is having lined the clubhead on the target you line up your feet, hips and shoulders left of the target or parallel to the target line.

If you succeed, a good swing should follow. Take advantage of all work you have done beforehand. It should be quite easy to do all this as you are in a static position (unlike the swing).

Swing. Take, for example, the wooden clubs. Knowing the type of implements they are, and understanding their limitations, and having aimed the clubhead at target and organised the body in such a way as to accommodate these limitations, you have to encourage yourself to make the right swing – by moving left side back and developing an "in" to "out" swing. The big advantage I find in the night schools

21

I run is that I have for the first four sessions the golfers indoors. This removes the impulse to hit the ball, without having prepared. It allows the golfer to settle down and to look like a golfer standing to the ball and to develop a decent shape on his swing, before going out to play.

You must develop a "feel" for the game and learning to play like an experienced player.

As we cannot see our swing we do not know what it looks like and we cannot see our faults and have no idea if we are actually correcting them. We have to rely on other parts of ourselves to master the game and it is not logic, nor our conscious mind but developing an awareness, a feeling for the clubhead, its importance – that it is the head that moves the ball – and become aware of where it is during the swing and more especially at impact.

As in modern society we are used to being brainwashed or spoonfed with information. I stress the need for the use of our imagination and especially our senses. **We build up a relationship with the clubhead, and developing a "feeling"** for it and knowing where it was at impact even though it is moving so fast that we cannot see it – "swing with our feelings", and so on.

It does not mean theorising, probing or experimenting with the swing. We realise that the swing is the one aspect of the game that we have very little control over. And at any rate it is controlled not by what we say we will do during the swing but by the way we organise ourselves beforehand. As I said if you want to change the shot you change the way you stand to it, and added to this you must be aware of what is happening to your hands through the hitting area.

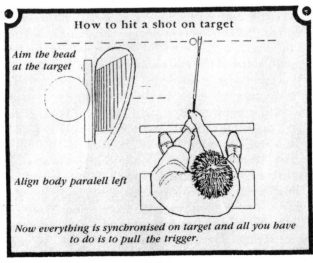

How to hit a shot on target

Aim the head at the target

Align body paralell left

Now everything is synchronised on target and all you have to do is to pull the trigger.

Having learned how to play in the simulation we bring the Potentially Good Player (PGP) to the real situation; to the ball. I stress the need for **the progressive approach.** That is, to use the easy clubs first and then progress on to the harder ones.

I suggest you use an eight iron to eliminate the problem which is to hit a ball with a difficult club and you are free to concentrate on developing a sound technique.

Why is it there is a tendency at the driving range to take out the driver? If I were to blindfold the golfer somehow he would still manage to reach for the driver as a magnet. He is taking on the most difficult club, the hardest to swing to the maximum distance. A battle ensues, shots become like machinegun fire, steam comes out from the bay before eventually the PGP is practically taken out from the bay by the heels, having learnt nothing, in **an exhausted and frustated state.** This is not the way to do it, don't be a donkey. Golf is like a lot of things in life you have to sneak up on it.

Take the eight iron instead. This is a great club to work something into your game. What you have to do is to repeat the swing you learned without the ball, now with the ball. Once you get the swing to repeat with the ball it only follows that you can progress onto the more difficult clubs – 7, 6, 5, 4.

Always start the practise session with an easy club.

Of course the tendency will be for the swing to disintegrate when the ball goes down while you try to be the first man or woman to drive to the moon. But this is where the awareness, the feeling for the clubhead comes in and the realisation that it is the clubhead that moves the ball not your body and so let the club do the work.

Use the same easy tempo of the eight iron even with your driver. It was designed for the longer shot, as it has a longer shaft and a straighter face. You will drive the ball 240 yards with an eight iron swing tempo.

The sequence you should follow is:
(1) Know golf geometry;
(2) Study the implements you must use;
(3) Have the perfect set-up;
(4) Learn how to aim;
(5) Develop a good shape on your swing with a club and no ball, and then progress on to hitting a ball with the easier clubs. Finally, use it with the driver. At this stage you should not be thinking of which way you are swinging but rather where you want the ball to go. Imagine the shot you are hoping for and allow all your hard work to come to fruition.
(6) Observe ball flight and react accordingly.

Synopsis

It is very important to develop a fluid swing with a good tempo, and not to be swinging from position to position. This is why it is important **to know the mechanics but not to swing mechanically.**

"I meant this head, you idiot."

On the golf course when you strike a bad shot always hit the next shot **soft,** with an easy club. Do the opposite to what you instinctively want to do.

CHAPTER 4

Understanding the game

I will start by asking you to take a distant look at the game and to approach it in an intelligently patient way. Let us begin by looking at what you have in your golf bag.

(1) Getting a better understanding of the clubs you use.

(2) Understanding how your ordinary life militates against you making progress at the game.

(3) Realising that the potentially good player, who is trying to improve through practice, is usually looking or facing in the wrong direction.

(4) Finally, that the only real way to progress is through the set-up. The set-up is the key.

It is all simple to understand. There are no gimmicks. I hope that after your reading and study of the following pages, I will have helped you along the right road to more successful golf play.

Great events, we often find,
on little things depend,
and very small beginnings,
have oft a mighty end.

The clubs we use

You are allowed only 14 clubs. The particular clubs you choose are entirely up to yourself.

The woods generally used run from No. 1 to No. 5. The irons from No. 2 to sand-wedge (No. 11).

Let us start with the low numbers. By this we mean the woods from No. 1 to 5 and the irons from No. 2 to 6. these are the really difficult clubs to use. However, **in order that you master them, you must first have a basic understanding of the limitations of these clubs.**

To explain we will use the extremes

A driver or No. 1 unless made to order, has 11° loft; the face is very **flat.**

A sand-wedge or No. 11, has 55° loft; the face is very **lofted.** *(See diagram 12).* This is the easiest club with which to hit the ball. The sand-wedge is designed for a high shot using an upward and downward swing. *(See diagram 13).*

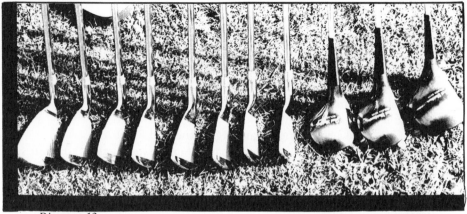

Diagram 12
The lower half (1-6) are for distance and accuracy. The higher clubs (7-Sw) are for
ACCURACY only.

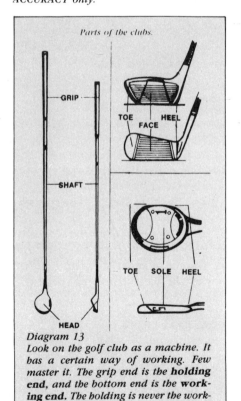

Parts of the clubs.

GRIP

TOE HEEL
FACE

SHAFT

TOE SOLE HEEL

HEAD

Diagram 13
Look on the golf club as a machine. It
has a certain way of working. Few
*master it. The grip end is the **holding***
end**, and the bottom end is the **work-
***ing end**. The holding is never the work-*
ing end but with many it is
unfortunately!

Diagram 14
Aim to move a round object
in a forward direction with a
flat face.

The driver – The point is that you are trying to move a round object in a forward direction with this flat-faced club, and because there is no slant on the face (unlike the sand-wedge) to get the ball airborne you **cannot hit down on the ball.** This is the most difficult club to use. *(See diagram 14).*

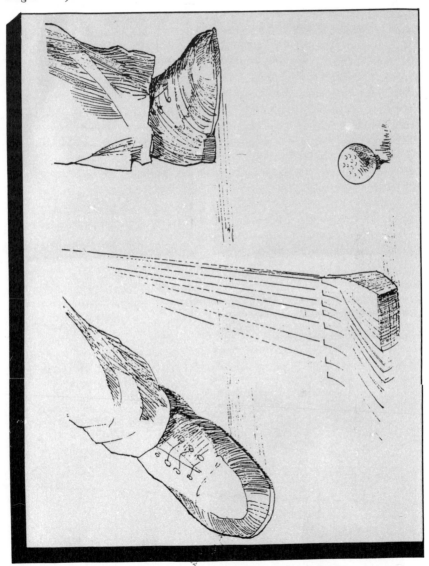

*Note: The clubhead coming in **parallel** to the ground towards the back of the ball from a **shallow** angle.*

Diagram 15
You need a wide swing for a shallow approach.

Diagram 16
and to be able to drive the ball forward.

---

*The majority of amateur's left arm collapse at impact. You should learn to **release** the clubhead into a **solid left arm.***

Indicates shallow sweeping swing

Diagram 18

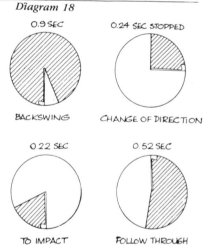

0.9 SEC	0.24 SEC STOPPED
BACKSWING	CHANGE OF DIRECTION
0.22 SEC	0.52 SEC
TO IMPACT	FOLLOW THROUGH

TOTAL SWING TIME IS 1.88 SEC
From the top of the backswing to impact is one-fifth of a second.

Listen to the clubhead going back

The only way to make a successful stroke with the driver is **to focus on the back of the ball,** not the top. (The arms react to the message from the eyes which are focused on the back of the ball and will tend to guide the club in that direction. See Special Lesson 4 "Chicken-eye the ball.") Push the club back along the ground on n the inside for the first part of the back swing. Ideally, one should be trying to sweep the ball off the tee. The objective should be to actually **leave the tee in the ground** – as all top pros do. In other words, the **power** of the swing is **directed forward,** not downwards. *(See diagrams 15, 16, 17).*

The power in the swing must be used in a forward direction, not downwards; after all you do wish to see the ball go forward! There should be no question of hitting at the ball; in fact, the ball should be incidental to swing. It just happens to come in the way. The same principle applies to any flat-faced iron.

One point which I consider to be vitally important is the fact that the **swing is largely reactionary.** If you pick up the clubhead quickly on the back swing, on your downswing you will come down on top of the ball. While this strategy will work sufficiently well with lofted clubs, i.e. 7, 8, 9, 10, it will prove to be disastrous with flat-faced clubs. (A player having this particular problem will have noticeable damage caused to the top of woods.)

Look in the right direction

(1) The average swing is over in less than two seconds. *(See diagram 18).*

(2) The potentially good player cannot see his swing.
Therefore:
(a) He cannot see his faults.
(b) If he thinks he is actually correcting them, he can have no idea that this is so. He is in effect working in the **"dark".**
(c) He makes an automatic response to ball flight.
For example:
If he is slicing – he aims to the left (anticipating the slice).
If he is hooking – he aims to the right (anticipating the hook).
If he is getting too much height – he hits down on the ball.

The problem really is that the more you aim away from paradoxically (instead of curing the ill, what is happening in effect, is an extension of the problem), the more likely will it be that the ball will end up in real trouble! The great majority of golf courses are designed in an anti-clockwise direction with boundaries on the right. As a conse-

29

quence the beginner will always have difficulty on this side as he will aim off to the left away from the boundary and the result is a tendency to slice the ball to the right.

(d) Finally, and most important of all, as the swing is over in a "flash" what has been happening has already been determined by the set-up.

To sum up:

(1) He is looking in the wrong direction.

(2) He is responding incorrectly to ball flight.

(3) He is always trying to correct his swing.

The set-up

Bad golf, poor shots, originate in the set-up.

If you are going to do any job in your ordinary life, you must set it up before you do it. The secret of its success is in its setting up no matter what job you are going to do. For example, if you are lucky enough to have bought a hotel, you will follow the well-tried system: manager, assistant manager, receptionist, head chef, and so on. There are systems for every job. You will put your particular mark on the proceedings. However, you will rely on well-tried systems.

The most important part of the system in golf is the set-up. There is great uniformity in the set-up of all top players.

Hoping to improve without perfecting your set-up is like going on a strange journey without consulting a map.

The distance in yards an average golfer should reach with each iron and woods is shown in diagram 19.

"If your set-up correct, there is a reasonable chance you will hit a decent shot, even if you make a mediocre swing. However, **if you set up incorrectly, you will hit a lousy shot, even if you make the best swing in the world**" (Jack Nicklaus).

The point to be made here is, you may feel a fault in the strike, and you may well hit a very bad shot. It was of course caused by a bad swing, but the faulty impact originated further back than the swing – at address. You must dig deeper. **Top-class players always change the flight patterns by altering their set-up positions – rarely their swing.** The altered set-up positions affect the swing change for them. Bad golf, flight changes and above all good golf starts at the beginning of your set-up. It is a very much attainable goal for you. Peter Thompson once remarked: **"Every player should look like a champion standing to the ball."**

30

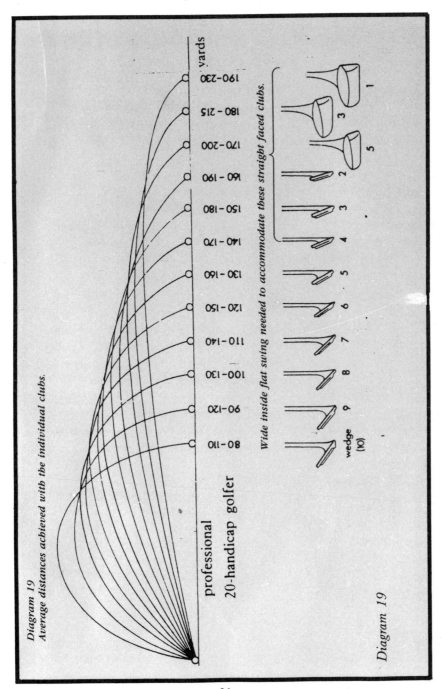

Diagram 19
Average distances achieved with the individual clubs.

yards

190-230
180-215
170-200
160-190
150-180
140-170
130-160
120-150
110-140
100-130
90-120
80-110

professional
20-handicap golfer

Wide inside flat swing needed to accommodate these straight faced clubs.

1 3 5 2 3 4 5 6 7 8 9 wedge
(10)

Diagram 19

THE UPSWING PLANK

If you are having problems with your woods, or you cannot hit a low club well, and most especially your driving is off, you should try the upswing plank.
The idea is to encourage an upswing through impact and discourage a downswing. A large majority of golfers swing down towards the ball steeply and wonder why the ball is not going forward for them. Once you set up for this shot you will automatically cock your left shoulder higher than your right, and position most of your weight over on your right foot. You will begin to develop a swing where you will swing the clubhead in paralell to the ground. Extend and lift your arms up after impact, ending in a high finish. Having trained with the upswing plank, you should place the ball on level ground, but try to retain the muscle memory, that you have learned and use it to improve your driving

Note: Left shoulder tilted up.

Think you are still using the upswing plank and the swing you must use to accomodate it

Note: Weight on right foot.

Wood on upswing.
Wedge on downswing.

CHAPTER 5

Set yourself up for life

The set-up

There are two parts to the set-up: (1) Preference. (2) Aim.

The naturally-weak left side must be given the preference in the set-up, if it is going to play a major role, which it must, in the actual swing when it takes place. (For left-handed players please reverse left for right.)

The left side

(a) The left hand

As the hands are the sole contact you have with the club, it is important that this contact is correct. **The power of the swing is transmitted through our hands.** Consider your left hand.

(1) You must **start the grip in the fingers,** not the palm of your hand. Through the finger grip, you will become well aware of the muscles in your left arm and back, and these larger muscles will become active in the swing as a result.

(2) You close the left hand over the club, so that the V which is formed by the base of the index finger and the thumb points just inside the right shoulder. This is the most important move you are going to make in golf. **You can practise this anywhere.**

(b) The left arm

As a result of the grip, the left arm will fall into a position where it is **more or less in line with the shaft of the club.** The feeling you should be looking for is that from your left shoulder to the clubhead, there is one, continuous straight line more or less. *(See diagrams 20, 21, 22, 23).*

The consequences of achieving these positions are:

(1) **Through the finger grip you will bring the larger muscles of the left side into play and it will have every advantage over the stronger right side when you swing.** *(See diagrams 24, 25, 26).*

(2) You will automatically move the left side back in the back swing keeping the clubhead low to the ground as desired with the low-angle clubs (preventing the right side from picking the club up quickly), and therefore increase your chances enormously of coming in at the back of the ball and moving it forward. In this way the angle of attack is taken care of.

33

Diagram 20
Avoid this grip.

Diagram 21 The distance grip.
Diagram 22

Diagram 23 Left side connected to clubhead.

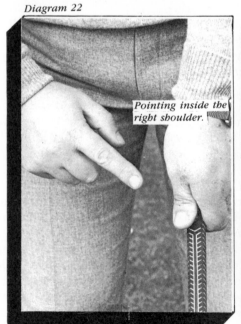

Pointing inside the right shoulder.

LEFT SIDE EXERCISE

Straighten the fingers on your right hand – train your naturally weak left side to do most of the work when you are swinging.

Diagram 24
Your left shoulder is connected to the clubhead.

HOW TO DEVELOP A WIDE BASE TO YOUR SWING

Extend your weak left arm

EXTEND YOUR LEFT ARM ON YOUR BACKSWING

Diagram 25
You move the left shoulder and the clubhead together.

Swing your left arm forward towards the back of the ball from the "inside"

Diagram 26

(3) Power.

It automatically follows that from this initial take-away, a full 90° shoulder turn is easily obtained. Finally, and most important, through this left hand finger grip, you will develop a feeling for the clubhead and so be able to develop clubhead speed and impact. The distance a ball travels is directly the result of the speed that the clubhead is travelling at impact. Clubhead speed equals distance. **The left side set-up is accepted and used by all great players today. It certainly makes sense, doesn't it? Use it!**

The correct movement happens automatically and subconsciously as a result of the correct set-up.

Ways to practise

Practice positioning your left hand on the club so that the V formed by the base of the index finger and the thumb point just inside your right shoulder, and get used to the feeling of having the left arm in line with the shaft of the club, more or less; then practise swinging the left arm only. **In other words, the left side (your naturally weak side) must be trained to do most of the work and when you are swinging** try to maintain the line you have created from left shoulder to the clubhead – do not break left arm. This is easily done by avoiding excessive wrist work and keeping back swing short.

Another important point should be noted with regard to being able to use your left side. The left side is unaccustomed to playing a leading role in everyday life, but in order to make progress at the game it must be encouraged to do so.

Become left side orientated
Henry Cotton's tyre drill system

It is well known that Henry Cotton believed in improving and strengthening the left arm with a tyre drill. It simply involved placing an old tyre on the ground, holding the club by the grip, and placing the clubhead inside the tyre. The exercise was of a backward and forward movement of the left arm, short, quick taps, the clubhead striking one side of the tyre without hitting the other at speed. There are many similar drills which you may use, when once your realise that any of them can actually be practised during the winter months in your garage or back-garden.

The right side. The completion of the set-up

It is important also to realise that the **right hand plays a "passive" role in the back swing.** It only goes along for the "spin". To ensure that this actually happens:

36

Diagram 27 Consistent golf.

Extend your left arm
out after impact

Build up a solid left arm
through impact –
one that will be able to stand
up to the forceful right arm.

(a) The naturally weak left side must be given preference in the address position.

(b) This situation must be capitalised upon, thus creating the correct sequence, i.e. the club being pushed back by the left shoulder, arm, hand and left knee. However, the right hand plays the most important role in the golf swing in the hitting area. **You hit the ball with your right hand. You release the clubhead with your right hand.** This will happen automatically and naturally; you will now have to think about it.

(Diagrams 28, 29, 30, 31).

A grip I always recommend to the player who has a problem "finding" the clubhead is the two-handed one. The problem may relate simply to a lack of distance, or to the slice or even the dreaded socket. If the right hand is overlapping the left or interlocking with the left hand, it is very easy to "block" the shot. This means the body is coming through leaving the clubhead behind and usually wide open (pointing right). **If the player is advised to release the clubhead this is usually misinterpreted and results in his effort to speed up the clubhead in a faster swing with the body coming through even more ahead of the clubhead.** The problems deteriorate, at which point you have to explain that this is what is called "repressive progress" meaning you get worse before you get better, so free the right hand from the left by separating the two hands (on the grip). The results are twofold – by freeing the right hand it will automatically encourage a wrist cock at the top of the back swing and, because it is "away" from the left hand, it will turn into the shot and so release the clubhead for you. In other words the three problems relate to the one fact of not being able to use the right hand in the swing. By separating the two hands in the grip the results will change as the right hand is free to work its own.

P.S. If the problem is acute and persists increase the gap between the hands.

Now the full set-up from start to finish

You address the ball with your left shoulder, hip and knee, considerably higher in a position of dominance over the right-side counter part. Why? In order to create an upswing hit the feeling you should get is that of one straight line with your left arm and the clubshaft. You will automatically position your left hand slightly ahead of the clubhead. The shaft should appear to be pointing towards the right foot. The reason for this optical illusion is because your eyes are not directly over your left shoulder.

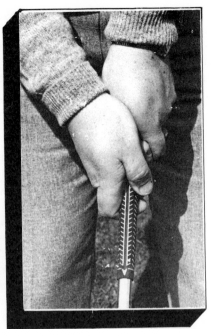

Diagram 28 Right hand barely sitting there.   *Diagram 29 Two hands form a unit.*

Diagram 30 Left arm extended – creates a   *Diagram 31 The Vardon overlap.*
wide swing.

You place the right hand on the club, so that the shaft lies across the fingers. You close the right hand over the grip so that the V formed by the thumb and the base of the index finger point at the right shoulder. **The finger grip promotes maximum "feel" and "touch"** and allows the right hand to whip the clubhead through the ball with a powerful swing reaction.

The two hands have come together on the shaft and will act as a unit. All the great players have their hands very close together on the shaft. *(See diagram 32).*

With your right shoulder slightly lower, you tuck in your right elbow. The feeling you should be looking for is that of the right arm in the **"soft"** position or relaxed and ready to **fold naturally** in the back swing. *(See diagram 33).*

Your left arm is in the extended or straight position and the right arm is slightly bent inward. The reason for this is that if the right arm is slightly bent at address it will fold naturally in the back swing. You are setting-up so that the right things will happen automatically and easily. **You are setting-up the correct chain of events.** The naturally strong side is in a weak position and the weaker left side is now ready to take over, pushing the clubhead back low along the ground. This causes all the right things to happen. To practise this you can use the club shaft as a check-up between arms.

You have broken your daily sequence and are now ready to play golf.

How to practise your set-up in the livingroom
(see **Make the right statement**)

First of all, when you have placed the ball on the ground, you should hold the club in the left hand approximately half an inch from the top of the grip. Having lined up the clubhead square behind the ball to an imaginary target, you should now position both feet at right angles to a line btween the ball and the inside of your left heel. Now continue by using an underarm movement, positioning right hand on to grip. *(See diagram 34).*

This has the effect of pulling down the right shoulder, thus facilitating a correct swing pattern, which should always be used towards the back of the ball, but not changing the direction of the shoulder line, which is parallel to the target line. You will see how this simple routine clearly **emphasises the dominance of the left arm** and also affirms the strictly subordinate and supportive role provided by the right. In fact it can clearly be realised that the right side is only an addition to an already organised set-up. *(See diagram 35).*

Right arm relaxed inwards.

Diagram 33
Creating the right statement I
am really saying "this is the
position I would like to be in at
impact".

Diagram 34
Cock your left shoulder higher
than the right – this helps create
an upswing hit and prevent a
downswing one.

Diagram 35
Tuck in your right elbow.

RELAXED

READY

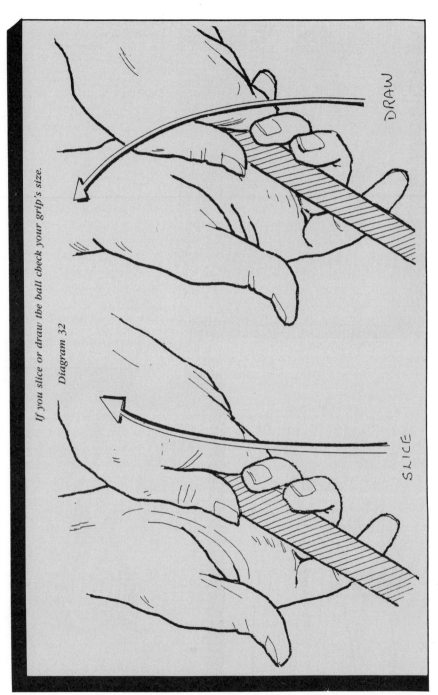

If you slice or draw the ball check your grip's size.

Diagram 32

42

Creepy crawlies can distract you!

Evolution of the Vardon grip *(See diagram 31)*

The Vardon grip is largely a finger grip, a light grip, and it is interesting to study how it came to be.

Harry Vardon was born in Jersey of farming stock. In the same way that the youth of Ireland often make their hurley sticks, his golf implements were hewn from branches of trees. This made for a rough gripping surface which was extremely damaging to the hands when held in the hitherto accepted fashion. By a stroke of genius Vardon decided that **a finger grip** would be much less damaging to the hands. He later saw the **benefit of moulding both hands together on the club,** and so created the overlap grip, as we know it today.

Despite all the many changes in equipment and techniques that have taken place through the years, the Vardon grip remains an integral part of the modern game.

43

Make the right statement (An easily attainable goal)

When you address the ball, you are really making a statement. You are saying this is the position I would like to be in, when I'm striking the ball. If you care to study the illustrations, you will immediately see that there is a great similarity. It is the same in every swing, good or bad. You will always tend to return to your address position at impact.

1

If the great players wish to alter the flight of their shots they will do so by changing:

• Their address position i.e. by standing more open or closed or....

The point to be made is that you

7

may feel a fault in the hitting area which is caused by your swing, but it originated way back in your set-up. The correction is also to be found there. From setting up to impact takes approx. 1.5 sec. If you are able to position yourself like a top class player

1) You have a very good chance of returning to it at impact. Compare address and impact. Note • Head position. Behind the ball, focusing on back of ball.
• Weight back on right foot
• Left arm extended • Left shoulder higher than right • Right elbow tucked in.

What you do in 1 will determine how you will be in 7 and if you wish to improve 7 you must improve your position in illustration 1.

Note

● Eyes focusing behind ball.	This focus will help direct the swing towards the back of the ball. Also helps shoulder turn.
● Left arm extended.	Creates wide arc to swing.
● Left shoulder tilted up.	Helps create a similar position at impact – right moves down as left moves up (an upswing hit).
● Right elbow tucked inside hit.	Helps flat shoulder turn.
● Weight back on right foot.	Much easier to get behind ball.
● Closed stance.	Encourages "in to out" swing.

Here is a routine you can practise at home. Stand erect, place club in fingers of your left hand and close so V formed by thumb and base of index finger points to right shoulder. Extend your left arm fully. Widen stance to shoulder width. Hold your back straight up and bend your knees and hips in order to get down to the ball. Lift up your chin and turn your head to the right.

Place your right arm behind your back. Drop your right shoulder down and, using an underarm movement, place your right hand on the club so that the V formed by your thumb and index finger points in the direction as the V on the left hand (towards right shoulder). Flex your right elbow inwards. This movement ensures that your stronger right arm is placed in a totally submissive position. Even though right now you may feel like an octopus, you should begin to look like the set-up in the photo.

CHAPTER 6

Posture and ball position

Stand tall and into the ball

All the great players have good posture. "Good posture" simply means standing your height. There are very good reasons for this. It is said that the great players use a minimum of effort to get a maximum result, what we call economy of movement. An upright position will indeed generate more power for the same effort.

A practical demonstration to explain "leverage" in golfing terminology can be illustrated in the following way: Let's suppose you are driving along in your car and suddenly you get a flat tyre. Having taken your spare tyre from the boot, you have, say, just two wrenches, one long, one short. You try in the first case the shorter one only to discover that, no matter how hard you try, you fail to initiate movement of the nuts. On the other hand, if you try the longer wrench you will have immediate success. Why should this be so? Simply you will find that the longer one will have more leverage and more power and you are able to exert more pressure on the nuts. You will see from this that there are so far two reasons for standing your height:

(1) You need less body movement.

(2) You generate more power or leverage.

Here's how you go about having good posture.

Practice:

(1) Standing your height to the ball.

(2) Keeping the weight centred back towards the heels so when you bend down to reach the ball you don't bend over.

(3) **You should not bend over to the ball but bend slightly at knees and hips, keeping back straight.**

(4) You must keep you head upwards. The top of your head (that bald patch) should not be visible to someone standing opposite you. The reason is that this particular position enables you to have room to swing allowing **the left shoulder to move freely under the chin on the back swing;** it also allows better vision and a wider arc to your swing.

(5) Generally speaking, you stand into the ball. It should be said you cannot stand too close to the ball.

46

Bad posture – Bad golf

Diagram 36
If you stand with knees straight,
back bent, *weight forward . . .*

Diagram 37
. . . you will have a steep, tilty, outside
backswing, and play bad golf.

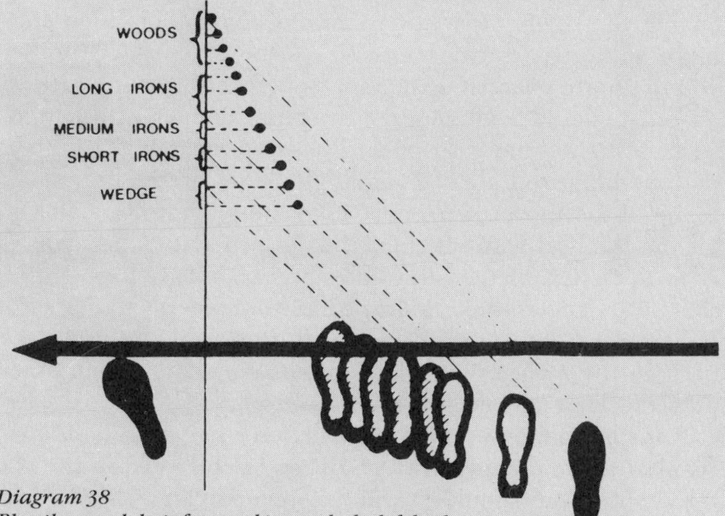

WOODS

LONG IRONS

MEDIUM IRONS

SHORT IRONS

WEDGE

Diagram 38
Play the wood shots forward towards the left heel
and the high irons opposite your right foot (back in stance).

Too crouched
Tilted back swing
Consequences of crouching in swing terms

If you bend over as shown you will lose on two fronts. *(See diagrams 36, 37)*.

(Explained in detail in Chapter 8 "Turn your shoulders at the same level in order to create a square hit.")

(a) You need more movement for the same power.

(b) You lose power and, as a result, you cannot possibly turn away from the ball in your swing. You will only "tilt" (like a boat anchored on a windy day, tilting to and fro on its mooring) if you find yourself in the crouched position; your left shoulder going upwards. In effect what this means is that the right side will pick the club up steeply, rather quickly on the back swing, resulting in a downward blow being struck on the ball. The result will be a high shot as you make contact with the bottom of the ball using the top of the club, causing too much backspin. After all you do wish to move the ball forward, so the power of the swing must be directed in a forward motion, not downward.

Ball position

It is important to remember that you should position the ball inside your left heel for driver and woods three, four and five. However, in relation to higher iron play, the ball should be placed back in the stance as in diagram 38. This ball position will enable you to use your iron in a more dynamic fashion and with more authority. Furthermore, it will be of assistance in helping you to square yourself up at address before you swing, preventing an open shoulder alignment. In actual fact, it will help you to strike a slightly more downward blow on the ball as is imperative in good high iron play (seven, eight, nine, wedge, sand-wedge). Some of the top professionals advocate playing the ball forward off the left heel with all clubs, but in order to do so, you would need to be as athletic as they are, and be able to use your legs as they do. You should follow the example of the great Seve Ballesteros, who, on the other hand, invariably positions the ball back in the stance with the irons, as do many of the other top players. They are what I call "hand players". *(See diagram 38)*.

A further point in relation to ball position, which has disastrous **results, is the placing of the ball too far forward in the stance.** Inevitably, your shoulders will be aligned in an open position and the shaft of the club will point towards the right shoulder or in line with your right arm. Your grip will automatically be weaker.

Let's think for a moment about the impact zone, seeing it in terms of a semi-circle. Having positioned the ball towards the end of the semi-circle, or forward in your stance, the inevitable consequence is that you swing off towards the left, or in the direction of the tail-end of the semi-circle to which it is pointed. *(See diagrams 39 and 40).*

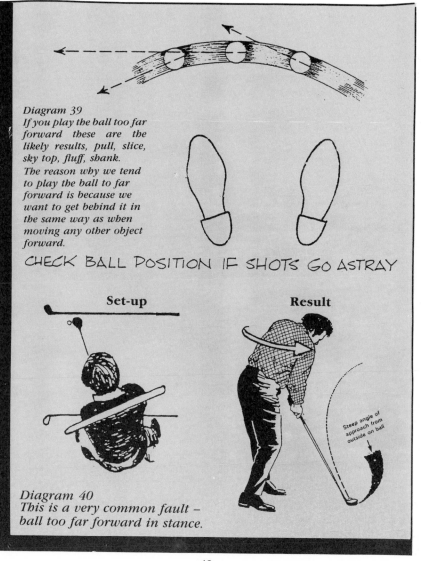

Diagram 39
If you play the ball too far forward these are the likely results, pull, slice, sky top, fluff, shank.
The reason why we tend to play the ball to far forward is because we want to get behind it in the same way as when moving any other object forward.

CHECK BALL POSITION IF SHOTS GO ASTRAY

Set-up

Result

Steep angle of approach from outside on ball

Diagram 40
This is a very common fault — ball too far forward in stance.

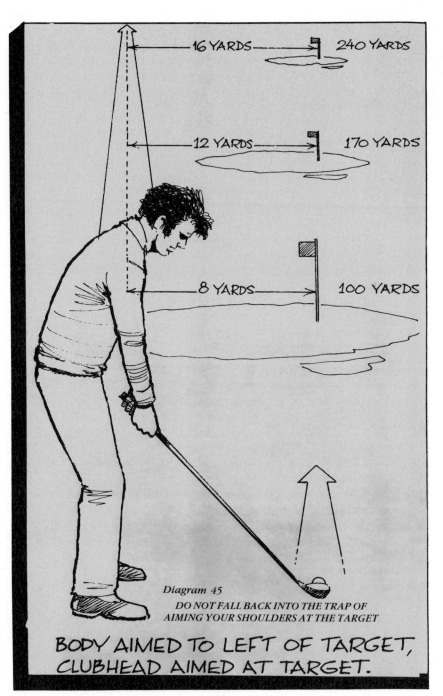

16 YARDS ← 240 YARDS

12 YARDS ← 170 YARDS

8 YARDS ← 100 YARDS

Diagram 45

*DO NOT FALL BACK INTO THE TRAP OF
AIMING YOUR SHOULDERS AT THE TARGET*

BODY AIMED TO LEFT OF TARGET, CLUBHEAD AIMED AT TARGET.

CHAPTER 7

How to line up

You aim with head

This is the most neglected area in the game. Most PGP (Potentially Good Players) **never bother with alignment,** yet they wonder why the ball does not go where they want it to go. If golfers were to behave in their ordinary life as they do on the golf course, there would be many more accidents on the road, and certainly it would be a very dangerous society to live! When you are driving your car you try to aim the front of it where you want it to go. It is the same thing if you are firing a gun you try to aim the front of it where you want the bullet to go. Now it is exactly the same with golf. Yet when I have golfers for lessons and I see that their practice swings are very good, but when they actually go to hit the ball the swing disintegrates. The reason for this is that, when they are taking the practise swing, there is nothing at stake, nothing involved. However, when the ball goes down, and when they line up to hit it instead **of aiming at the target they may be aiming 50 yards right of the target.**

If there happens to be a boundary on the course, (and there are boundaries on most courses) instead of aiming at the target, they actually aim at the boundary. Instead of swinging where they are aiming – across the fence – **they try and correct their bad aim by swinging back around themselves to the target.** They start with a fault which is aiming miles to the right of the target, and then try to correct it and end up with another fault in their swing.

It is like the engine of your car, if one part goes wrong it will affect other parts in the engine. If you start with a fault it will affect your whole swing and cause a lot of things to go wrong in your game. If, on the other hand, **you start with one thing right, a whole chain reaction follows – a whole lot of rights – all the other pieces fall into place.**

What I am saying is, if you learn how to aim at the target, you do not have to make **any correction in your swing.** All you have to do is swing where you are aiming. There is a very good chance of it coming back to exactly the same position at impact. In fact it will be difficult for it not to hit the ball towards the target.

How to hit a shot on target

Diagram 41 Approach with the head.

Diagram 42 Aim the clubhead at the target.

Diagram 43 Align body parallel left of target.

Diagram 44 Swing clubhead towards target

What do you aim with?

When I ask a golfer this question he invariably says "I try to aim my shoulders at the target!" and I ask them "Do you hit the ball with your shoulders, your knees or your hips?" "No." "What then, do you hit the ball with?" He says "With the club". "What part of the club? "The clubhead."

And then we come around to the idea that if you want the ball to travel towards the target, what you hope will happen is that the **clubhead will be moving down towards the target when you are hitting the ball.**

If you ask yourself these questions you will learn to aim the head of the club, not your body, **at the target.** The secret is you aim the **clubhead first** and **your body second.**

There is a well rehearsed routine that all the professionals in the world use. Unfortunately when golfers go to a tournament they will watch mostly the flight of the ball or the swing of the superstar. They don't watch the small things, for example the way the professionals hold the club, the way they line-up and set-up to the ball.

Now you can follow the *diagram numbers 41 and 42.* You can practise it to imaginary targets. Get your friends to help you, to see that you are lined up on the target. In the early stages, it takes time because you are doing it mechanically. However, if you practice, you can do it very quickly on the golf course.

In fact you can do it as quickly as anybody placing a ball normally. This is the routine to practice until it becomes automatic.

Having placed the ball on the ground, move back behind into a position where the ball is directly between you and the target ensuring you **can see the line that you want the ball to go on.**

You **have to get a mental picture of the flight of the ball.**

Holding the club with your right hand, walk in and, while still facing the target, **place the clubhead behind the ball, and aim it at the target.**

You do not line up your body until such time as you are happy that the head of the club is facing the target. *(See diagrams 43, 44).*

Work your body into a position where it is left of the target or **parallel to target line.** *(See diagram 45).*

The only thing you aim at the target is the head of the club – nothing else.

If you don't think this is important consider the fact that Jack Nicklaus, Bernard Langer and Severiano Ballesteros, the top players of today all use this routine. They have their own variations. But they are all very careful how they line up to the ball. The next time you go to a tournament or watch one on television, look out for this and open your eyes to what is important.

If you are really interested in playing the ball down to the target have the patience, the determination, the singlemindedness to follow the routine. Most people don't!

This same routine holds for all the clubs in the bag. You have a distinct advantage with your wooden club because on most of the heads there is a brand name and generally this name is printed in a straight line. If you place the head in such a way that the brand name is facing the target the head will also be.

Chipping

It is also true for your chipping, even if you are very close to the flag – on the fringe of the green. *(See diagrams 46, 47, 48, 49).*

Here is the formula for the high irons.

Position yourself in such a way that the ball is directly between you and the target or the flag.

Holding the club in your right hand – **you aim the clubhead at the flag on the part of the green you want the ball to land.**

Aim body well left of target so that there is room for the arms to swing through.

Visualise before you take the shot that the clubhead and the flag are one or that the flag is like a magnet to the clubhead. When you then swing the club you will be amazed at the results you will get. You will become very accurate. Your clubhead, because it was lined up on target, will automatically come back to the target through the hitting area.

I cannot over-emphasise this point. It is very frustrating to watch golfers expect good results When they have aimed yards to the right or left of the target.

Summary

(1) **Aim the clubhead at target.**

(2) **Body left or parallel to target line.**

(3) The swing happens in two seconds – and you don't have the time to make alterations in your swing.

It is the same for every shot in the game. For example, the sand shot, aim the clubhead at the target and your body well to the left of it. Once again the clubhead and flag are one, or drawn to one another.

There are some variations on this which we touched on earlier. If you are playing a tight or narrow fairway when there is an out of bounds on the left hand side of the it, then you have to say to yourself

Diagram 46 Approach with the head.

Diagram 47 Aim it at the target.

Diagram 48 The secret is to swing the back of your left hand towards the flag.

Diagram 49 Extend and lock your left arm after impact.

– "I don't want to hit this left." Line up on middle of the fairway, then make a slight adjustment by opening the clubhead up or aiming it down right hand side even though your body is lined in the middle. As well as this, you can encourage yourself to the weaken left hand grip by turning it in an anti-clockwise direction. The left hand will want to move back to its natural position and so cause the clubface to open.

To repeat, if you **are afraid of the left-hand** side of the fairway and there is room on the right and you don't want a disaster, **open the clubface** so that it is aiming at the right hand side. Opening the clubface will weaken the grip. You can more or less guarantee that, no matter where the ball goes, it will not go left and will therefore be in play.

Reverse the routine if the trouble is on the right hand side as it is on the majority of golf courses that were constructed on the St. Andrews model and run in an anti-clockwise direction with the boundaries on right.

Instead of aiming the clubface down the middle of the fairway it is a help to "toe it in" slightly (this will automatically strengthen grip) and use a stronger left hand grip and so make sure that ball will not go right as the clubface won't be open through the hit. These are very minor alterations that you make during a round of golf. There is no harm in having these weapons in your battle against the course. It's all about the clubhead. The clubhead will do it for you.

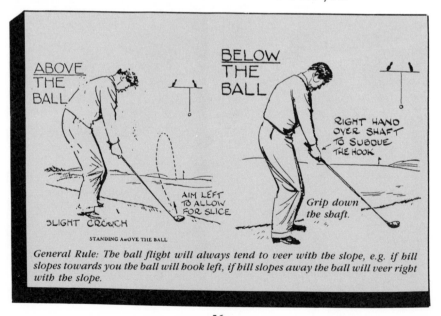

General Rule: The ball flight will always tend to veer with the slope, e.g. if hill slopes towards you the ball will hook left, if hill slopes away the ball will veer right with the slope.

SPECIAL LESSON 4
Chicken-eye the ball

Note head turned right and his eyes are focused on the back of the ball.

LOOKING AT THE BALL
What your eyes see and how your body responds
÷

If you focus on the top the result will be steep swing with the power directed towards the ground

Focus on inside result will be swing from inside

Focus on outside result will be swing from outside

You should focus on on inside back of ball (not the top), move the clubhead back behind the ball and swing in from a low angle to the inside back in order to move it forward.

Inside hit

Good golf

Inside hit.

Outside hit

Bad golf

Pull, Slice, Top, Sky, Fluff, Shank

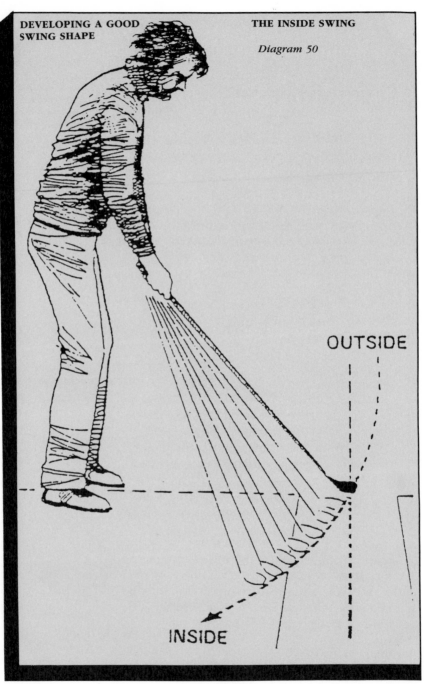

OUTSIDE

INSIDE

CHAPTER 8

Developing a good swing shape

In the early stages of learning the game, you need to have two extra aids in your bag – patience and perseverance. As it is an old and essentially simple game that has evolved slowly, it has a lot of depth to it. It is also true to say that once you have a good set-up, you have to go about acquiring a decent "shape" to your swing. In many ways in these early stages the ball is a menace. You will be so concerned with making contact with it that you will forget to swing. The question you have to ask yourself, however, is: "Have I the patience to persevere without hitting a ball, until such time as I have a good shape?" Accepting that the ball is an inhibiting factor in the execution of a fluid swing, regular practice without the ball can build up a worthwhile and lasting rhythm. A tee stuck in the ground can be an adequate "target" at this stage of your swing development.

"In" to "out" and you can't go wrong

What then, is the basic swing shape? The one that you need to develop **is an "in" to "out"**. A line straight back from the ball and straight through the ball indicates the direction to the target. The clubhead is moved **inside** this on the back swing and outside on the forward swing.

As we examine the swing, it is not my policy to give you "paralysis by analysis". After all, the swing is over quite quickly – in less than two seconds. It is not to your advantage to entertain too many swing thoughts. This could lead to a mechanical and less effective action. However, once you set-up correctly, you will start it right.

(a) Back swing – take-away *(See diagram 50)*

Many people are under the misconception that the club should be taken straight back from the ball. This is not so. **You should push the clubhead back along the ground on the inside. You push using the left side, the left shoulder, arm and hand with the right hand side only going along for the "spin".**

Very important

Diagram 50a should be examined carefully.

59

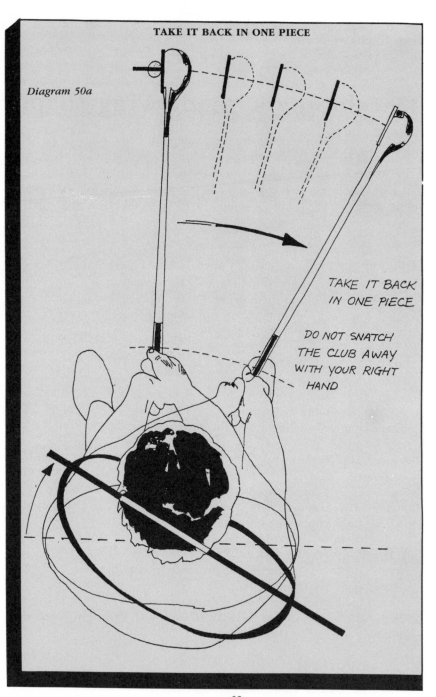

Diagram 50a

TAKE IT BACK
IN ONE PIECE

DO NOT SNATCH
THE CLUB AWAY
WITH YOUR RIGHT
HAND

Result of this take-away

Your left shoulder automatically begins to turn, thus coiling the muscles in the back and creating power. You are also moving the clubhead **around and behind, providing width, preventing the "steep" back swing and thereby creating a proper angle of attack on the ball from behind.** You should really concentrate on this first few inches of the back swing. If you get it right, everything else will fall into place and good shots will result. Remember: **"back along the grass on the inside".**

(b) Forward swing – "so the word is out"

In the forward part of your swing, you must develop a feeling for swinging **out to the right of the target;** even though you wish the ball to go towards the target, it is far too easy to swing across yourself and finish around. This is the most common fault and of course can have devastating result. What it actually means is that you are swinging with your shoulders and, as the ball is not shoulder high but on the ground, it is a fruitless exercise.

There are four points which relate to back swing and forward swing which I will deal with here. These points reinforce the need for the dominance of the left side in the set-up and explain why you should encourage your left side to work in the swing. The four main reasons are:

(1) Power
(2) Plane
(3) Consistency
(4) Development

(1) Power

A short back swing with a full follow through is much better than a full back swing with a short follow through. In general terms, the forward swing is the "power" part of your swing and that which you should concentrate on. Many people fail to realise that you do not "hit" the ball on your back swing. Many believe that you need a long back swing in order to get power – this is not so. If you go back too **far everything collapses, breaks down and you "fall"** into the ball. If you go back too far and too fast, you have what is called a **"right-sided" turn** and there is no coil. The idea of a back swing is to give you "power" and "position". In order to get power, you have to push the left side against the right knee and coil the muscles in the back into a tight spring. If you take the club back with the right hand and arm, the whole right side turns and you have no coil. It is like trying to coil

61

Diagram 51
*A steep back swing with no width results in a **down** chopping blow on the ball.*

Diagram 52

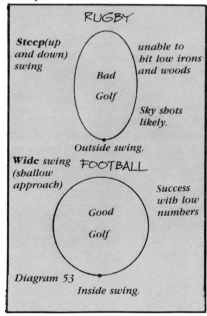

RUGBY

Steep(up and down) swing

unable to hit low irons and woods

Bad

Golf

Sky shots likely.

Outside swing.

Wide swing (shallow approach)

FOOTBALL

Success with low numbers

Good

Golf

Diagram 53

Inside swing.

a spring by pushing it against something that moves. You lose the coil and you lose power.

You should always start the back swing from the left shoulder. By the "left shoulder" **I mean that part of the body left of the spinal cord, not just the shoulder alone.**

(2) Plane

The right-sided take-away also affects the plane of the swing. Think for a moment of the pendulum of a clock and the way it swings back and forward. Suppose that pendulum were to go back that little bit further and then further, it would, as a consequence, go higher and higher until such time as it would stop moving forward but would fall downward. Remember the aim is to move an object in a forward direction. What you are looking for **is a backward and forward movement not an upward and downward one.** Let me make another analogy involving a rugby ball. **The right-sided take-away reminds you of a rugby ball where there is no width and very little chance of attacking the back of the ball from behind.** It is a "lifting" type of swing. The left-sided take-away which is, of course, the correct one, is a wide "pushing" one, mindful of the broader football in make-up and shape. *(See diagrams 51, 52, 53).*

(3) Consistency

In the early stages you need a compact swing, basically an arm swing which will give you consistency, not necessarily distance. From a consistency point of view, too many are so fond of going back too far, that they get lost and are not able to return the clubhead to the ball. Regard learning to swing like learning to drive; take a long drive in your car and yo may get lost, take a short one and you know where you are and you are able to get back safely.

(4) Development

In general swing-terms, remember to practise "pushing" the clubhead back on the inside, keeping the left heel on the ground, and once your left shoulder touches your chin, then it is time to come forward. You must feel that you are swinging out through the ball, finishing with your hands high and your right heel off the ground.

Feel as though you are taking the ball just as it happens to come in the way, forward, that the ball just happens to come in the way of your swing. There is a reason why the right heel should be off the ground at the finish. It is not because of the fact that it looks good – which it does – but because it allows you to hit through the ball.

A "high finish" is a sign of a good swing. Have a "mental picture" of finishing with your hands high and your right foot off the ground. Remember all the top players have good swings. If you play with an "ugly" swing, even though you may do quite well, you will do so "despite" rather than "because". *(See diagram 54)*.

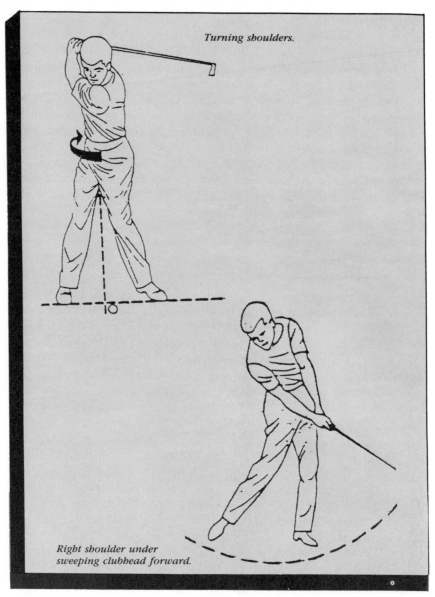

Turning shoulders.

Right shoulder under sweeping clubhead forward.

Diagram 54
Developing a good temperament.

SPECIAL LESSON 5

Respect the earth

At address do not ground the driver

TAKE THE BALL OFF THE TOP DECK!

looking at back of ball

Swing from the inside towards the back of the ball

Left arm resistance

Sweep ball clean off tee

Respect the earth

Jack Nicklaus and Greg Norman are two very famous golfers who never ground their clubs. If you have a tendency to sky the ball, hold the clubhead off the ground as you prepare for the drive.

RESPECT THE EARTH

Wood on upswing.

*If you are given an advantage in life you should always take it. The ball is already off the ground and the aim of your swing is to drive the ball forward, i.e. to put as much distance between you and the ball. There is no **earthly** reason why you should strike the ground while you are hitting the ball.*

Tee the ball high and take it off the top deck even into a strong wind!

Tip: Take the ball off the top deck. Do **not ground the club** as the ball is already sitting on the tee, approx two inches off the ground. **Don't make contact with the ground at any stage during your forward swing.**

**BACK SWING
TURN YOUR SHOULDERS
CREATING POWER**

Diagram 55

RELAXED

Turning shoulders
against the resistance
of right knee

You must
keep your left
foot planted
on the ground during
your backswing

CHAPTER 9

Playing low-numbered clubs well

You must turn your shoulders at the same level in order to create a square hit. *(See diagram 55).*

What is a turn on the backswing? It is when your shoulders are parallel to the target line at address and then at the top of the backswing have turned around ninety degrees to the right. A good way would be to use the motto "Turn, turn, turn." The best example I have seen was that of Tommy Bolt. He just stood there at address and turned on the spot. Nothing seemed to move except the shoulders turned. "You are allowed only one move on the backswing and that is turn."

Why do you need to turn your shoulders?

(a) **Position.** Get around behind the ball so that the clubhead will approach from behind the ball, not above. If you do not turn you will pick the clubhead up on a steep swing.

(b) **Power.** If you turn your shoulders you will coil muscles in your back and these muscles create power in uncoiling in the downswing. **Turning the shoulders against the right knee is like pushing a spring against a wall. The top class player turns his shoulders straight away.**

If you were to roll your wrists on take away or your hands were to move away and leave the shoulder behind the link would be broken. If you move the small muscles only – it leads to a loose swing with a lack of control, and gives away the power to the right side and generally results in an overswing and inconsistency. The classic example of this is Ben Hogan. In his early days he had a dreadful overswing, in fact he did not become a great player until he was over thirty years of age. He would ruin an otherwise good round with a terrible "duck hook". You see from the overswing the tendency is once you lose control at the top of the backswing and let go, the first move on the down swing is to cast the clubhead down at the ball or in golf terminology, to hit too early. The result is that the clubhead comes in before the hands causing a hook. If your swing collapses at the top of the backswing it will also collapse at impact and you will have no extension to the ball. Hogan invented a secret recipe for this problem but he was not going to tell the world for a number of years. Naturally that made everybody twice as anxious to find out what this was. In the end all that it amounted to was a rather awkward word called pronation, which meant simply that you held your left hand in a slightly cupped position through the hitting area and so held the clubface slightly open (prevented the hook).

Let me say of course that this should happen automatically from a good set-up position. What do I mean by this? If your weaker left side is in the dominant position when you are standing to the ball it will automatically start the turn. The stronger right side is paralysed by putting it in a soft or relaxed position and the whole left side will begin the move. By the whole left side I mean not only the shoulder but down the back – the left side of the back. There are different ways of looking at this, one is to keep everything in synchronisation – meaning **the left side, left arm, left hand, left knee, all turn together as a unit.** Another way is to call it **"connection".** The clubhead is connected to the shaft which is connected to the left hand and the left hand to the arm and the arm to the shoulder and the shoulder to the left side of the back. **The clubhead and the left side are connected and the way to get the turn is not to break the link.** *(See Diagram 56).*

How to practise the turn

Understand that the way you organise yourself before you swing determines your swing and the resulting shot. You should organise yourself in such a way that it would be very easy for you to turn your shoulders. Remember that your strong side is your right side as it does most of the work for you it naturally wants to assume control of this situation. **You are probably holding this book with your right hand.** If I was to give you a club, more than likely you would put out your right hand in order to receive it. You have to go against a normal daily routine when you are organising yourself. It is very important to put your weaker left side in a strong position and your strong right in a supporting role. Another way is to have your shoulders slightly preturned to the right (stand closed).

It's nearly impossible to stand too near the ball. One of the causes of not being able to turn is faulty posture. If you have bad posture, which means have your knees in a straight position with your back bent, the weight will automatically be forward on your toes, and you will be standing too far from the ball. If you are in this position your right side is in a much too strong position and a tilted backswing is certain. A tilted backswing is one where your left shoulder goes down and your right shoulder moves up. A right sided turn means that the left side is not turning against the right knee, and creating coil of the muscles, but the whole right side is turning. Pushing your left side

70

Diagram 56
Weaker left side in a dominant position.

Diagram 57
*If you stand with knees straight, **back bent**, weight forward . . .*

Diagram 58
. . . you will have a steep, stilty, outside backswing, and play bad golf.

71

against your right knee is like pushing a spring against a wall. A right sided turn is like pushing the spring against the wall and the wall moves back – there is no coiling action, "no wound up power". *(See diagrams 57, 58).*

To prevent this happening you have to adopt the motto that you cannot stand too near the ball. Stand into the ball, stand your height to get down to the ball. Do not bend your back, simply bend at the knees and hips, keeping the back straight. You should also forget the advice of "keep your head down" as this is the most misleading bit of advice ever given, mostly by people when they do not have a clue what they are doing wrong. Do not bend your head down, keep it up so that your whole face is visible from one opposite you. The reason for this is if your chin is down on or near your chest, it will prevent your shoulders from turning freely on your backswing. Keep your chin so that your left shoulder will be able to move freely under it.

Finally make sure your weight is back on your heels. If you succeed in having good posture like all successful golfers a turn becomes much easier. A turn where your shoulders are turning at the same level against the resistance of your right knee is essential. *(See diagram 59, 60).*

Another way is to have your shoulders slightly pre-turned to the right. This means when you are setting up the ball, having aimed your club at the target, you aim your body slightly right of it. (This ensures that your left side is in a very good position.) **The first movement of backswing should then be with the big muscles of the left side – your left shoulder moving back to your chin and your right shoulder turning around behind you.** There are variations, however, if you happen to be slim and supple you will not need to pivot your hips on the backswing as much as if you were big boned and heavier. You can judge this for yourself. If you have a heavy build it is important to ensure that your left knee moves with your left thigh and so **cause the right hip to move out of the way,** and allow the full shoulder turn. This is called a **pivot** of the hips. What it means is that the **right hip is clearing out of the way and allowing you to turn your shoulders.** If your right hip does not pivot, it will block the turn of the shoulders. *(See diagram 61).*

Swing your arms up as you turn your shoulders on a flat plane.

One important precaution in the turn is not to allow your arms to follow the turn of the shoulders. If you do, your backswing will be very flat indeed and the club will more than likely be laid off at the top of the backswing. One of the things all great players have in common in the down swing is what is called "separation", which means that your

72

Diagram 59
Keep your weight back on your heels

Diagram 60
For a Flat Turn and square hit.

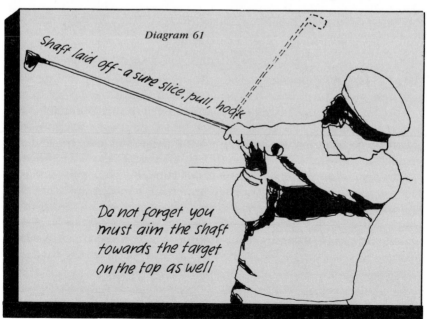

Diagram 61

Shaft laid off – a sure slice, pull, hook

Do not forget you must aim the shaft towards the target on the top as well

arms are moving away from your right shoulder on the down swing
into the hitting area. In other words, your hands are quite near your
right shoulder at the top of the back swing, but on the down-swing they
move quickly away from the right shoulder, i.e. your arms separate
from your shoulders. In the bad golf swing unfortunately what happens
is that both come down together, the arms and the shoulders together.
(See diagram 62) what this means is that the right shoulder comes outside on the down swing resulting in a swing that comes across the ball.
The reason why it is important for your arms to move on a slightly different plane to your shoulders, **is if your arms move slightly up** on
the back swing while your shoulders are turning they will automatically
move away on the down swing, and so separate because they have
already separated on the back swing. The other reason why it is important that your arms do not follow the shoulder turn is that you have
to position the shaft of the club on the top of the back swing in such
a way that it is pointing to the target or slightly to the right of it. If your
arms follow the turn of your shoulders, as I've said, this will result in
a flat back swing with the shaft of the club laid off to the left or pointing
to the left of the target at the top of the back swing and that is the direction in which you will swing. Without going into too much detail to
help you position the shaft towards the target and prevent the ''laying
off'' of the club, you should be aware of your hands being underneath
the shaft of the club at the top of the back swing with your wrists in
a cocked position in such a way that if you look up at your left wrist
you will be able to see some wrinkles on it.

Ways to practise

Turn, turn, turn Take the stronger right out of the set-up.

(1) Organisation – having organised yourself in such a way that your
weaker left side is in a strong position and your stronger right side in
a soft or relaxed position, **you open the fingers of your right hand**
in such a way that only the thumb and the base of the index finger is
on the grip. Now you have total left side control – your right side isn't
there at all. **You ''drive'' your left side back while at the same time
holding your right hand fingers in a straight position.** In this way
you are preventing your right side from playing any part in your back
swing. Be careful to position the club properly on the top of the back
swing – towards the target, with your hands underneath the shaft. *(See
diagrams 63, 64).*

(2) Another way of practising the turn (used by the tour professionals) is having taken up your strong left side address position, move
your hands directly upwards into such a position where they are

74

Staying behind the ball

Diagram 62

In the good player's downswing the right arm straight very quickly in downswing.

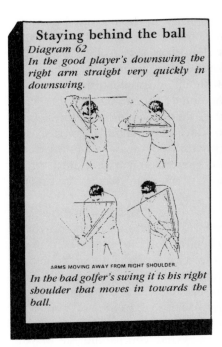

ARMS MOVING AWAY FROM RIGHT SHOULDER.

In the bad golfer's swing it is his right shoulder that moves in towards the ball.

Wrong

Steep angle of approach from outside on ball.

Right shoulder outside on downswing.

Diagram 63

A very good way to practise left side control.

. . . by straightening fingers on right hand.

Diagram 64

. . . using left side to turn.

75

directly opposite your chin with your arms in the extended position. Now simply turn the shoulders and position the club. This is a very good way to help you to **turn your shoulders at the same level,** your left shoulder and your right shoulder are turning on the same level and preventing a tilt, i.e. where your left shoulder dips down and your right shoulder moves up. Touring professionals sometimes use this when their swing becomes a little tilty, they take their normal address positions, move their hands straight up into the position, then turn their shoulders and hit the ball. In other words, **turn away and swing down on the inside.** If you could use this exercise it is a very good one to help you get a feeling for the turn. Use an eight iron as the practise club. *(See diagrams 65, 66).*

(3) It is possible to practise it in your home. You have to be able to get into position where you can see your reflection – in the mirror or even where you can see your reflection in the window at night. Remember the motto "you are allowed only one move on your back swing, that is turn". Stand opposite your image, watch your shoulders, watch them turning. You should not see any other movement than your left shoulder moving back to your chin and your right shoulder moving around behind you be careful to position the club at the top of your back swing correctly. What you should see in your reflection is your back turned towards the target at the top of your back swing. *(See diagram 67).*

Concentrate on your right shoulder. Try to turn it out of the way on your very first move of your backswing. To achieve a square hit you must swing the clubhead around and behind the ball on your back swing. I am certain you have noticed how **slow** the great players swing the club. Yet from their seeming lack of effort they are able to drive the ball enormous distances. The main reason for the slowness is because they always start their back swing with their bigger muscles. They start turning their shoulders from take-away. By the time their back swing has reached hip height their shoulders have nearly fully turned. They finish off their back swing by lifting their arms and positioning the club shaft on target. The high handicapper tends to snatch the club quickly away with his/her right hand and tries to continue turning at the top of his back swing. The result is an out of tempo back swing with an over swing. You must start your turn with the L, that is, your left arm, your left and right shoulders, turn the complete "L" together.

This is a very good way to practise a flat turn, hands opposite chin,
turn shoulder at same level.

Diagram 65

Back turned on target.

Diagram 66

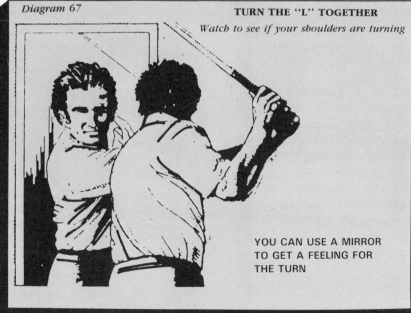

Diagram 67

TURN THE "L" TOGETHER

Watch to see if your shoulders are turning

YOU CAN USE A MIRROR
TO GET A FEELING FOR
THE TURN

SPECIAL LESSON 6

THE ARC OF THE DOWN SWING

The arc of the down swing must be inside the arc of your back swing.

If you are able to visualise your own golf swing in this way, you will nearly always hit a good shot. To drive the point home you must understand that there are only ten possible bad shots in golf and seven out of a possible ten are struck **from outside across.**

Strike from the outside is undoubtedly the single biggest fault in golf! Why is it that the vast majority of golfers return the clubhead down on an outside path to the ball?

It is of course because of the **crucial change over that occurs at the top of the swing.** The majority make the wrong pass at the top, **out pops the right shoulder and this throws the whole swing plane outside.**

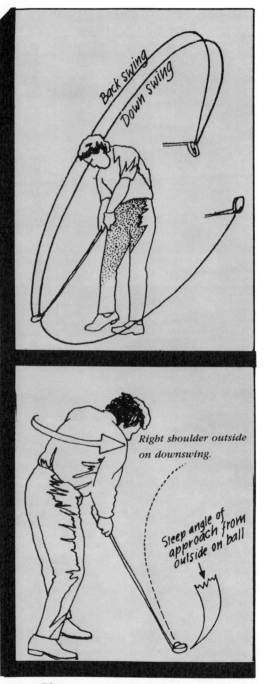

Right shoulder outside on downswing.

But why does it occur?

Simply because the good golf swing is a paradox. You are told you must turn your shoulders a full 90° on your back swing, **yet on your down swing you are warned you must not turn into the shot.** You are told you must turn on your back swing yet the very opposite going forward.

Why is this seemingly contradictory advice good for you?

The reason of course is the little ball. It is on the ground. If it were shoulder high it would be extremely wise to turn the shoulders into the ball like the baseball player. However, as the ball is on the ground and the clubhead **is approximately five feet** off the ground at the top of your back swing the clubhead has to descend **from five feet to two inches in one-fifth of a second without actually descending as it strikes the ball.**

At the top of your back swing imagine there is a heavy weight pulling your arms straight down towards your right pocket first and from this shallower angle you swing your arms forward towards the back of the ball.

Extend your arms out towards the target.

The direct route down is taken by many from five feet to two inches without first levelling out. If you are able to keep your down swing arc inside the back swing one you can only do so by starting down by driving your hips forward and thus (1) creating an initial pull which automatically brings your arms and right shoulder down inside (2) to a shallow angle from where you are able to strike the back of the ball and drive it in a forward direction.

RIGHT SHOULDER GOES DOWN

Imagine that there is a very large pane of glass just outside the ball and if you swing down on the outside you will smash the pain of glass.

DETOURING HIS DOWNSWING

HANDS INSIDE.

RIGHT ELBOW BACK TO HIP

Keep the down swing inside.

THE ARC OF THE DOWN SWING MUST BE INSIDE BACK SWING ONE

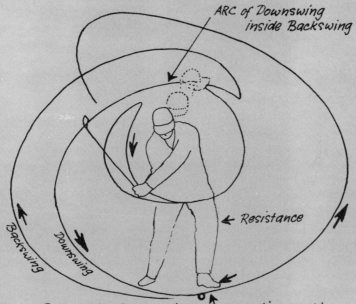

ARC of Downswing inside Backswing

Resistance

Backswing

Downswing

Descending Power with an ascending motion

HIT THE BACK OF THE BALL FROM THE INSIDE

CHAPTER 10

Get it right on top

You must aim the shaft of the club towards the target at the top of your back swing if you are to swing in the direction of the target through impact. *(See diagram 68).*

From four points of view
(1) Not able to hit the low irons.
(2) Hitting the three and seven irons the same distance.
(3) Hooking high irons and slicing low irons.
(4) The correct position at the top of the back-swing.

You must be able to use it
The only important thing about the top of the back swing is that it should be a position that you can use – "you must be able to use it".

What do I mean by "you must be able to use it". Basically you have to be in a position at the top of the back swing from which you will be able to release the clubhead at the ball and have it travelling at a maximum speed in the right direction and also facing at the target when you are hitting the ball.

If you are in a wrong position at the top of the back swing there is nothing you can do about it, because you are not going to get it right at impact, when you consider the fact that from the top of the back swing to impact is one-fifth of a second. **It is true to say that if you are wrong at address your swing will be wrong,** and certainly if you are wrong at the top of your back swing there is no time to make the corrections in your down swing. That is the first point. It is a fact that **I could put a top tournament player in a position at the top of the back swing from which he would never break 80. Unfortunately, it would be one of the many positions one would see on the first tee on Sunday mornings at any of our clubs.**

What do we mean by the right position at the top of the back swing and how you have to be able to use it?

It is where the shaft of the club is pointing at the target, the clubhead square, and hands underneath on the shaft, with the wrists fully cocked ready to release the clubhead through the ball at impact. *(See Bobby Jones diagram 68).*

Aim 1: the clubhead at the target.

GET IT RIGHT ON TOP **Note left wrist position**

Diagram 68

Aim the shaft towards the target at the top.

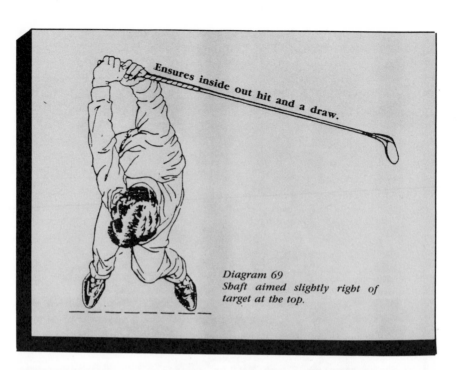

Ensures inside out hit and a draw.

Diagram 69
Shaft aimed slightly right of target at the top.

Top of backswing

He will definitely swing left.

Diagram 70
Laid off on top – a sure slice

Result

Steep angle of approach from outside on ball.

Outside-in swing.

Aim 2: the shaft of the club at the top of your back swing at the target.

Now if you want to err, you might as well err on the right side, many of the top players do not have the shaft of the club pointing at the target. **They have the shaft of the club pointing to the right of the target.** In this way they are encouraging themselves to hit the ball from the inside and "away" from themselves, or along the line of the shaft. *(See diagram 69).*

If you look at a diagram of the golfer, you will see that the shaft of the club is not pointing at the target but pointing well to the left of the target. The question is where is he going to swing? *(See diagram 70).*

The answer is where the shaft is pointing. It is pointing to the **left** of the target. Where is he going to swing? He's going to swing to the left of the target.

What does this mean? He is going to **swing across the ball from the outside.** It also means from a very, very **steep angle** down on the ball. The low number clubs have one thing in common, they have a flat face. They do not have very much loft on them. The type of swing you have to use is one where the head of the club approaches from behind the ball to take account of the lack of loft. **A steep swing will not work with low numbers.**

(1) Let us now take the first part of the question – why you cannot hit your low irons well. Invariably be because your swing is too **steep, too much "down"** on the ball. You can be sure, if you are having trouble with your low irons, and your swing is too steep at the top of the back swing, **the shaft of the club will be in a "laid off position".**

If you are in the laid off position, what is means is the shaft of the club is pointing left of the target and you will swing **left of the target.** You will swing out to in or "across". The point here is that you will not be able to use your low iron while you **will have success with the high numbers** because they have the angle on the face. The "loft" is there and no matter how much you hit down on the ball, there will be **plenty of loft left on the face** so that the swing will "work" with the high numbers.

(2) It is true that it will work so well with the high numbers, that you will tend to hit them the full distance and in some cases you are turning your seven iron into a five iron.

With the low numbers you will hit them so badly that you may end up hitting your three iron the same distance as your seven iron. This is because at the top of your swing the shaft of the club is in the "laid off" or "locked" position pointing left of the target, as a result of which you will swing down and across the ball.

"You wouldn't believe it, I forgot my keys."

Hitting high irons left, low clubs right from same swing.

The flat face creates sidespin if face misbehaving, the ball will swerve with these clubs.

The lofted face creates backspin, hence the ball will fly in same direction as swing line.

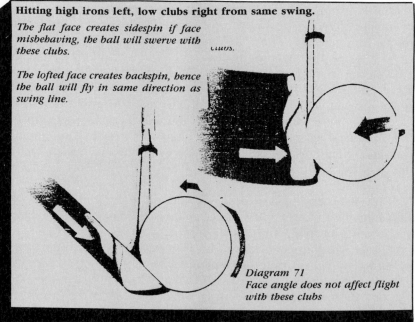

Diagram 71
Face angle does not affect flight with these clubs

(3) The third point is why am I hooking my high irons and slicing the low irons? *(See diagram 71)*.

The effect you think you are **getting is probably a "pull hook"** – one where the ball has already started left and tends to go more left during flight. If you look at the diagram you will see that on the high numbered clubs because of the angle on the face (the loft is there), where your clubface meets the ball (even if open), it is the bottom of the clubface that makes contact with the bottom of the ball so creating a lot of backspin. The result of this – you do not have much sidespin – is that the ball tends to go where it is hit. In other words you could say the ball has no brains! If you are **swinging left** with the **high numbers** the ball will tend to **go there.** Let me say that this is a good indicator of the direction of your swing. Let me say that a good indicator of the direct use of your swing – the line of your swing – is your 9s, 8s or wedges. If you are continually striking these shots left of the green, this line of your swing is left – and "out" to "in".

On the other hand if you are using the low numbered club with the flatter face, and you make the same swing – across with the clubface open – **because the flatter face contacts the middle of the ball and impacts mostly side-spin** (not back-spin) the ball will start left but very soon that will **veer wickedly to the right.**

The result will be completely different. The difference is the head of the clubs, the loft of the face. The lofted face (even if open) at impact creates back-spin while an open flat face encourages more side-spin. The Nos. 8 or 9 will tell you about your swing line (towards the left) and the Nos. 3 or 4 about the clubface angle which is open (towards the right).

To conclude, the reason we are we getting the two types of shot is because at the top of the back-swing the shaft of the club is in the "laid off" position, it is pointing left of the target. If the shaft is in the "laid off" position, with your three iron you are going to swing across the ball with clubface open and going to create sidespin and slice it. With your eight iron, you are going to swing across the ball but this time create backspin and the ball is going to go straight left.

This is the one cause. The **"laid off position" and is to be avoided at all costs.**

(4) The question is how do we get into the right position and what is the right position?

It is the one, as we have said, when the shaft of the club is pointing at the target, the face square, and your hands in a "soft position" underneath the shaft and ready to release the clubhead for you.

Let me say straight away that you have to: (1) line up the clubhead

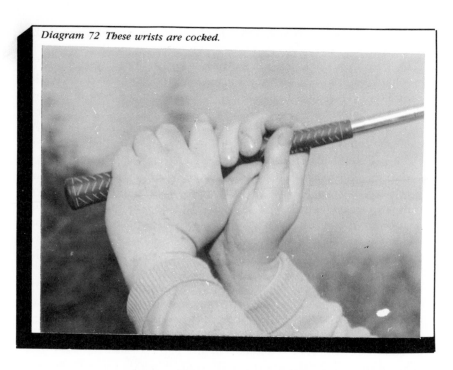

Diagram 72 These wrists are cocked.

Diagram 73
Note left wrist position.

with the target; (2) get your feet, hips, and shoulders parallel to the target line.

This is very important if you are to get the right position at the top of the swing.

If you want to err, do so on the right side – line up slightly right of target. The drill is to "turn the shoulders and position the shaft towards the target."

It is also important that you have a decent turn on your back-swing and not only that but that you have a good wrist-cock. By that I mean that your **hands are underneath the shaft in such a position that you will be able to see wrinkles on you wrists on the top of the swing.** *(See diagrams 72, 73).*

In this way your wrists are "hinged", wrists cocked or hands in soft position. The best example I have ever seen was that of the immortal Bobby Jones. *(See diagram 68)*. This is an ideal position for the golfer who wants to hit the ball a maximum distance with a minimum of effort.

Ways to practise the wrist-cock
Start the wrist-cock early in the back swing

You may have to do it mechanically first if you are to do it naturally later. One of the ways is when you have your hands hip high on the back-swing, instead of moving your hands up and any higher, start to hinge the wrists by turning your right up and, at the top of swing, your wrists should be fully cocked. (If you feel pressure on left wrists at top this is correct.) *(See diagram 74)*.

Remember if your wrists are cocked on the top of your back-swing they will automatically uncock through the ball and produce the clubhead speed for you.

On the other hand if **your hands are in the "hard" position** *(See diagram 75)* if your left hand is in **a locked position** at the top of the swing it will be **locked through ball** and produce a blocky type of shot **lacking distance and control.**

If you were to try to play with this position where the left hand is in "locked" position you would need to be as strong as an ox to produce any result.

There is another way to exercise, having taken your address position. Once again do not move hands upwards, just keep them in position and just hinge wrists by moving clubhead upwards. Through this exercise you will be able to get a "feel" for the wrist cock.

I cannot over-emphasise the importance of the position you have your hands in at the top of your swing. If your hands are in once again

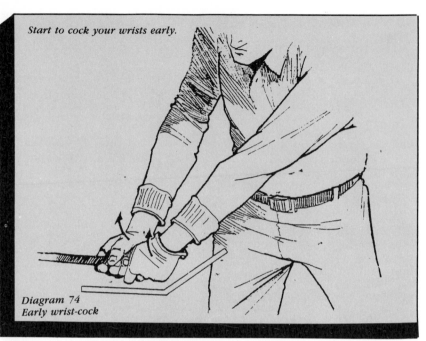

Start to cock your wrists early.

Diagram 74
Early wrist-cock

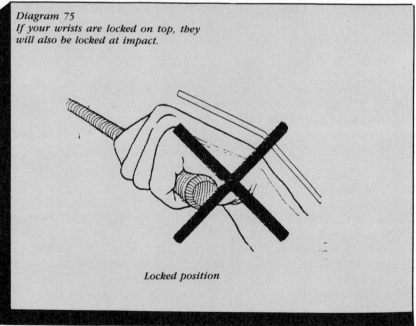

Diagram 75
If your wrists are locked on top, they
will also be locked at impact.

Locked position

a locked position, if your wrists are locked, the shaft will be laid off, with the clubface "closed" and, more important, you cannot release the clubhead.

The other way to develop the "soft" position is when you swing back, instead of holding very tightly with your left hand, actually let go or open the fingers – the famous Piccallo grip *(See diagram 76)* – which would be frowned on by many as being an absolute disaster. The point here is that if you want to get a "feeling" for the top of back-swing position, a feeling for the softer position, if you let it go slightly with your left hand, suddenly you get into a lovely soft position, where you get an excessive wrist-cock and certainly be able to release the clubhead very quickly on down swing. If you are locked you will never be able to release it. If you practise swinging letting the club go with your left hand, you will develop a feel for the soft position. When you are playing because the ball is there you will automatically firm up at the top of the swing. There is no need to worry about the loss of control, **because the problem with most golfers is not that they release the club too early but they do not release it at all.**

Another cause of not having the **wrist cocked comes from playing tight courses** with trouble on left and right where subconsciously you may have decided to keep the ball in play and **to "steer" it.** In other

NEAT DRESS ESSENTIAL

"FOR CRYING OUT LOUD, MR. MURPHY, WE CANNOT TOLERATE YOUR COMING INTO THE MEN'S BAR WITHOUT A TIE. IT'S JUST NOT ON!"

The excessive wrist cock – Soft position

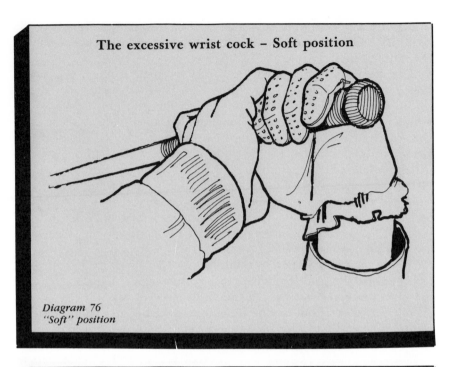

Diagram 76
"Soft" position

You must be able to see wrinkles on your left wrist at the top as a result of the hinging of the wrists.

Diagram 77
Back of left wrist cocked inwards

words you are hitting the ball quite well but you **are not generating the clubhead speed** in order to get the distance. You can be sure that the problem arises from the fact that you have no wrist-cock, and are not generating any clubhead speed – and you never will as long as you continue to push the ball.

The problem goes back to the top of the backswing that you are just **leaving the club back there. You are not really cocking or setting the wrists,** so that they will release the clubhead automatically for you and produce the clubhead speed giving you the maximum distance for the minimum effort. *(See diagram 77).*

The other way of practising is to simply separate the hands. Put right hand on the grip in such a way that there is a gap between hands on the grip and swing the club back. By virtue that your hands are separated your right hand will automatically pull down against your left and so create the wrist-cock.

A synopsis

If you are right on top, the shaft will be pointing at the target with your hands underneath, and face square. You will be able to release the clubhead towards the target, with it facing in the right direction and travelling at the maximum speed for you.

The three problems relate to the one position, that of the shaft "being laid off" at the top of the swing. It is set up to the left of the target and is not suitable for low numbered clubs, and means **that you will pull high numbered clubs. Not for you!**

(1) **Aim the clubhead at the target at address.**

(2) **Aim the shaft of the club at the target at the top of your swing (or even slightly right of it) with your hands underneath the shaft and your wrists fully cocked.** *(See diagram 68).*

SPECIAL LESSON 7

THE SQUARE HIT

How you can achieve a square hit.

The high amateur finds it very difficult to achieve a "flush hit with the middle of the face. The majority of shots are hit off centre. Yet we all know that feeling when the ball comes off the **middle of the club face.**

The key to all this is to develop a swing where there is **no tilting action with your shoulders on the backswing.**

If you **dip your left shoulder down on your backswing** you can be certain there will be **a compensatory dip on your forward swing.** *(See diagrams below).*

If you experiencing too much height as well on your shots, or you have a tendency to pull the ball with the 7, 8 and 9 or W you have a **faulty shoulder** turn which causes **you to swing steeply.** The correction is to stand much nearer to the ball, and place the weight back on your heels. **Practise turning your shoulders at the**

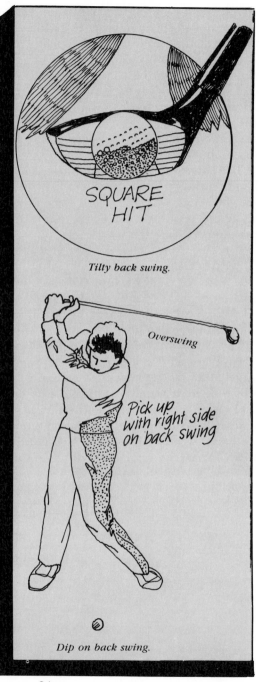

SQUARE HIT

Tilty back swing.

Overswing

Pick up with right side on back swing

Dip on back swing.

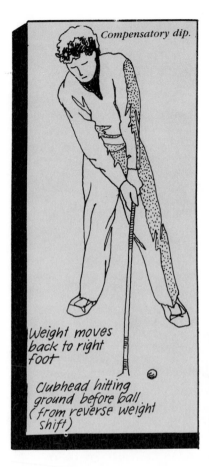

Compensatory dip.

Weight moves back to right foot

Clubhead hitting ground before ball (from reverse weight shift)

McNulty who won 11 tournaments in 1987 was asked why his game improved so dramatically replied ''I put it all down to one thing a flat shoulder turn. I concentrate on ''turning my shoulder on the same level.

Turn flatter.

I must turn my shoulders at the same level

Think of flat swing

same level – a **Flatter shoulder turn.**

Concentrate especially on your right shoulder. See if you are able to start your backswing by turning it around and out of the way.

This flatter turn will create a shallow plane and a square hit. Mark

Swing the clubhead into the ball parallel to the ground.

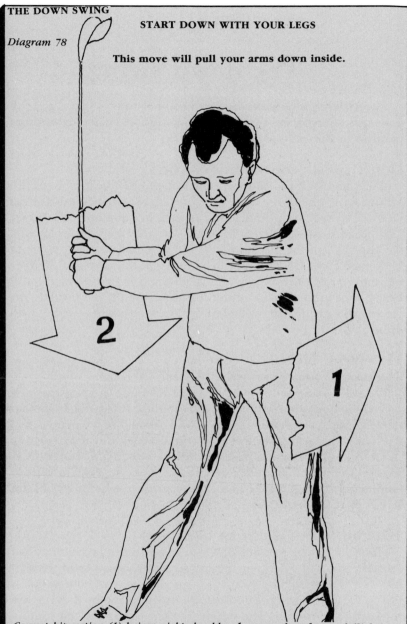

START DOWN WITH YOUR LEGS

Diagram 78

This move will pull your arms down inside.

*Correct hip action (1) brings right shoulder **down** and **under** and (2) brings hands down to hip high point with hands, arms and club ready to move **forward** and sweep the ball clearly off the tee.*

CHAPTER 11

The down swing

The difference between bad and good swings is that the clubhead descends sharply on the ball or, in a good swing, it approaches parallel to the ground. *(See diagram 78).*

Don't spoil your shoulder coil!

What part the body plays in the down swing? The driver has 11° loft on the face (unless made to measure). It is a flat faced club and it requires a **shallow approach on the ball.** For example, if a driver has 11° loft on the face, that is the angle you are allowed to come into the ball at – 11° off the ground or 11° from behind the ball, if you are to hit a good shot. On the other hand using a standard sand-wedge with 58° loft you will get away with approaching from less than that angle from off the ground or 11° when you are swinging into the ball. In simple terms a steep swing will work with a sand wedge but not with the driver.

Flat-faced clubs
The start of your down swing is vital

We are looking for a swing that will take into account these limitations. What part does your body play in the down swing? On reaching the top of the back swing the down swing should be a reaction. In other words if your back swing is okay the down swing will also be. However, if, on reaching the top of the back swing, the **top half starts the down swing, the right shoulder will come outside and so throw the clubhead on the outside path and therefore a steep attack on the ball – an out to in swing.**

Hit the ball with your bum!

How can this be prevented? Once again I have to say that the body should respond to the swinging of the clubhead on an in to out line, but what you should be aware of happening is your bottom half working on the down swing. **You start the down swing by driving the legs forward, and moving the weight back towards the left foot as you begin to clear the left hip out of the way on the through swing. This forward thrust with the legs will bring the clubface down on an inside path** (and the right elbow back to the hip), as the legs are nearer

Diagram 79

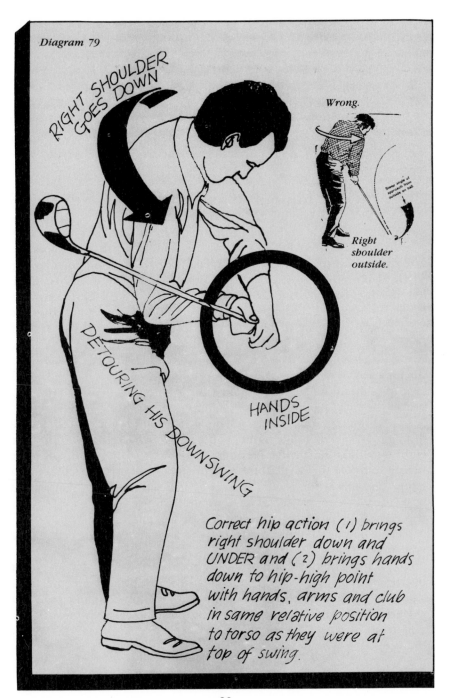

RIGHT SHOULDER GOES DOWN

DETOURING HIS DOWNSWING

HANDS INSIDE

Wrong.

Right shoulder outside.

Correct hip action (1) brings right shoulder down and UNDER and (2) brings hands down to hip-high point with hands, arms and club in same relative position to torso as they were at top of swing.

the ground and so create an in to out swing or a shallow approach to the ball. A good indicator of faulty footwork is when your shots begin to fly straight left. It often happens when you are unfit, overweight, or legs are tired. Indeed you may be unaware that you are not using your legs on the down swing, and so transferring the body weight into the shot. It is also true to say that by drawing the bottom half forward you will change the swing line **from across** to **straight through** because, by driving the bottom half forward, you change the start of the down swing from starting down **outside to starting on the inside.** *(See diagram 79).*

Clear the left hip out of the way on forward swing

The reason why you must clear the left hip is so that your arms will move through freely and you will hit through the ball and not at it. If you do not turn your left hip out of the way, you will block yourself or be in your own way on your forward swing. Start the down swing by **thinking of driving your right knee into the shot and turning left the hip so that the middle of your belt would be facing the target at impact.** This movement will, as I have said, bring the clubhead on an inside path to the ball. In the same way if you are big boned or heavily built it is important to pivot your hips on your back swing (to allow full turn) so it is **important to clear your left hip on the forward swing.** If you have strong legs and weak hands you should play to your strengths and rely on your legs to give you the power to propel the ball. Jack Nicklaus is a very good example of this.

It also follows that this movement will allow you a full follow through. **If, on the other hand, you keep your weight back on your right foot, it is like as if somebody was holding you when you were trying to move forward.** If the weight stays back it is very difficult to follow through as the weight is holding you. At the finish you should be aware of where the weight has completely moved over to the left and **the right foot is out of "the bucket of cement".**

Take a photograph of this position and hang it over your bed in case you forget it! *(See diagram 80).*

While it is extremely important to get this movement I am against overuse of the body in the swing as golfers can become caught up in "positions" etc., and **forget to swing the clubhead at the ball and release it through the shot.** In other words the body swings the clubhead (never the body) at the ball.

Diagram 80   **STRIKING FROM THE INSIDE**

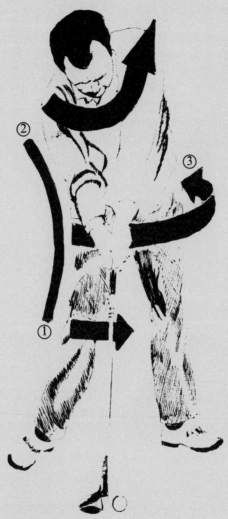

① *Right knee driven forward.*
② *Right shoulder goes down.*
③ *Left hip moving clearly out of way.*
④ *Finish with middle of your belt facing the target.*

SPECIAL LESSON 8

Think of the golf swing this way
UPSTAIRS DOWNSTAIRS

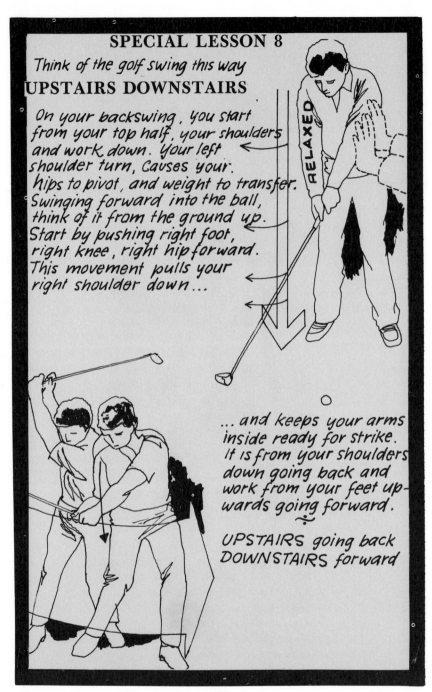

On your backswing, you start from your top half, your shoulders and work down. Your left shoulder turn, causes your hips to pivot, and weight to transfer. Swinging forward into the ball, think of it from the ground up. Start by pushing right foot, right knee, right hip forward. This movement pulls your right shoulder down...

RELAXED

... and keeps your arms inside ready for strike. It is from your shoulders down going back and work from your feet upwards going forward.

UPSTAIRS going back
DOWNSTAIRS forward

CHAPTER 12

Your wrists are your engine

(See diagram 81).

I am often asked what is the most important thing in the game from the teaching point of view, or if I was given five minutes what would I choose to talk on, or, alternatively, is there one thing above everything else that is most important in the game.

I always keep coming back to one point. It is this that you have to learn to hit the ball first and control it later. Most of the established tour players have already conquered the first aspect and are seeking to refine the other. Hence, their coaching is based around this control concept most of the time. On the other hand the majority of potentially good players who **come to me for tuition are seeking the first – to hit the ball a maximum distance with less effort.** The problem arises from their natural interest in improving and this actually works against them, for they generally speaking, read up on any material they feel might help them. This advice is written by tour professionals whom the magazine owners feel will sell copies for them. The distance factor does not enter this class of player's theorising. It is also true to say that they are at their physical peak at the top of their professions.

All this leads up to the fact that there is **a huge gulf between the tour professional and the potentially good player,** and even more between **the tour professional and the novice.** He can have no idea of how little the novice knows, or how he actually feels when, for example, stands on the first tee and wonders is he going to hit it right, left, sky, top or even hit a corker. To quote Henry Longhurst, "I sometimes wonder whether the likes of me – I will not say us – can really be helped by the likes of Jack Nicklaus. He cannot have any conception, fortunately enough, of what it feels to be like me. Tuck a pillow in front of his trousers, enfeeble his left eye, drain three quarters of his strength from his hands and fingers, make him pant when walking up slopes and cause the blood to rush to his head if the ball falls off the tee and he has to bend down to pick it up again, and he might begin to get the idea." It is hard for the tour player to comprehend the situation where every shot is a "one-off situation". Now I know we all have "inflated" ideas about our game. That is why it is said that "golf is the greatest game of all to play badly". Your partner in a fourball could after a few "sweetners" at the bar start to describe some of his

YOUR WRISTS ARE YOUR ENGINE

Diagram 81

"Think of the stone on the end of the string."

ignore the shaft . . .

feel the head.

In the same way as you feel a stone at the end of a string, you should feel the clubhead at the end of the shaft.

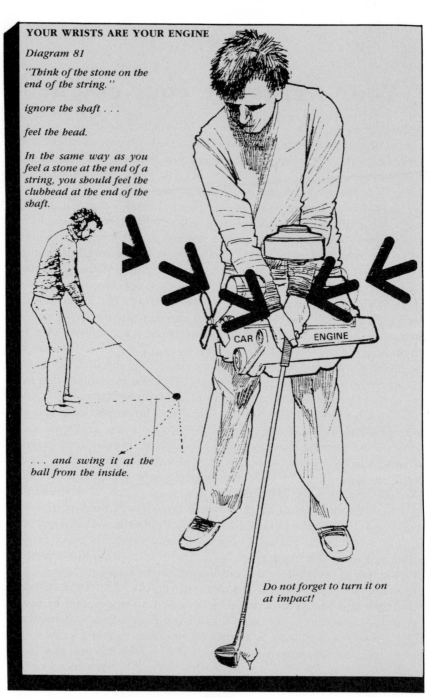

. . . and swing it at the ball from the inside.

Do not forget to turn it on at impact!

more classical strokes, to the extent you begin to wonder if you were in the same fourball as him at all or if he was talking about someone else. To quote Tommy Armour, the legendary Scottish golfer, "The expert player manages to hit between six or eight good shots in every round, the rest are good misses . . ."

We manage to disguise it through the handicap system. (When have you last heard a club player talk of his gross score, he always refers to the nett.) The problem relates to the fact that the vast majority do not come to the game until they have reached their late twenties, early thirties or even later. The tour player on the other hand, is in his twenties, at the peak of his fitness, and generally wants "width" in his swing with a good "extension" through the ball – to keep it on line. This **body teaching works very badly for the potentially good player** because, first of all, **he does not have the physical fitness, the strength, the agility – the engine of the other.** In fact many times he is a successful businessman who in his quest for success in the business world neglected his physical fitness. His whole life is conditioned towards success so he proceeds to attack golf like he did his job. With the **untrained and neglected body which has been the price he has paid for his long struggle for success, he attempts to play like the top tour players!**

The net result is that the potentially good player often misinterprets what is written and goes away with something like "hit the ball with your legs" – with the result that his body tends to move ahead of the clubhead on his down swing, or "extension on the back swing" – he starts his back swing on the outside.

Delegate the clubhead to work for you

"**The engine or power part of your body is your wrists**". It boils down to one thing, the potentially good player, once he has organised himself for the shot should forget the body talk, and turn away on the back swing, but when he is hitting the ball realise that his engine or the power part of his body is his wrists. They are where you are going to get your power from. In many cases, the theorising from still photos causes one to come upon the idea that one must hold one's wrists still when one is hitting the ball or, to lead with the left all the way. *(See diagrams 82, 83)*.

The most important thing in the game is to use the wrists when striking the ball. If you don't, what happens is that the clubhead and your arms are travelling at the same speed through the ball. This results in a lack of distance and no control. **The ability to "crack the whip", "skip the stone over the water"** (using an underhand movement) **or**

105

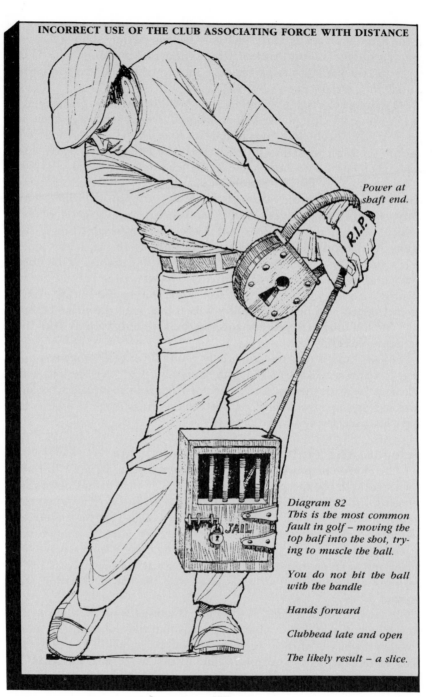

Power at shaft end.

Diagram 82
This is the most common fault in golf – moving the top half into the shot, trying to muscle the ball.

You do not hit the ball with the handle

Hands forward

Clubhead late and open

The likely result – a slice.

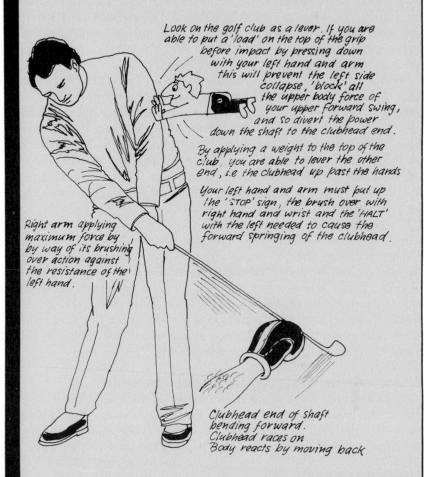

Look on the golf club as a lever. If you are able to put a 'load' on the top of the grip before impact by pressing down with your left hand and arm this will prevent the left side collapse, 'block' all the upper body force of your upper forward swing, and so divert the power down the shaft to the clubhead end.

By applying a weight to the top of the club, you are able to lever the other end, i.e the clubhead up past the hands

Your left hand and arm must put up the 'STOP' sign, the brush over with right hand and wrist and the 'HALT' with the left needed to cause the forward springing of the clubhead.

Right arm applying maximum force by by way of its brushing over action against the resistance of the left hand.

Clubhead end of shaft bending forward. Clubhead races on Body reacts by moving back

You must learn to work the right hand against the left in a scissors movement, with the springing of the clubhead on the ball.

give the clubhead a swish with your wrist against the resistance of a solid left arm is the most important. Suddenly the ball begins to "fly" with no effort. *(See diagram 84)*.

Don't force the feel, feel the force of the clubhead
Swing slow but let the clubhead go!
There are a few pitfalls however. **Don't confuse fast hands with a fast swing.** They are completely different. **You could be swinging very fast and your clubhead might not be moving nearly so fast.** If you want to really move the ball you will have to move the clubhead and it is your wrists that will move it for you. The secret is in the wrists.

Another pitfall is to try the routine with the "big sticks" on the full shots. Like a lot of things in life you have to "sneak up on it". Try doing it this way. **Take an eight iron and practise chipping the ball** using a short back swing. Be careful not to roll the wrists on the take-away. Keep everything quiet going back – not too slow, in tempo. Do not speed up coming into the ball, **just use your wrists to propel the ball forward, give it a flick with your wrists like tossing a line out to fish.** Don't look for distance and for the first time in your life, **"feel the power of the clubhead".** Think clubhead.

When you have experienced it with one club you can use it with them all. Practise with the easy ones, then you will have eliminated one problem – hitting the ball with a difficult club. You are then able to concentrate on working **"release the clubhead with your wrists"** into your game. Use this with all clubs – look at the face of the driver, look at the name on the head whatever it may be, Lee Trevino, Jack Nicklaus – take a motto **"Make Jack do the work"** – **give him a swish with your wrists and once again not a fast swing** – final motto **"swing slow but let the clubhead go".**

Ways to practise release of the clubhead
(1) One way is by turning the club upside down and gripping the club by the head. While you are swinging try **to make a "whipping" noise** with the shaft through the hitting area. If the shaft is moving at the same speed as your arms, there will not be any whipping noise.

Flick clubhead with your right wrist
(2) Practise placing the clubhead in heavy grass, then make a normal swing but **practise swinging the clubhead through the heavy grass.** The golfer with the best hand action in the world is undoubtably Severiano Ballesterous. It is interesting to note that he was not allowed to practise on the fairways as a young man. He had to practise in the

rough and **so developed great hand action.** If you are on the fairway and want to **impersonate** the feel, imagine you are in heavy rough and are trying to **whip the ball out of the grass.** Develop the mentality that if somebody was to put a hand in to stop the clubhead, you would whip the hand off.

(3) **Put a stone on the end of a piece of string and practise swinging.** In the same way as you feel the stone at the end of the string, you should try to feel the clubhead at the end of the shaft. *(See diagram 85).*

(4) A fourth way is to look on it like as if you were hammering a nail into a piece of timber, you would not swing your whole body at the nail, instead you would use a wrist action to release the head of the hammer at the nail. An even better example is splitting a log with an axe. **You have to let the head of the axe do the splitting for you** in the same way as the clubhead moves the ball. Look on the clubhead like the head of the axe. Feel that just as you **swing the head of the axe at the piece of timber you are swinging the clubhead at the ball.**

(5) A fifth way of practising the release of the wrists is to look on it as if the hands are the centre-point. Imagine that they are not moving laterally but only the wrists and the clubhead are. It is like pulling elastic and then letting it go, but not going with it.

Diagram 84
Strike with the right hand. Use your strong hand when striking in order to prevent a slice and obtain your maximum distance.

Repeat this action when striking the ball

109

Separation: free the clubhead from your body swing

Releasing the clubhead means freeing the clubhead in your swing from your overall swing. In other words you do not go with the clubhead through the hitting area but you let the clubhead go. Remember the locked swing is one where there is no wrist-cock and the body moves into hitting area leaving clubhead behind. Releasing the clubhead starts by realising that it is the clubhead and not yourself that moves the ball, and becoming aware of it. In the swing, **start by waggling the clubhead and make certain of the wrist-cock on the top of the back swing and on the down swing just let clubhead go.**

Try this drill. Get a piece of elastic, stretch it between your hands and let it go from your right hand, it will immediately smack off your left hand. Now stretch it again and as you release the elastic from your right hand let the hand go with it. The speed with which it smacks off your left hand is greatly reduced. It is the same with the clubhead, you either let if off (release it) or go with it and so reduce clubhead speed. **Release the bottom end of the club against the resistance of your top end, i.e. left hand, arm and left shoulder.** *(See diagram 86)*.

A way of practising this while you are in a sitting position is to place your arms along your knees and practise moving your right hand over

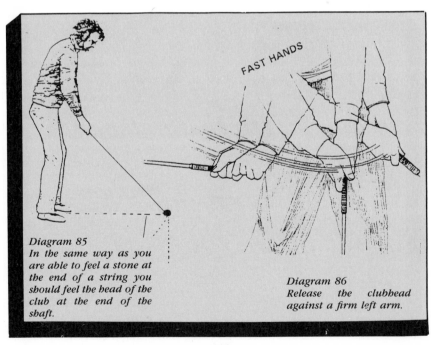

FAST HANDS

Diagram 85
In the same way as you are able to feel a stone at the end of a string you should feel the head of the club at the end of the shaft.

Diagram 86
Release the clubhead against a firm left arm.

your left without moving your arms. This position prevents you from moving your arms. Unfortunately, if somebody mentions releasing the wrists the golfer tends to speed up his swing, and get even more ahead of the ball at impact. It is not until he realises that a fast clubhead has nothing to do with a fast swing that he or she understands what releasing the wrists really means.

While you are there, try out this exercise (without a club)

EXPERIENCE THE SUCCESSFUL RELEASE OF THE POWER OF YOUR SWING EFFORT

THINK CLUBHEAD

There is no need to stand up for this exercise as it can be practised from a sitting position. Extend your left arm, relax it slightly. Repeat that exercise a number of times. Think of "impact".

As you think of impact extend it again. Associate a firm left arm with your impact position.

Hold your left arm in an extended position. Relax it slightly.

Place your right arm behind your back. "Swing" your right hand forward from well inside and as you swing it "past" your left hand immediately stretch your left arm down towards the ball area (a scissors move).

The sensation you should begin to experience is that of striking with your right hand as your left arm is resisting. A collision of "forces" with clubhead the real "beneficiary".

Finally, grab a club and take a "simulated" correct two-handed grip as if about to take a shot. Think of "impact" again. Lock left elbow as you speed up the clubhead.

Swing your arms back a short distance (in one piece, of course, and very much inside). Whip-lash your right hand wrist forward as you "resist" with your left elbow. Your right hand brushes over your left, as the left wrist hinges back. (Note it is not a turn over of your right hand it is a "releasing" of your wrists.)

You have experienced "resistance" high and "power" low. Henry Cotton once remarked: "You must train your right hand to be **clever** - not strong."

111

On the practise ground

Try this with a number eight iron (hitting short shots), using the one-piece inside very short back swing, resisting high on the forward swing and suddenly your clubhead will begin to explode with "power" through impact. Not only that, but you will also have a firm left arm at impact and an extended follow through.

Finish your swing with a very short follow through – holding your left arm in a locked-up position, fully extended. The drill is to release the bottom of the stick (clubhead) against or "into" a solid left arm.

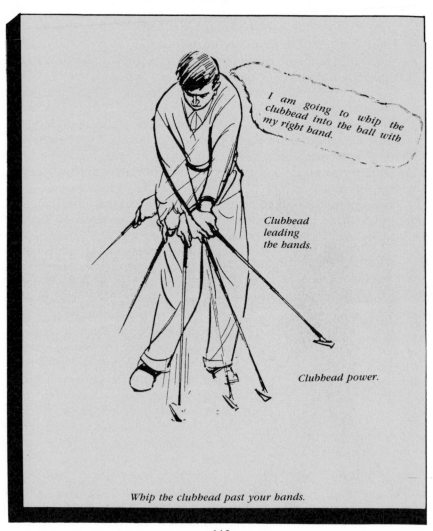

Whip the clubhead past your hands.

SPECIAL LESSON 9

PAROLE THE CLUBHEAD

The secret to the strike.
How to get rid of your slice.
How to gain distance without effort.
Why is it so **difficult to produce clubhead speed and so easy to produce body speed on your down swing?**

Because you must reverse everything you have done on your back swing on the down swing. The vast majority of golfers, unfortunately, repeat everything on both sides of their swings – he/she turns the shoulders going back and turns going forward – a normal reaction.

Ben Hogan once remarked that for **every natural instinct you have, you must do the opposite** and only then will you come near the perfect swing. It is a game of opposites.

If you swing left, the ball tends to go to the right. If you swing down on the ball it tends to rise. If you swing low along the ground and strike the ball high up, it will have a low trajectory. If you swing hard you lose distance.

The vital point is that if it feels right to you it is probably wrong. If it seems wrong to you, it is probably right in a golf context. It is like the medicine of long ago, the worse the taste the better it was deemed to be. **In other words, you must never try to apply normal every-day logic to golf.** Forget it.

Why is this so? One reason is that we are put in a dilemma in golf. We are given a stick and told – there is the ball on the ground; now go and strike it. But how? We cannot go directly behind it and croquet style it forward. No, **we must stand to one side and try somehow to "angle" it forward.** This "side standing" changes a whole lot of things. It creates a lot of angles we must consider. Couple this with the introduction of dimples and inevitable spin – now we have a difficult game.

Let us now consider the strike.
What is the whole idea of your back swing? It is of course to set up a shallow angle of approach and above all to **store energy and produce clubhead speed not body speed.** You must therefore concentrate on the **outer extremity.** The farthest away point from you is the clubhead.

To be blessed with the faith to trust it – way out there – to do the job for you. (The clubhead is three feet approx. away from your hands and two months from your **Brain!**). No! You want to do it yourself. Your natural reaction is to **move your shoulders into the down**

113

WRONG

PAROLE THE CLUBHEAD

*Swing power escaped –
thus weak-clubhead-power.
Power here is at wrong
end of shaft – grip end –
as left arm has collapsed.
There is no solid base for
the lower end of club
to be released.*

CORRECT
*Resist at handle end,
strike at head end.
the ball . . .*

*Power stored
and used
at clubhead.*

*Note: The one reason why
the vast majority of golfers
never improve is because
the energy they create in
their swings is allowed
escape by the collapse
of the left side through impact.*

*Note: Left hand pressing
back against the emerging
force of the upper body
and so blocks upper body force,
levers it down the shaft
and creates power at
clubhead end where it
is very useful.*

*This illustration shows
clearly the player
deflecting the power of
his swing away from
his shoulders down the
shaft by blocking the
forward thrust of his
swing with his left arm
and hand and so causing
the shaft to bend on the ball.*

*You should try to
bend the lower
end of the shaft
on the ball.*

swing. The result is that the clubhead arrives slovenly on to the ball and a sloppy strike results.

Your back swing is all about turning your shoulders against the resistance of your right knee. **Your down swing is all about resisting the impulse to turn your shoulders into the shot. It is about transferring the stored energy from your back swing down to the clubhead end of the shaft and so produce a clubhead speeding.** If the clubhead must speed, it only follows that the body – i.e. the top half of your body – must slow down and resist the impulse to turn into the shot in order to provide a solid base and to allow the actual outer extremity to come forward.

Release the clubhead against a solid left side. Use your left side as the launching pad for the clubhead. The launch pad must provide a solid base.

On your down swing you must start down with your legs – this forward move with your legs pulls your arms down inside. From this position **you must do all in your power to hold your left shoulder back and allow the clubhead to come up for the strike.** You must do the exact opposite to what you consider to be normal. You must hold your left shoulder turn, and as you are swinging forward use **your left hand as a resistance and push it back against the grip** in order for the other end, i.e. the clubhead, to move forward. Use your left arm as the resistance. **Block the forward power of your swing and transfer the power down the shaft** – and allow the clubhead to catch up. **Press your left hand down the shaft, use your right hand against the press to bring the clubhead up.** It is like pressing the top end of a crowbar to increase the power of leverage at the bottom end.

Remember if you are in a car travelling at 70 mph another car must be travelling at 70 + in order to pass out. **The faster your top half moves the less chance the clubhead has of catching up.** Hit against a firm left side, left knee, a firm left arm, and left hand at impact. **Use this resistance to parole the clubhead end of the shaft – to release it. If your left arm collapses at impact there is no resistance,** nothing to release from. Use the left hand as a base for the release.

Every golfer, ever the beginner, creates great power in his/her swing. This **power, alas, usually stays at the wrong end of the club, i.e. the grip or body end, for the duration of the swing.** If you are to become a top class player, you must be able at impact to **transfer all your swing power, to compress it down the shaft on to the clubhead.** Remember from the top of your back swing, there is always going to be a race between your hands and the clubhead as to which of them reach the ball first. Your hands have a huge advantage at the top of your back swing as they have much less of a distance to travel. You must be **able to hold your hands back and allow the clubhead**

115

come forward and pass out your hands with flying colours through your hitting area. This is the one secret of golf. To achieve it you must react against what nature has conditioned you to do, **to swing the clubhead forward and keep the top half back.** Resistance is low (right knee) on your back swing and high (left side) on forward swing, i.e. to deflect the power to the working end of your golf club. Think of an elevator – the power is stored on the second floor, on your back swing – however, you must drop it all down to the first floor if you are to benefit from it at impact. **Most golfers spend their time fooling around the wrong floor.**

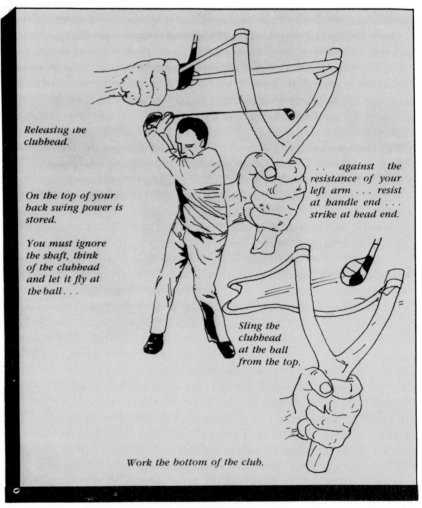

Releasing the clubhead.

On the top of your back swing power is stored.

You must ignore the shaft, think of the clubhead and let it fly at the ball . . .

. . against the resistance of your left arm . . . resist at handle end . . . strike at head end.

Sling the clubhead at the ball from the top.

Work the bottom of the club.

CHAPTER 13

On the golf course

1. How to learn experience.
2. How to develop experience.
3. How to gain experience with the easy clubs.
4. **How to be an experienced golfer.**

The established player cannot explain experience to the novice. It may have taken him years to acquire it. The experienced player has certain knowledge of how he is going to perform, a definite feel for the game and is free to express himself. The novice is "locked" out.

The game itself in its traditions works against the novice. The people who played golf in the earliest days were from the privileged classes. Consider that a gutta percha cost four and six pence or twenty-two and a half pence way back in 1848. They had plenty of time on their hands and they did not have to answer to anybody and maybe this explains why the game takes so long, mainly because they were not in a hurry anywhere. In the modern world the novice does not have as much time on his hands. **Most of the time he is trying to practise when he is playing.** His motto should be – **don't play to practise, but practise to play.** *(See diagram 88).*

Who needs a handicap

The second big influence on the game was the British army who spread the game through the colonial world. The emphasis was on rules, regulations, standards, and so on. Almost immediately on joining the club the novice is given a handicap and is initiated into behaviour code. This handicap sets a certain set of expectations from him. For example, with a handicap of eighteen, he is expected to play to eighteen above par. If he exceeds his expectations and plays well he is on a "streak", labelled a "bandit". His handicap is reduced and a new set of standards are set for him. If on the other hand he plays worse than his handicap he is labelled a "hacker" and is to be avoided by other members until he improves. He becomes increasingly taken up by the system of standards, competitions and the handicapping system that goes with it. **As a result he has so many worries about keeping up to what others expect of him and what he expects of himself that his fears are preventing him from performing.** In other words most of his energies are taken up with what can go wrong, what others will

Diagram 88
It was at one time a game for the elite only at St. Andrews.

Charles Lees R S A   C. E. Wagstaffe, Engraver

1. Sir John Muir Mackenzie of Delvin, Bart.
2. Sir John Murray Macgregor, Bart.
3. O. Tyndall Bruce, Esq., of Falkland
4. Sir Charles Shaw
5. Col. Playfair of St. Andrews
6. The Earl of Eglinton
7. Robert Lindsay, Esq., of Straiton
8. James Hay, Esq., Leith
9. Earl of Leven and Melville
10. A. Robertson, golf-ball maker, St. Andrews
11. Sheriff Gordon
12. John Sligo of Carmyle
13. Hamilton Anstruther, Esq.
14. John Whyte Melville, Esq.
15. Lord Berridale
16. F. Blair, Esq., of Balkhayock
17. The Master of Strathallan
18. John Grant, Esq., of Kilgraston
19. J. Wolfe Murray, Esq., of Cringlettie
20. J. Ogilvie Fairlie, Esq., of Coodham
21. John Hay, Esq., of Morton
22. Sir David Baird, Bart., of Newbyth
23. Major Playfair of St. Andrews
24. Thomas Patton, Esq.
25. Sir Ralph Anstruther, Bart.
26. John Balfour, Esq., of Balbirnie
27. Hon. David Murray
28. John Stirling, St. Andrews
29. James Condie, Esq., Perth
30. Col. Murray Belches of Invermay
31. James H. Dundas, Esq., W.S.
32. James Blackwood, Esq.
33. James Oliphant, Esq., W.S.
34. Charles Robertson, Esq.
35. Sir N. M. Lockhart, Bart., Carnwath
36. Robert Chambers, Esq.
37. Col. Moncrieff
38. Lord Viscount Valentia
39. John Campbell, Esq., of Glensaddel
40. Henry Macfarlane, Esq., M.D., Perth
41. W. Pirrie—a caddie
42. Sir John Campbell of Airds
43. Hon. Henry Coventry
44. George Cheape, Esq., of Wellfield
45. W. Dun, golf-club maker, Musselburgh
46. Captain David Campbell
47. W. Peddie, Esq., of Black Ruthven
48. W. Wood, Esq., Leith
49. G. Dempster, Esq., of Skibo
50. W. Goddard, Esq., Leith
51. Robert Patullo, Esq., St. Andrews
52. Sandie Pirrie
53. Ginger-beer girl
54. St. Andrews

118

think, that he has little time left himself. For instance if you put a plank down two feet wide and ten feet long, and ask somebody to walk it, there is no problem. Now put the plank from one skyscraper to another under the same conditions and ask him to walk the plank. That person would be so taken up with fear of failing or falling that he would be unable to put one foot in front of the other. **In a competitive situation the fear of failing prevents the golfer from performing.**

If he is to break this barrier he has to challenge the whole system of competitions and handicapping. He must realise that the secret of living is to stop **competing and to stop thinking of other's expectations.** Only when he or she discovers that the vast majority are caught up in themselves and really don't give a hoot about him except if he **interferes with their enjoyment,** is he released from web. In other words stop trying to live up to other's expectations and even your own expectations. Forget about the **worldly aspect of the game,** the prizes, the praise, the things we are conscious of. Say to yourself they are not for me. It is a fallacy to say you have to compete at golf. In ordinary life you have to compete in order to survive, and when you are in the home you have to encourage your family to compete, **if they are to become like you!** Doesn't it make sense then that when you come to the club you don't bother competing. Relax, play to have fun!. When somebody asks what is your handicap you should say I don't have one, **I just play the game.** Immediately there are no expectations, no standards for yourself or others. You have moved your game down from the skyscraper to the ground and with it **the fear of failing is gone.** All you have to do is walk the plank, just hit the ball, and you will have the energy to develop a feel for the game, and the freedom to express it.

119

Diagram 89
Grip the club loosely and develop . . .

for the head of the club.

When hitting a full shot imagine you are hitting a big chip.

Diagram 89a
Educating the hands about the clubhead

How to develop experience

How do you develop experience? First you have to understand the basics. For example, an open club face causes a slice and a closed one a hook . . . Learning the way you organise yourself before you swing determines the way you swing. If you want to change the shot, change the way you stand to it. You cannot see your swing, so it is very hard **to develop a swing as you do not know what you might be developing!** There are two ways in which you can. One is if you can manage to see your swing **on video.** Now you know where you are. For example, if it is an upright swing you flatten it and so on . . . Most people will readily admit that they can see the fault in the other fellow's swing but they don't know what they are doing wrong themselves. When you are looking at your own swing on video, **you are looking at the other fellow's swing!** The other way is **imitation, just watch a good player swing and learn from him.**

Most of all what the experienced player has over the beginner is a feel for the game. It is a knowledge of where the clubhead is during the swing, and more especially at impact. What you have to do is to think clubhead, **try to feel where it is during your swing and more especially when you are hitting the ball.**

"Feel is an awakening, an awareness about the clubhead." The way to experience "feel" is having rid the mind of expectations, results and so on, realise it is the lump of metal at the end of the shaft you are swinging that moves the ball. Get rid of all the jargon, the positions, the theory, get a feeling for swinging the clubhead and letting it go at the ball. An experienced player from Lahinch was once asked by an American tourist how it was he could draw the ball or hook it at will. He was expecting a very technical reply but he said: "To tell u the trut I dust tink hook." Just think clubhead, and you will develop a feel for it and experience hitting the ball with the head of the club and you will be on the same level as the established player. *(See 89, 89a).*

How to gain experience

You have to educate the hands to feel the clubhead. To do this you have to work the clubhead with your hands, or move the ball with it using your hands in different ways. Take out a number nine iron or a wedge and practise chipping the ball, not forgetting that the way you organise yourself beforehand determines the way you swing and the shot you hit. If you want to change the shot you change the way you stand to it. There is, however, a little more to it than this and it is to be aware of what is happening your hands when you are hitting the ball. Take, for example, the "cut-up chip shot" where your hands hold

121

Diagram 90
It's the head you
aim at the target.

Diagram 91
Approach with the
head . . .

Diagram 92
Be aware of the
head aimed at the
flag.

Diagram 94
Swing back of left
hand to flag.

Diagram 93
Ball back in stance
weight on left foot.

Low punch shot!

the clubface open when you are hitting the ball. The shot is played with a steep out-to-in swing using an open clubface making contact with the bottom of the ball and thus creating plenty of back-spin on it.

How to experience the chip and run shot

The chip and run shot is a miniature draw or hook shot. In this shot you roll the clubface through the ball with your hands. The technique is to turn right hand over left as you are hitting the ball. The shot is played using a shallow in-to-out swing where your hands turn the club face closed through the hitting area, creating little or no back-spin on the ball. First we must organise for it.

Aim the face of the club at the flag.

Adopt a slightly stronger grip.

Stand slightly closed or in-to-out, which creates a shallow angle of approach to the ball.

Swing along the line of your body.

Be aware of working your right hand through the ball by turning it over the left, and so turning the club face closed. *(See diagrams 90, 91, 92, 93)*.

How to experience the low punch shot

The low punch chip shot is a cousin of the draw. The only difference being that, instead of turning your hands over, you hold **your left hand facing the target for longer or keep your hands ahead through the hitting area.** First you must organise for it.

Aim the club at the target.

Position hands ahead of ball or simply play back in stance towards right foot. This closes down the position of the shoulders, feet and hips creating a shallow approach on ball. To help you to keep your hands ahead through the hitting area move your weight forward onto your left foot.

Swing straight back and be aware that you are **keeping your hands ahead when you are hitting the ball.** You will get a low flying ball with little movement on it. It is a great three quarter shot in the wind. You have to move up two clubs in order to play it. *(See diagram 94)*.

How to experience the cut-up chip shot

Aim the face of the club at the flag.

Weaken the grip as this equals an open clubface.

Stand open and this will result in a steep out-to-in attack on the ball.

Swing along the line of your body (out-to-in) holding the club-face open or pointing skywards which will create spin.

Diagram 95 Approach with the head

Diagram 96 aim it at the flag. Aim body
with left.

Diagram 98
. . . slide it under ball holding club-
face open (pointing skyward).

Diagram 97
Take club back on the outside

Be aware of the feeling of sliding the clubhead under the ball "cutting the legs from under ball", or holding the clubface open with your hands when you are hitting the ball. *(See diagrams 95, 96, 97, 98).*

How to play like an experienced golfer *(Diagram 99)*

Once again the same rules apply for long game as for the short game. You must have a good grounding in the basics understanding that the way you organise yourself determines the way you swing and therefore the resulting shot. If you want to change the shot all you have to do is change the way you are holding the club and the way you are standing to the ball. **For example the way you put your hands on the grip determines the way the clubface will be at impact and the way you stand determines your swing line. The shot is a result of the direction of your swing-line and the angle the clubface is at impact open, square or closed.** *(See diagram 99a).*

The square club – shot on target.

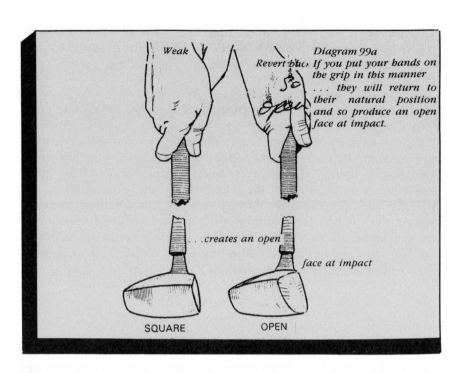

Weak

Revert back

Diagram 99a
If you put your hands on the grip in this manner ... they will return to their natural position and so produce an open face at impact.

...creates an open

face at impact

SQUARE   OPEN

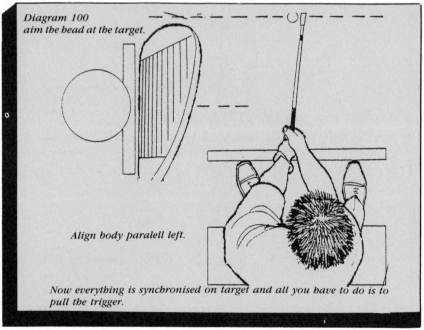

Diagram 100
aim the head at the target.

Align body paralell left.

Now everything is synchronised on target and all you have to do is to pull the trigger.

How to experience a shot on target!

Central must be the realisation that the whole game is based around the clubhead. The need is to aim the clubhead at the target and if you do this all the bits and pieces will tend to fall into place. **If you have your clubhead pointing at the target and your body parallel to the target-line at address, you will have a good chance of swinging along the line of your body and having the clubhead pointing at the target at impact.**

To summarise: Preparation is understanding and organising.

Aim the clubhead at the target. Stand parallel to the target-line or swing line. You grip in such a way that the clubface at impact will be pointing at the target.

Let us now play a shot on target

Preparation equals understanding the importance of the clubhead and the need to aim it at the target because, if the ball is going to fly to the target at impact, the clubhead must be moving towards and pointing at the target. *(See diagram 100).*

Aim. Following the routine **aim clubhead at the target.**

Address. Taking a grip that will bring back the face square or pointing at target.

Giving weaker left side a preference and having strong right side is a supporting role.

Positioning face, hips and shoulders parallel to the target line.

Everything is now synchronised on target. All you have to do is "pull the trigger".

Swing along the line of your body, being aware of moving the left side back and **release the clubhead through the ball against the resistance of a solid left side.**

Have an awareness of clubhead, where it is during your swing and especially at impact. It is a protection against "useless" theorising because awareness of what the clubhead is doing leads to developing a relationship with the clubhead from which you will develop a game.

Let us experience the draw shot

Preparation – a draw shot results from an "in-to-out" swing with the clubface slightly closed to the swing line.

Aim clubhead at target.

Ensure that your left hand is on grip in such a way that the clubhead will be slightly closed at impact (use three knuckle grip).

Align body – feet, hips, shoulders pointing in an in-to-out direction or stand "in-to-out".

127

Swing along line of body and be aware of turning away at the start of take-away and clubhead returning to the ball **with right hand working, rotating through impact and left hand resisting.**

A draw shot results from an in to out swing with clubface slightly closed to swing line. If you prepared in such a way that you aim the **clubhead at target and align body slightly right of target,** you now have lined your clubhead slightly left of where you are aiming and so have set the angle needed for the draw shot, i.e. **the clubhead slightly closed to swing line.** *(See diagram 101).*

To conclude, if you are to play a more experienced game, you have to rid the mind of all expectations, fears and **understand the implements you will be using,** the way they work and their limitations. Play the game in the knowledge that the **way you play** is determined by the way you **organise yourself** beforehand, and above all have an **awareness** of what your clubhead is doing during your swing. Develop a ''feel'' for it and ''mould'' a relationship with it.

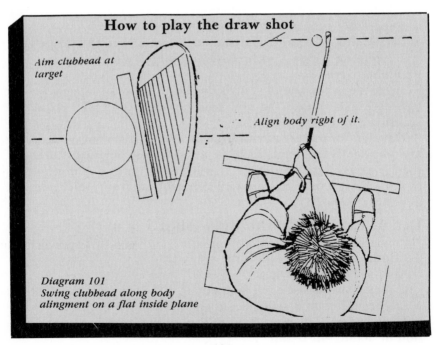

How to play the draw shot

Aim clubhead at target

Align body right of it.

Diagram 101
Swing clubhead along body alingment on a flat inside plane

128

Diagram 103
Play your own game.

IF IT WORKS USE IT!

Aggressive person.

Cautious person.

You should play to your **tendencies!**

CHARLES
MACNEILL

CHAPTER 14

If it works use it

There is a great golfer waiting to come out in me
(See diagram 103).

Let us say that we all rely on basic principles of a system no matter what job we decide to do. Of course the secret is getting a system that works. Take for instance the McDonald hamburger chain; it is just one system that worked and was repeated over and over again. It is the same with golf. However, even though we rely on a well tried system we will always put our own mark on the proceedings. Once we have **established our play and are having success with it we should not change our way of expressing ourselves.**

I am often amazed at established players even the very top professionals deciding to change the way they hit the ball in their quest for perfection. What they are sure to get is imperfection.

While we depend on basic principles in dealing with the game we should **never forget that we are unique in physical and mental make-up. This is why personal idiosyncrasies should be guarded like the crown jewels.**

For example, the idea of changing nearly always comes from a rational judgement. "Wouldn't he be a truly great player if he did not have a very strong left hand grip!" He may play very well with a strong left hand grip. If he is foolish enough to listen, there is one thing he can be sure of, that is a loss of form from which he may take years to recover or indeed never. There are numerous examples of this. Hal Sutton had a bad year in 1985. The previous year he was the leading money winner on the U.S. Tour. The reason was, he decided to weaken his grip and his form slumped. He was called a one year wonder. He was, however, fortunate enough to be paired with, arguably the best player in the world, Bernhard Langer in a 1985 Ryder Cup match. Langer absolutely thrashed him in the match but he did notice Bernhard's grip. It is a very strong left-hand grip. He decided to revert to his old grip even though it wasn't exactly according to the book and his form returned. **The secret of success is firstly self-discovery and then to express yourself. If anything accentuate your differences.** *(See diagram 104).*

Star player!

DON'T FOLLOW LIKE SHEEP, DEVELOP YOUR OWN GAME

Andrew McKellor was the first golfing maniac. He became so obsessed with the game that he neglected his business. He played all day and at night with the help of a lantern light. His wife brought his meals to him on the course. He died in 1813.

It also makes sense to say "why change?"

If you have something that works it does because of previous experience. You have brought your work to a fruition and you should trust your past. **Your past knows more about you than anybody else.**

Through endless hours of practise your body has found a **way of expressing itself physically and mentally.** This you should continue to do.

When you reach a higher level the pressure is on you to try for perfection to change what looks like a fault in your set-up or swing but **you could lose it all.**

We have our own way of doing things, and have groomed our own way of hitting the ball. We have also a certain temperament. It may be **cautious like Ben Hogan or bold like Severiano Ballesteros.**

Mentally you may be aggressive and this is your style, so you go for it. **That is the way you play.** Take the legendary Arnold Palmer. He was an attacking player. In the late 60s and early 70s he was going through a slump. So, he began to think that maybe his approach was wrong. He decided to change, to model himself on Ben Hogan, a cautious player who played the percentages. **If he was in a slump he soon realised that it had not bottomed out** and he became like a novice on the tour. His form did not return until he reverted to his old ways of generally going for everything.

It often happens that something becomes fashionable and is deemed the way to do it. I am reminded of eminent child psychologist Dr. Spock, who wrote that the way parents should rear their children was to give them a free hand. If they learn from breaking a window then let them go ahead! A whole generation was affected, and millions of people (a lot of glass). He married late in life, but his second book was an apology for his first.

The point I want to make is that you should never follow along like a sheep. Trust yourself, your own mind and physical way of doing things. A good example of this was when the swing was first broken down by the camera. It became obvious to the experts that all the top players were in what is called, **a late-hitting position** before they hit the ball. This, they said, was where they were getting the power. In other words their hands had nearly reached the ball while the clubhead was back at hip height. The power came from the release of the clubhead where the hands moved forward only inches while the clubhead moved feet and caught up with the hands in a whiplash effect through the hitting area. This was the secret, "the late-hit". The result of the still photos was misleading. All the potentially good player

132

succeeded in doing was thinking at the top of his back-swing that no matter whatever else, **he must not swing the club or release the clubhead at the ball. He must go for the late-hit.** If you consider that from the top of the back swing to impact is one fifth of second and if you are trying for the late hit all you will succeed in doing is get a blocked body type shot. **It is accepted now that the late hit is a fallacy, a camera illusion.** Yet many readers were influenced over a period of years and still are to an extent. *(See diagram 106).*

Yet another fashion in the early 70s, was the "fade"'. The motto was "you can talk to a fade but a hook won't listen". Jack Nicklaus played it and he was the best player then, and probably the best ever. If you were to be successful you literally had to use it, especially off the tee, to join the "club". There were many good players who were natural "drawers" of the ball and were influenced and changed around. The result was their game slumped. Sometimes these players **were shorter hitters or small in stature and their bodies told them the way to compete was with the "draw for distance" shot.** One example of this was Bernard Gallagher who had many lean years because of it. He was a natural drawer who tried to play the fade and suffered the consequences. *(See diagram 107).*

At the same time the **upright swing** plane was being put forward as the way to do it. You would need to be as strong as an ox and have all day to practise it. Yet because it was put forward by some leading players **many were influenced and tried to do it.** *(See diagram 108).*

If you are on the practise ground hitting shots well you should not change. Yet another way of killing originality is, as often happens a top amateur turns professional and tries to learn the professional way. He may decide to spend the winter with a renowned teaching professional, who more than likely has his own ideas about the golf swing and even imposes it on the aspiring professional. For example, if the teaching expert had a notion about playing the game with the hands and the pupil was a young, supple, athletical player who played the game with a body-swing, he could be destroyed. I have seen good amateurs with a beautiful long flowing swing spend a winter practising and come back with a short jerky and imperfect one. Remember the good teacher will develop your strong points and not mould you into his own idea of what a golfer should be.

Develop yourself not somebody else

It is like the painter. Many of the great ones perfected a style of their own. It could be landscapes, portraits or buildings. That was their speciality. You must be the same, **what you have working you work to its full potential.**

133

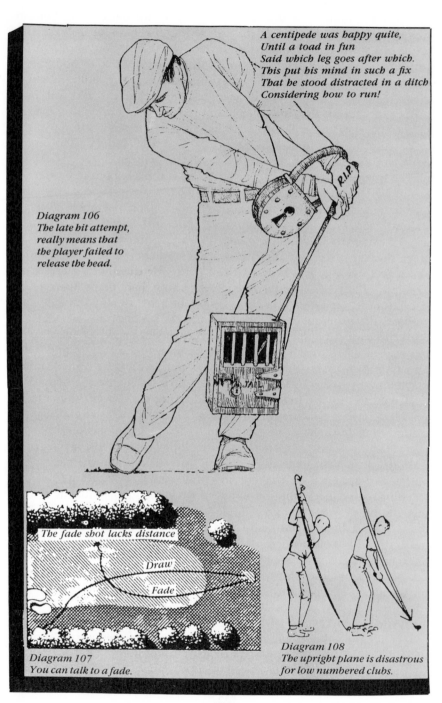

A centipede was happy quite,
Until a toad in fun
Said which leg goes after which.
This put his mind in such a fix
That he stood distracted in a ditch
Considering how to run!

Diagram 106
The late hit attempt,
really means that
the player failed to
release the head.

The fade shot lacks distance

Draw

Fade

Diagram 107
You can talk to a fade.

Diagram 108
The upright plane is disastrous
for low numbered clubs.

The best example of this was the great South African golfer Bobby Locke who had his own peculiar way of hitting a ball. He could play all the shots, but **he stuck to one that he had perfected.** It was the hook shot. He would stand inside very close to the ball and hit hooks. He even hooked his putts. (A putt is a miniature golf shot.) All the methods of playing the game and the teaching were "square to square" and one piece take-away. Yet here was this fellow standing with his back to everything and hitting these massive hooks and, what's more, winning. One day, while he was sitting in a locker room some of his adversaries who resented his style and his nasty habit of putting his hands into their pockets, remarked within earshot: "Isn't it a pity about Locke's left hand grip." He replied: **"Don't worry I am able to take the cheques with my right hand." He would not change his winning ways.** (See diagram 109).

How to avoid going off on useless tangents!

Let us look at the novice first, and see what can go wrong. A great number who take up the game achieve remarkable success at it in the earliest days. There are people who played another ball game and are natural hitters of the ball, and take to golf like a fish to water. They hit the ball a "country-mile" not really knowing how they are doing it. They then decide to learn the right way, and they get lost in the theory game. The novice must know his strengths and develop them by seeking a teacher who will develop what he has rather than something that he has not. Above all, avoid theorising, probing and experimenting. Do not listen to everybody who gives advice. You will end going from one professional to another in the hope to be told something that **will bring about a revolution in your game.** I am reminded of a club player who remarked: "I want to play but I don't want to learn" – meaning he didn't want to have a whole **plethora of instructions hurled at him. You have to be single-minded in what you have and selective in what you want.** If it is a case that you are not happy with your performance, you have to be able to find out where the problem is and correct it. Discover yourself and develop your strong points. Have as your motto "there is a great golfer waiting to come out in me" and **find a teacher who will reveal something you already have and not to try to give you something he has.** (See diagram 110).

Something you have may be outside the classical mould but you are not unique in this. Even Jack Nicklaus and Bernhard Langer, whose golfing talent is awesome, have their idiosyncrasies – Jack's flying elbow and Bernard's left-hand grip, or Paul Azinger's left-hand grip.

135

Bobby Locke's unique swing.

Paralysis by analysis

"You can't divide a swing into parts, a cat is a cat, if you divided it you'll have blood and guts and bones all over, but you won't have any cat!" (E. Jones).

While it is important to have the confidence to hold on to something that works, it is just as important to change what is not working. There are some elements that are outside the natural realms of control. If you have a problem that it outside your control you have to be man enough to admit you have it and that the normal corrective measures simply won't work. It is like the alcoholic who will not admit he has a problem with drink. For example, Bernhard Langer had a real problem with short putts. It was nothing to do with technique. **It was "psychological".** He had the confidence to admit he was not able to do anyting about it, so he had to make a drastic change in his approach, a change that would signify to the world that he had this problem. He took the unusual step of moving his left hand down below his right and it worked.

There are many who have similar problems and won't to them. They go on tinkering with them – changing putters, making imaginary changes in stroke but the problems remain. Missing short putts finished off the careers of many a great golfer.

I remember a priest who was a beautiful striker of the ball, coming to me with a problem. He was "yipping" the putts. The attack was so bad that I could not believe my eyes and I thought he was joking. I asked him: "Have you tried correcting it yourself?" I was hoping for some sort of miracle to happen on the spot. He replied: "I always practise on the carpet in the house." I thought "practising the yip!" This was a case where it was outside his control and normal "cause and effect" cures were no use. I told him there was nothing for it but a whole change of approach – "you will have to putt left handed". I went and took out a new left-handed putter and gave it to him leaving his secondhand putter in my shop. He tried a few putts with the left-handed one and sure enough the jerk was not there. He was at least making a decent stroke with it. I left him on the putting green, thinking that my fame would have spread far and wide because of my curing the incurable, as he was a well-known golfer in the area.

The practise ground is adjacent on the ninth green and I was out giving a lesson one day when I detected in the distance my "prize" coming down the ninth heading in the direction of the green. He was not aware that I was watching him. With his second shot on the green he proceeded to search around his bag for a while. He eventually saunters on to the green with a putter. I was not sure which one it was, so I had to wait and see but lo and behold if he didn't go back to his old yipping ways using the same old putter which he had sneaked back out of the shop in my absence. **His putting was as bad as ever but he wasn't prepared to admit he had a problem that was outside his control, or to look a little bit unusual in order to cure it.**

137

In another game which I am sure you are familiar with, called snooker, there was a player whose eyesight was poor and it was exaggerated by the fact that when he bent down to play a stroke his eyes would be looking at the ball over the glasses. He decided to accept that he had a real problem and went about getting glasses made that were about three times the normal size. He looked odd playing the game – but, when he bent down to hit a shot, his eyes were looking through the glass. Even though he looked odd, he went on to win the world championship the following year.

If you have a real problem, be prepared to admit it and try a completely different approach. If you have chipping yips, be prepared to play with left hand below the right or even to play left handed because this is the only way you are going to cure it.

The mark of the true champion is the one who has the confidence to admit that he has a problem and if need be look a little bit unusual in order to correct it.

Unfortunately, some golfers become linked to a particular problem. Their reputation is linked with it and it often happens that in a strange way it becomes an insurance for the player. He is regarded as a great golfer if it was not for this little problem. In time the player becomes attached to the problem which he loves to hate and develops an obsession with trying to correct it. One could ask who does he really bluff.

Perhaps he is happy to live on with this ''limbo''. Golfers come to me for tuition and sometimes they say ''I have a good short game.'' I immediately suspect they have a bad long game. If I improve their long game their short game tends to disintegrate, partly because of technique but often because the person has found a level of scoring which satisfies the mind. If he was to score much better than before and to win all the time, too much pressure would be put on him mentally and physically, too much for the golfer to take. Hence, this safety valve, **he still has the reputation but not the realisation ''isn't it a pity he cannot chip''.**

If you have something that works, it is worth being single-minded in your resolve to stick to it. On the other hand, if you have a real problem, be man enough to admit it, and avoid it altogether by playing a completely different kind of stroke.

P.S. Special Lesson 10 is an example of how to cure a fault directly.

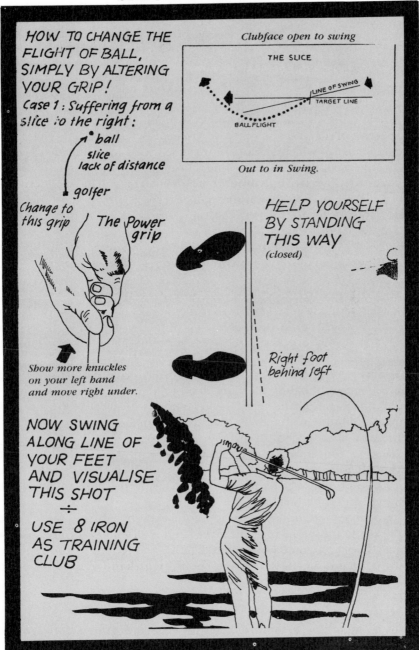

HOW TO CHANGE THE FLIGHT OF BALL, SIMPLY BY ALTERING YOUR GRIP!

Case 1: Suffering from a slice to the right:

ball
slice
lack of distance
golfer

Clubface open to swing

THE SLICE

LINE OF SWING
TARGET LINE
BALL FLIGHT

Out to in Swing.

Change to this grip

The Power grip

Show more knuckles on your left hand and move right under.

HELP YOURSELF BY STANDING THIS WAY (closed)

Right foot behind left

NOW SWING ALONG LINE OF YOUR FEET AND VISUALISE THIS SHOT

÷

USE 8 IRON AS TRAINING CLUB

CHAPTER 15

The short game

It was at the 145 yard, 8th hole at Prestwick in 1868 that Tom Morris achieved the earliest recorded hole in one, and an American Bob Metere is reputed to have recorded the longest hole in one in 1965 at a hole of 447 yards long slightly downhill.

In terms of match-play, one of the many fascinations of its character is the manner in which a competitor can extricate himself from a seemingly irretrievable position, simply through the execution of some devastatingly precise shots around the green. You will have noticed the way galleries at professional tournaments reserve their most enthusiastic applause for the player who can pitch or chip the ball "stiff".

The fact is that many players freeze over this shot, yet it is not in my view a particularly difficult one. **The key to success is the ability to achieve plenty of loft on the ball over a short distance.**

Are you getting height on your chip shots?

If your set-up is correct, this shot should become a formality. If, on the other hand, you are experiencing difficulty in this area, or with your short game in general, then it is time you had a **serious look at your grip.**

In earlier chapters we discussed the correct grip. We explained the consequences of holding the right hand in a hooker's grip, so producing a hook, simply because the clubhead will always be closed at impact. You should remember that hooking applies equally to all shots, delicate shots as it does to driving. *(See diagram 111).*

Another consequence of a closed clubhead is an inability to get sufficient loft on the ball. It can also result in fluffed shots because the angle of approach is too shallow, causing the club to strike the ground before the ball.

We will now consider the set-up for the chip shot. Just as the left side is the key to the long game, the right hand is all-important in the short game. The short game is all about delicacy and feel – the sort of gentle touch a pianist has in his fingers. **Your right-hand grip must be in the fingers.**

Set-up

It is important to ensure that the left-hand grip is through the fingers, while employing an open stance with the feet, allowing plenty

If you are having trouble around the green – it might be your grip.

If you want height and stop on green chip shots.

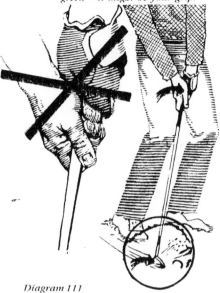

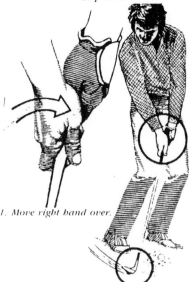

1. Move right hand over.

Diagram 111

THIS GRIP WILL CLOSE THE CLUBFACE AT IMPACT

Diagram 112 *2. This will create an open blade and backspin.*

CORRECT GRIP

SPECIAL BUNKER SHOTS

Chipping out
Use in shallow bunker with
good lie and room for roll.
Open stance, feet close together,
ball off right heel,
open clubface slightly.
Aim at pin, using wrists mostly,
striking ball before sand.

Fairway bunker
In shallow bunker with good lie,
use club with enough loft to clear.
Strike ball as you would off fairway,
hitting down and through.
Don't try to help ball out.

Putting out
Use in shallow bunker with
no lip and good lie.
Play ball off left heel,
strike crisply, don't touch sand.

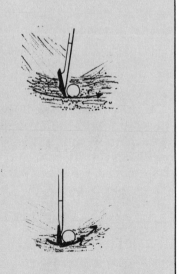

141

of room for the hands to move freely through the impact zone. Then place the clubface behind the ball and aim it at the target.

With the left hand very relaxed, you will play the shot with the fingers of the right hand and, because of the open stance, you are free to swing along the line you feel, slightly out and in. It is because of the weak grip, right hand well over the club, that the club will open automatically through impact, producing the necessary height. *(See diagram 112).*

The sand-shot – the bunker

The word "bunker" itself was first used by Sir Walter Scott to describe shallow hollows used by sheep for shelter and was later used on golf links, where similar hollows gathered the running ball. With the passing of time the bunker deepened and lost its grass mantle as a result of repeated escape shots, particularly when iron clubs became popular. These sandy hollows became the modern bunker and were placed on all golf courses.

The sand-wedge

Bobby Jones used a club which was designed specifically for sand-shots on his way to victory in the British Open at Hoylake in the grand slam year 1930.

It had a convex head and the Royal and Ancient later declared it to be illegal. It was claimed that a player could hit the ball twice during the same swing, because of the large convex face. Gene Sarazen contends that early in 1933, **while taking flying lessons,** he pulled the control stick back, as a consequence noticed the tailflaps go down and the nose simultaneously jut upwards. He immediately related these actions to the principle of sand-play.

If the trailing edge of the sole were lower than the leading edge, the club would cut through the sand more effectively, allowing for an explosion shot without the digging action of the conventional niblick. This is how the sand-wedge was born. Forty-one years later, at the 126 yard, 8th hole, known as the "postage stamp", on Troon golf course in the 1973 Open Gene Sarazen holed out his tee shot.

The bunker shot

With regard to bunker play, it is important to realise that sand, being loose in texture, will react differently than soil. The main problem with a bunker shot occurs when the clubface closes, so allowing the sand to accumulate in front of it causing a "fluffed" shot. Remember the sand-wedge was never meant to be used as a bulldozer.

THE EXPLOSION SHOT

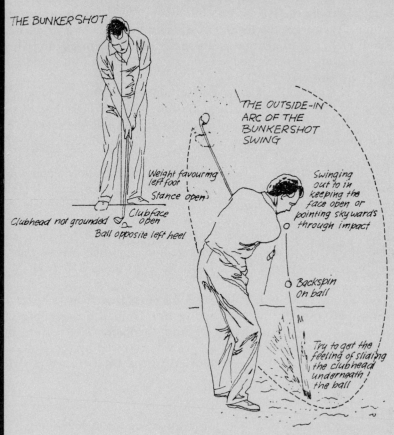

THE BUNKER SHOT

Weight favouring left foot

Stance open

Clubhead not grounded

Clubface open

Ball opposite left heel

THE OUTSIDE-IN ARC OF THE BUNKERSHOT SWING

Swinging out to in keeping the face open or pointing skywards through impact

Backspin on ball

Try to get the feeling of sliding the clubhead underneath the ball

Impact: Strike sand two inches before ball.

Diagram 113

With regard to the sand-shot, the same technique applies as to the short game. **You aim your feet and shoulders left of target, you only aim the clubhead at the target. In order to do this the clubhead must be "laid open".** You should aim the clubhead about two inches behind the ball. **The swing must be an "out to in" one,** or across the ball, keeping the face of the club open or pointing skywards all of the time. Try to get the feeling of the **clubhead sliding underneath the ball rather than against it.** Imagine there is an insect underneath the ball holding it up and you are going to cut the legs from underneath him. (Poor thing!)

There is a great temptation among handicap players to look at the outcome of a shot before it is actually completed. Where bunker shots are concerned, the need to keep the head still through the exercise cannot be overstated. "Look at the spot where the ball was" should be your motto.

Finally, the exercise of exploding a ball out of sand demands considerably more power than the inexperienced player might imagine. There is a tendency for beginners to consider only the relatively short distance the ball may be required to travel from a greenside trap.

Because of the high resistance inherent in golf sand, however, a full shot is absolutely vital. The explosion shot should be played with the same tempo that would be exercised to extricate a ball from heavy rough.

The distance the ball will travel on emerging from a bunker is determined, not by varying swing but from the point the club makes contact with the sand behind the ball. The texture and, thereby, the resistance of the sand, can be assessed by the movement that occurs when the **feet are shuffled into a final stance position.** *(See diagram 113).*

Synopsis

No matter what shot you encounter around the green use the system. **It is always worth remembering that it is accuracy you are looking for and not distance.** It is not a full golf swing you employ, but a short back swing with a wristy through swing. It is obvious that if you have a **long back swing** and you want the ball to travel a short distance, **the tendency will always be to slow down through the hitting area.** It is much better to have a short, compact back swing with an accelerating clubhead through the hitting area. It is more of a "flick" type of a shot. If you try to play around the greens with stiff wrists you will not be able to develop any "feel". All the good short game golfers are wristy.

144

The routine

Position yourself in such a way that the ball is directly between you and the target.

Holding the club in your right hand and approaching from **directly behind the ball, you aim the clubhead at the target.**

You align your feet left of the target, and so clear **left side out of the way,** to allow the arms to follow through. Move your **body weight on to your left foot and, at the same time, position the ball back in stance** (unless you want to cut a shot up into the air, in such a case you play the ball off the forward foot).

You swing the club along the line of your feet while, at the **same time, being aware of having the clubhead pointing at the target** through the hitting area (I always encourage a short back swing with an accelerating clubhead for chipping).

The secret of the short game is to swing the back of your left hand towards the flag. *(See diagram 114).*

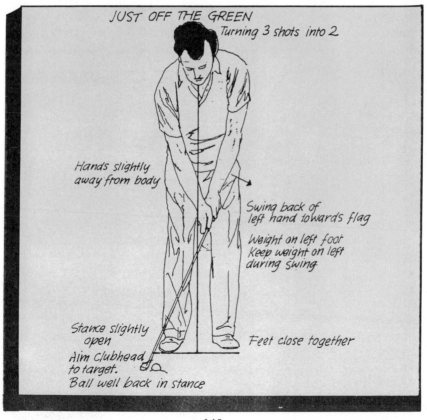

JUST OFF THE GREEN

Turning 3 shots into 2

Hands slightly away from body

Swing back of left hand towards flag

Weight on left foot
Keep weight on left during swing

Stance slightly open

Aim clubhead to target.

Ball well back in stance

Feet close together

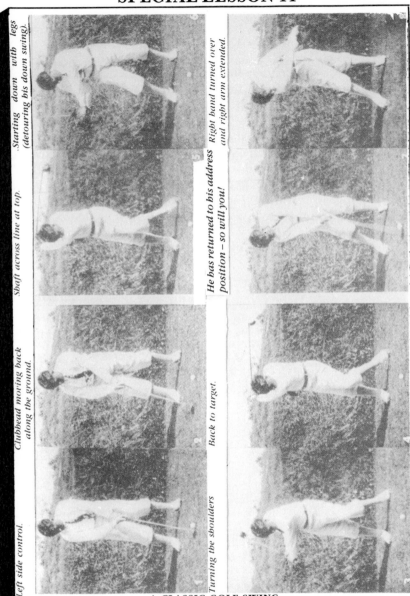

The following labels appear alongside the swing sequence photographs:

- *Left side control.*
- *Clubhead moving back along the ground.*
- *Shaft across line at top.*
- *Starting down with legs (detouring his down swing).*
- *Turning the shoulders*
- *Back to target.*
- *He has returned to his address position – so will you!*
- *Right hand turned over and right arm extended.*

A CLASSIC GOLF SWING
The Bobby Jones swing that most golfers should try to emulate.

Points to note: Compare photo 1 with photo 7. Note (a) Head behind ball; (b) Majority of his weight on his right foot; (c) Left arm extended; (d) Left shoulder higher than his right.

CHAPTER 16

Putting

A big follow through is essential with putting

The American players are noted for their ability to "hole-out" under pressure. European players do not appear to realise the importance of putting. One will frequently hear them lament about missed puts of three feet, two feet and so on. They clearly do not accept that to miss from two or three feet is to play a really bad shot. A friend of mine was over at the Curtis Cup on a windswept Royal Lytham. He noted with interest that the British and Irish girls were out in wretched weather on the practise ground hitting long irons and drivers and so on. The Americans, on the other hand, were using the shelter of the clubhouse to practise their short game, to get the "feel" for the greens. It was ironic because if the Europeans were not capable of hitting the ball from the tee to the green, they would not have been selected in the first place. Consistently good putting can be achieved only through consistent practise. **It is the one part of the game where you should be able to say to Jack Nicklaus – "Come here, I can take you on, on the putting green."**

How the hole came into being

In the Dutch game which was "kolf", the players aimed the ball towards a stick in the ground. In those far-off days, it might seem strange that **petty crime and vandalism were responsible for the invention of the hole.** The stick was continually being removed by unseen hands and, after a time having tired of replacing it, the kolf players simply played the ball into the hole that remained. There are many players today who wish that the stick that was in use at that time was a bigger one.

The importance of putting becomes immediately apparent when one **considers that approximately half the number of strokes which go to make up a par of 72** are designated for two putts on the green. So it is appropriate from the outset to adopt a very positive attitude to practise. Lee Trevino's words should be to the forefront of every golfer's mind – **"You have to feel that you are a great putter, to be one."**

I believe that the challenge can be approached under three main headings: 1. Set-up; 2. Routine; 3. The "hole-end attitude". *(See diagram 115).*

*Swing putter along and over the line to the hole,
holding the putter head square to the hole after impact.*

Set-up

All of the top players have good posture and, in this context it is important to note that the more one's putting deteriorates, the greater the tendency to crouch. **Don't be afraid to stand your height,** it will give you a better view of the line of the putt and also of the hole.

The greater the distance a player is from the ball, the wider will be the arc of the strokes. This will result in a minimum of hand and shoulder movement, so reducing the margin of error.

Body weight should be placed fimly on the left foot. If the weight is on the right foot there is a tendency to quit on putts, whereas the correct approach allows one to hit through the ball while keeping the putter head moving towards the hole, after impact. All of the game's good putters agree on this.

When making the stroke, **it is essential to have one's eyes directly over the ball.** By being out of alignment, it is inevitable that the line to the hole will be distorted. A simple way of testing your line of vision (during practise) is to drop a ball from eye level. If it doesn't strike the ball in play, then you are off line.

The choice of putter and the grip are entirely up to the individual. Select a putter that feels comfortable. Remember, if it doesn't feel right, it won't work right. Most people use the reverse over-lap grip, allowing the forefinger of the left hand to rest over the right hand. **Putts should essentially be struck with the right hand, so enabling the player to move the putter towards the hole after impact, thus keeping the ball in line.**

Routine

Decide upon a routine and keep it. Remember that repetition is the only way of ensuring that the stroke will work under pressure. An example of routine is the manner in which Jimmy Connors, the tennis player, bounces the ball four times before he delivers a serve.

Attitude

"Life's battles don't always go to the stronger or faster man, but in the end the man who wins is the man who thinks he can." This quote applies to all aspects of the game of golf, but particularly to putting. Sadly, there are many golfers who condemn themselves to bad putting.

If a player says "I am a bad putter" or "If only I could putt", etc., he will never master the art. **Putting problems are largely the result of a negative attitude.**

149

NEW MIRACLE PUTTER £1,000!

THE EASIEST SHOT IN GOLF, THE FOURTH PUTT

Don't be afraid of missing a putt

Consider the mental approach of the man who is asked to walk along a plank of wood which is placed on the ground. No problem. When the plank is placed between two skyscrapers (just like the full shot), however, his conscious mind takes over and the fear of falling becomes so dominant that he is unable to accept the challenge.

In other words, the fear of falling has dominated the situation, rather than the simple exercise of walking. Putting presents a similar problem. If a player allows himself to dwell on all the reasons why he must sink a certian putt – remember Doug Sanders's three-footer for the Open Championships at St. Andrews in 1970 – his chances of success are greatly reduced.

Do you think that Jack Nicklaus or Tom Watson could afford to think of outside issues when they are faced with a four foot putt for a major title? Obviously not. The fact is that they have trained their minds to concentrate on the immediate task of getting the ball into the hole – nothing else.

The best way of doing this is to think positively. The ball is going into the hole – it cannot miss. **Imagine a picture of yourself picking the ball out of the cup when the putt has gone down.**

Finally, the former Irish Ryder Cup player, Harry Bradshaw, one of the game's all-time great putters, summed up his attitude very succinctly when he said: "I see only the hole."

Practise your putting as often as you can

Practise your putting as it is considered to be 43% of the game. It does not require physical strength to become a good putter. You can also practise putting anywhere. Develop a routine and stick to it. Find a putter that suits you. Do not think of method as much as the result. In other words, do not think of the technique of how you are going to strike the ball, but just rely on your body to do it for you. There is just you, the ball and the hole. It is also worth remembering that a putt is a miniature golf shot. Bobby Locke, considered one of the greatest of all times, used the same routine for driving and putting. He also relied on his senses to tell him if he was going to hole the putt. He listened to the sound. When asked to explain it he went like this, "I listen to the noise the ball makes on the putter head – ping, ping, **pung,** ping." If you strike the putt well just like any other shot, the ball will go where you want it. If the ball makes a hollow sound (pung) it is not well struck. Locke was thought of as the loudest putter on the circuit. As a putt is a miniture golf shot, **it is just as important to release the clubhead at the ball through the hitting area you must release the**

151

putter head at the ball. Many a putt is missed by "dragging" it to the left or "pushing" it to the right, in each case the problems are that the body has moved on it. **The secret is to release the putter-head** (not the body) and not to go with it, in other words not to allow the body to move forward and especially your head. **Use the head but don't move the head!** Think of the elastic experiment – of stretching it and letting it go and not going with it. The release is achieved by using the right hand when striking.

Finally, if you have a problem with very short putts a slight "yip", adopt the hurling or the Langer grip. Place your left hand below the right and, as this encourages your left side control, your left hand will tend to continue on out towards the hole when you strike the ball and so prevent you turning on it.

Ways to practise

(1) A way to practise is to place a cigarette package in front of the hole and putt to strike it. As it seems quite easy, your success rate should be fairly high. The next step is to remove the package and putt to the hole. As the hole and the cigarette package are the same width, if you are able to hit the package you should have no trouble with the hole.

(2) Start practising the short putts and gradually lengthen the putt. Here is the routine. Take a six inch putt, once you hole it move out to twelve inches, and to two feet and so on. You continue putting until you fail to hole from one of the distances, and you start from six inches and work you way out.

(3) A way to develop "feel" for putting is to practise with your eyes closed, and once you have struck the putt you have to nominate where the ball finished. Whether it was left, right, short, long or even in the hole. This helps you develop a feeling for the head of the putter and will help make you aware if you are opening or closing the blade of the putter when striking the ball. It will therefore instinctively help you to keep the putter swinging towards the hole when striking the ball.

(4) A short back swing and a good follow through is, of course, the key to good putting. **Practise hitting putts with no back swing, just a follow through, and develop a stroke where you feel you are putting the putter head into the hole.** Always keep the line to the hole in your mind and in the putting stroke swing the putter head to the ball and after contact with the ball keep it swinging on and up over the line towards the hole.

(5) To ensure a smooth stroke, a pendulum stroke, a very good tip is **not to ground the putter.** Simply feel the connection between your arms, the shaft and the head. Think "triangle" and swing all together.

152

Are you an inconsistent golfer?
Build up a solid left arm through impact.
Detour your down swing! Take the ball clean!

The top-class golfer has a wide follow-through, the high handicapper has a narrow one.

The clubhead of **the good swing comes in parallel to the ground, while in the bad swing it is only descending as it makes the strike.** The bad golfer's swing has a narrow base while it is the opposite for the good golfer. Why? On the top of your backswing the clubhead is approximately five feet off the ground. The clubhead has in effect to travel from a height of five feet to two inches in one-fifth of a second and not be descending as it makes the strike. **The problem is the direct route (short-cut) from the top is straight down.** This is the

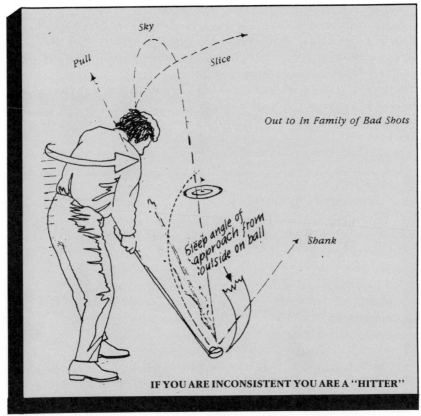

Sky

Pull

Slice

Out to In Family of Bad Shots

Steep angle of approach from outside on ball!

Shank

IF YOU ARE INCONSISTENT YOU ARE A "HITTER"

path many golfers unfortunately take. The **top-class golfer is able to detour his down swing.** From the top, he swings down and behind the body straight away to hip height and from this shallower angle of two feet approximately he eases the club down towards the ball. In other words he gives himself time and space by swinging down to his right hip first and then forward from the shallow angle.

Why is it so difficult to do?

Simply because **we tend to associate force with distance.**

(Release the clubhead against a solid left arm, hand and shoulder.)

The high handicapper may well start with an extended left arm, but with the hope of distance, the tendency to force, the inevitable right hand "lash" down on the ball this action ruins the control of the left arm. If you **are inconsistent you are a "hitter",** your left arm collapses at impact (as your arms happen to be attached to your shoulders they will always tend to want to swing around and never away from your shoulders).

Think of a **back** and **forward** movement.

Start by extending your left arm and placing the right hand on the club with the fingers extended or stretched. Push your left arm back behind the ball and start to swing down, around and forward towards the back of the ball. Do not swing from five feet to two inches direct, take a route around by your right hip. **Try to flatten out the middle section of your swing** by descending to your right hip first and swing forward from there. On your follow through **think of extending the left arm and finish in an extended position.**

At and after impact think of "locking up shop" with your left arm,

The top class golfer swings his/her left arm past the ball

The poor golfer's left arm is overpowered by the stronger right

LEFT ARM AND RIGHT KNEE FORWARD SWING

elbow and shoulder. Provide a solide base for the release of the head with the stronger right hand. This will prevent the spinning out of the shot with the shoulders to the left and keep the swing on line with the target. If your left arm crumbles, your left side collapses you will swing towards the left, and your swing power will also escape out high whereas the ball is low. Resist **high** in order to provide the power **low.** Block all the forward force of your swing high and allow it to escape low.

Think of it in this way, most high handicappers swing "into" themselves **with a collapsed left arm a "lottery" swing.** The good golfer hits "through" the ball keeping the back of his left hand moving towards the target. So should you. **Do not swing into yourself – swing away from yourself.**

P.S. This swing will help you controlling the ball – it may not increase your distance.

RIGHT ELBOW BACK TO HIP

Swing your left arm forward towards the back of the ball from the "inside"

Lock up your left arm at impact.

Forget the ball and swing.

*Try to avoid "**quitting**" on the shot and hit out "**through**" the ball extending your arms towards the target.*

CHAPTER 17

Strategy on the course

Playing a round of golf

- **Learn course management.**
- **Do not underclub.**
- **Count your putts.**
- **Tee ball high into wind.**
- **Encourage a positive approach.**

As we examine the strategy to successfully negotiate a golf course, it is important to look for the major influences on design, and on the way it has evolved.

The design of St. Andrews has become the standard and was adopted by all the early designers. *(See diagram 116).*

Up to 1764 there were twelve holes in all in use at St. Andrews with eleven played out and eleven on the way home again. Tees and greens as we know them, were non-existent. It was a case of playing for the hole and then playing the next one from two club lengths of that hole. It was decided to make the first four holes into two; and, as the same greens were used going out and coming back, the round was reduced to eighteen. This was to become the standard round. It was not until 1832 that eighteen separate holes were cut and today there are eleven greens in all in use, seven of which are used on doubles and four as single greens.

The course itself is run by a St. Andrews trust management committee on which the Royal and Ancient and the local authority have equal representation, having previously being owned by the townsfolk of St. Andrews who had free golf on it up to 1946.

The influence of St. Andrews is also apparent in other areas. The majority of our older courses follow the pattern set by St. Andrews and **run in an anti-clockwise direction with the boundaries on the right-hand side.** Royal Dublin is a good example of this in an Irish context. It is no mere coincidence that the "slice" is very much a feature of the Irish game because of this design factor. **The instinctive reaction is to aim away from the boundary, have an "open set-up", encouraging an out-to-in swing (or towards the left) and resulting in the inevitable slice.** Ironically, an emphasis on driving the ball away from the trouble has the effect of exaggerating the golfer's plight.

157

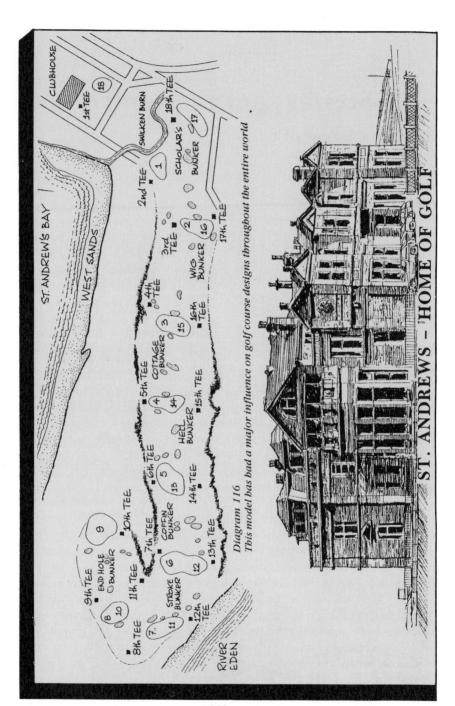

Diagram 116
This model has had a major influence on golf course designs throughout the entire world.

ST. ANDREWS – HOME OF GOLF

The great appeal of links courses to the leading professionals is that they offer a totally natural challenge. Lee Trevino put it so succinctly when he said: **"They just walked into a field and said let's play golf."** Contours of the land are preserved and sometimes embellished, creating a challenge entirely in keeping with the original concept of the game. This can be true to a lesser extent of inland courses, obviously featureless land would require structural adjustments in an effort to enhance terrain and consequently the challenge.

On the older type courses there are **"blind"** **holes** (a hole where you have to play a shot without being able to see the target), of which the "Dell" and the Klondyke at Lahinch Golf Club are good examples. The surface on these seaside courses tends to be uneven (Johnny Miller remarked that he thought there were elephant footprints on the fairways at Muirfield), often resulting in an unlucky bounce.

On the other hand, there is a tendency among many of the American designed courses to be artificially constructed with many of the features created by the designer.

Traditionalists like Peter Thompson are very much against these designs especially those containing large man-made water hazards. Thompson himself was able to play delicate pitch and run shots using the natural terrain to deadly effect while winning five British Opens.

The Russian connection!

The American designs, on the contrary, encourage the player to carry the ball to the pin. It is sometimes referred to as target golf or dart board golf. They believe that it should be a fair game and are taking the luck out of it. They are, naturally, very much against the blind shot. Arnold Palmer reflects the sharp difference of opinion which exists with the leading players about this aspect of course design when he said during his visit to the new Tralee course: "I have no objection to blind shots, provided they are in somebody else's design."

The doyen of modern golf course architects is Robert Trent Jones, whose courses are to be found throughout the world – even in Moscow. An interesting aspect of Jones's "Russian experience" is that only one hole of the planned course has been built. The idea for the venture arose in the 1950s in an attempt to ease tension between East and West. The Russians decided to build a golf course which that great enthusiast of the game, Dwight Eisenhower, might one day enjoy. The cold war intervened, however, and the project had barely begun when it was summarily abandoned.

Trent Jones, who designed the second eighteen at Ballybunion, is probably best known for his fine work on the Costa Del Sol in Spain.

Outstanding among his courses there are Andalucia, Mijas and Sotogrande old and new.

The most interesting aspect of Jones's designs is that he can provide the learner golfer with a highly-rewarding insight into course management. **For instance, he almost invariably offers the player two routes to every green – the option of an easy drive with a difficult approach shot, or a hazardous drive which is rewarded by perfect position for a shot to the flag.** This design feature is also true of many British Irish courses.

Playing the course

Playing a round of golf is like going on a journey. **The golfer approaches every game with renewed optimism in anticipation of the magic touch. He is born again every time he stands on the first tee.** It is every player's ambition in the early stages to break the magic **100 barrier.** It is interesting to note that it was broken for the first time in **1767 by James Durham,** who won the Silver Club at St. Andrews with a 94, and this score was to remain unbeaten for eighty-six years. On the lower scale, it was Allan Roberts who was first to break 80 on the old course at St. Andrews, and he is credited by some as the player to have invented the iron shot to the green. They were previously played with a baffing spoon. **Al Geibelger was the first to break 60** in a competition round on the U.S. circuit in 1972.

It is often said that the measure of a great competitor is his ability to score well while playing badly. This is the classic example of an individual operating within his limitations. A key factor in this context is a sound short game, which will allow a player through one perfectly hit chip or putt to compensate for mediocrity with his tee or approach shots.

In the final analysis, it is always the score that counts. It often happens that you may hit the ball from tee to green and putt badly and the next time you play, you may play badly but putt well.

If a potentially good player comes to me for a lesson and comments that he has a good short game, I expect his long game to be poor, as he has been scoring with his short game and now he wants to win with a good long game allied to his short game.

However, to score well you have to be mentally strong. It is easy to hole a putt for a one over par or a par, but difficult to hole the same putt for a birdie.

What is your putting average

Potentially good players often mislead themselves. They may

161

162

become obsessed with their putting average. They read about the great American putters – Trevino, Crenshaw, Watson – whose types of figures are realistically taken only with greens hit in regulation. The high handicapper may feel he is doing well to average thirty-two putts per round which is four less than the acceptable two per hole, but how many greens has he missed? And how many times has he chipped from the fringe of the green in two? Honesty is absolutely vital for the player. He must be prepared after a good score to analyse his game and accept the weakness where apparent. If he putted well and shot a moderate score, his long game must have been suspect. And the same applies in reverse if the long game was precise and produced only a reasonable return then the player obviously encountered problems around the greens.

Players sometimes look for a way out, subconsciously they do not want the pressure of winning, and develop some release valve. It may be anything. I often see potentially good players look for an excuse not to score. It may be the "loose change" in his playing partner's pocket, the colour of his sweater, the glare of the sun on his putter and so on. (One is reminded of this extraordinary hypersensitivity on the golf course by the story of Butcher from Lahinch who was a fanatical golfer, remarking "The day was so fine, the sun was melting the tar and **you could almost hear the bees belch.**")

You should not look for an excuse not to score and never be put off by a noise or anything else your playing partners create. In truth, you are only looking for an escape. Remember it is only a "fun thing", an extenuation of your youth and, when the cruel breaks occur such as a lipped putt and bad lies, always remember Nicklaus's famous remark: **"Nobody ever said golf was a fair game."** You are there because you enjoy it, and if you make new friends on the way round so much the better. As Walter Hagen said: "Don't forget to smell the flowers on the way round" – and if you play well look on it as a bonus.

The course itself

The "starting" hole varies; however, it is generally not too hard nor too easy, allowing for the fact that the player needs time to warm up. The really difficult holes will be encountered later in the round, to use an example from the 13th to the 17th at Rosses Point Golf Club, allowing for the fact that the player is in the heat of the battle and ready for these holes.

On each hole, the designer may give the player a relatively easy drive with a difficult second shot, or vice-versa, a difficult drive followed by an easier shot. Clontarf Golf Club, in an Irish context, is an interesting example of a course where the drive is tight and the approach shot is easier.

There are obstacles on every hole. **In many cases the obstacles are placed in such a way as to mislead you.** It may be trying to push you on a wrong line for the hole. The correct line for the hole may well be directly over the obstacle and, if successfully negotiated, will reward you with an easy second shot.

It should be accepted that there are ways of playing each hole, and places where the drive should be "hit". **Try to find out how the holes on your course should be played and where you should aim the drive in order to set up an easy second shot.**

There are par five greens and long par four greens, which are receptive to the long iron or wood shot. These tend to be long in design. On the longer par fives the greens may be smaller allowing for the third shot which is likely to be a short iron or a wedge. It sometimes happens that these are converted into long iron or wood shots.

There are also par three and short par four greens. The short par four may offer you an easy drive with the second shot to be played to a small green with the pin tucked in tight behind a bunker. The ninth hole at Cypress Point is an example of this. Christy O'Connor played the hole by driving into the bunker and pitching on to the green. He birdied the hole on each occasion.

The short par three may offer you a small target which if missed will leave you with a very difficult pitch. The "postage stamp" at Troon is a very good example of this.

On playing to a green it is important to know the pin position. **This may be checked by observing where the holes run parallel, e.g. if fourth oppoosite seventh you can check seventh while putting on fourth.** You should also look for other pointers, for example, if the pin is set towards the front at the first hole it may hold that position for the round.

It is true to say that there is always a safe side to miss a green and unless you are very confident of hitting at the pin you should favour that side, as it will leave you with a less difficult pitch shot. Missing the green on the wrong side may prove costly in terms of recovery shots.

The famous road hole at St. Andrews is an example of this, as it encourages the player to play left off the tee and to play left of the green as the out of bounds is on the right. The touring players see the second shot in many instances as one iron "chaser" that come up just short of the green leaving a relatively straight-forward pitch or a long putt.

On the other hand the player could be "pin high" left of the green, very close to it and have no hope of a pitch and putt, without endangering disasters because of the bunkers in the way and the undulations on the green.

In many instances the golfer under-clubs for the second shot with the result that the shot is played with too much force. **Players should at all costs avoid becoming caught up in the "power syndrome".** By this I mean the comparing of notes after a round as to which iron was used for his approach at either a short hole or a par four. I often hear a player comment: "I hit a drive and a nine iron" – **with emphasis on the "nine iron".** You should consider the fact that because it is a 130 yard pitch it is not necessarily an eight iron or for that matter a wedge from 100 yards. **You don't have to hit the perfect shot with the perfect club.** That 130 yard shot may well be a six iron down the shaft. This is the way the professionals play, and if you have a shot like this in your armoury, it will always be useful in match play situations as it may help "fox" your opponent into taking too much or too little club. *(See diagram 117)*.

You should always use the club that you are confident with and play the shot that you feel will leave you closest to the pin whatever that may be.

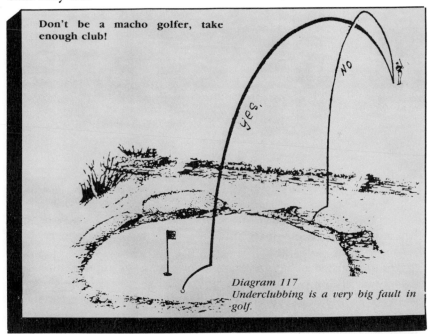

Don't be a macho golfer, take enough club!

Diagram 117
Underclubbing is a very big fault in golf.

An obvious example is a 90 yard pitch into a strong wind, a shot which should be played with an eight or nine iron "down the shaft" keeping the ball down and preventing the wind from interfering with its flight.

No medals for distance

When confronted with the 70 yard shot to the green it is important to realise that you **are not looking for distance but accuracy,** and the swing you employ should be one that lends itself to the exercise. I often see a potentially good player using a "driver type" back swing (over swing) for a short pitch and a **decelerating forward swing.** This is his way of trying to reduce excessive clubhead speed. The outcome of the shot is disastrous more often than not, as it results in a fluffed shot. A short, compact back swing is essential here encouraging an accelerating forward swing.

You should also bear in mind the position from which you would like to putt when playing this shot. If the green, for example, is sloping towards you, you should try to leave your approach shot short of the pin, leaving you with an uphill putt, if you charge it you will be left with a tricky downhill one. A very good practice to adopt is, **if the hole is above and there is no obstacle in your way, to putt; but if**

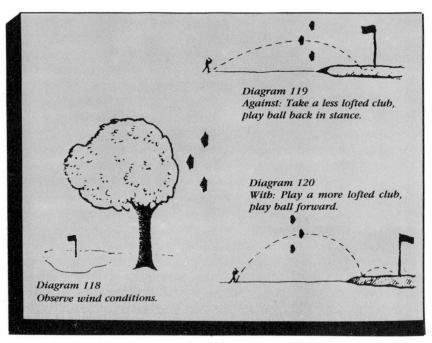

Diagram 119
Against: Take a less lofted club, play ball back in stance.

Diagram 120
With: Play a more lofted club, play ball forward.

Diagram 118
Observe wind conditions.

you have a downhill shot, to chip. The idea being that if you chip downhill the ball should not roll too far past the pin, while if you putt uphill it will not go too far past either. Chip downhill, putt uphill.

On reading the greens if you are undecided on a particular fall, always check the surrounding incline, as the "fall" will always follow the natural terrain.

You should also observe your playing partners' putts, and note the line, use their putt as a guide to your own if it is the case that you don't have to putt first.

The tendency of amateur players to leave putts short of the target is well documented. Less frequently emphasised, however, is the reaction of the players to a putt that is hit too strongly. Almost invariably he will turn away in disgust, instead of noting the line of the ball past the hole, with a view to simplifying the putt back.

How to score in windy conditions

(1) Observe trees, flag or pin, or toss a pinch of grass in the air, or learn from other players' shots. *(See diagram 118)*.

(2) Into the wind. Take a less-lofted club than usual. Aim the clubhead at the target. Position your body ahead of the ball. Move the weight on to your forward foot. Lead the shot with left hand through impact. Try to play the ball past the pin. *(See diagram 119)*.

(3) With the wind use a more-lofted club than normal. Tee the ball higher (if driving). Aim the clubhead at the target. Play the ball well forward in stance. Keep the weight back on your right foot. Hit the ball with clubhead on the upswing. *(See diagram 120)*.

(4) Cross wind. Take a less-lofted club than usual. Allow for the wind to affect the ball's flight. Aim the clubhead at the intended target.

Where it is the case that the wind is against you, try to keep the ball down and out of it, and where the wind is helping, try to use the wind to your advantage. Use a much wristier swing in the wind, employing an early wrist-cock and release of the clubhead. On the greens do not try to strike a putt but "tap it" once again using a wristy stroke.

Adopt the motto of Byron Nelson: "Make the wind your friend." Generally speaking adopt a wider stance than normal in order to anchor yourself. Try to swing less and hit more – adopt a wristier swing using more hand action and on the greens "top" your putts rather than employing your normal stroke putt.

In playing windy conditions, if you are able to use the wind, you will benefit greatly. For example, when playing into a strong wind the impulse is always to attack it, and swing hard at the ball. The opposite

GOLDEN RULE: WHEN IN TROUBLE
GET BALL BACK IN PLAY!

"SAND WEDGE, FINTAN."

is the correct method. You will find it more effective should you swing easier into the wind and harder down wind. If we examine aerodynamics you will notice when a plane takes off it always will do so into the wind as it does not need so much power to become airborne as when it has to take off with the wind. In taking off there is a need to use a lot more acceleration. It is important to realise that you hit the ball easier into wind and harder down wind.

Playing down wind a three wood off the tee will give more elevation and use as much carry as a driver and should be considered. Playing into wind one should try to keep the ball low. Try to "sweep" the ball off the tee and leave the tee in the ground. A downward blow on the ball should be avoided at all costs, as it will cause the clubhead to make more contact with the bottom of the ball resulting in excessive back-spin, and a "climber-shot". One is reminded of the story of my very good friend Tom Murphy practising in the "garden" at Royal Dublin Golf Club. He was hitting drives hard into the wind, alongside Christy O'Connor who was practising with a three wood. Tom's driver shots tended to soar somewhat towards the end of their flight while Christy's shots were penetrating through the wind and gaining distance. Tom was amazed at the result and inquired from the master as to the secret, whereupon Christy replied: "I am hitting halfway up the ball."

In setting up for the shot into the wind, you should anchor yourself in the ground by adopting a wide stance **and tee the ball high,** as this angle will help encouraging a shallow attack on the ball. Use the motto for the drive "tee it high and hit it low".

On playing **irons** into the wind always **place the ball back in the stance,** towards the right foot, as this will enable you to have a lower trajectory on the ball.

Trouble

If you perchance get into trouble the golden rule must be **"get back on the fairway"**. Bob Toski, the great American instructor, commented on the wisest shot he ever saw played in golf, a shot by Jack Nicklaus when he played straight back down the course in order to get the ball back into play. Accept the fact that you are going to drop a shot and play out.

It is interesting to note that Arnie Palmer used to play into trouble deliberately when practising in order to be able to play out of it when competing.

Let us finally look at contrasting course designs and how they affect strategy and also on the trends in course management.

At Augusta National where the U.S. Masters is played, there is no rough and the fairways are wide. There are plenty of trees, however. The idea behind this type of design is that it will give maximum enjoyment to the player, while if it is the case that you hit a bad shot you are penalised. You have to deal with the trees, however you are able to find your ball and you do not hold up play. (This is a very common design on municipal courses, facilitating maximum numbers.) Augusta National runs in an anti-clockwise direction, favours the player who draws the ball from right to left and, as the trouble is mostly at the front of the greens, it rewards the attacking player. Severiano Ballesteros loves this course, as he draws the ball to run with the dogleg par fives and he is a brave attacking player. Lee Trevino, on the other hand, has never done well at Augusta, as he fades the ball (from left to right) and this type of shot does not suit the course.

In contrast, the U.S. Open is always played at a course where the fairways are narrow and the rough is high. Severiano Ballesteros has never won a U.S. Open, while Lee Trevino has won twice. The answer lies in Lee Trevino's ability to keep the ball in play. The ''fade'' show he uses is a much safer shot as it flies higher and lands softly. His motto is: **"You can talk to a fade but a hook won't listen."**

Trends in course management

In the 1950s the so-called ''safety'' shot was pioneered by Ben Hogan and adopted by Jack Nicklaus, and was very much in vogue in the 1960s and 1970s. Arnold Palmer provided some light relief in the early 1960s. **Ben Hogan spent most of his career fighting the dreaded hook and finding ways of counteracting it.** His famous discovery ''pronation through impact'' resulting in the safe fade shot was to become the result. His book is sometimes referred to as an **"anti-hook book".** Jack Nicklaus adopted the ''power fade'' as it was to become known, to suit the tighter courses and it became very fashionable. However, the problem with it was that the players needed an abundance of strength to be able to use it. Players found that their normal shot was a ''draw'' and they were not scoring any better with this safer shot. It is interesting to note that both Jack Nicklaus and Lee Trevino both use this shot a lot more now.

The real secret in scoring is to develop a shot that repeats, whatever it may be. This demands single-mindedness. Bobby Locke used to ''draw'' everything from right to left. He used this shape on all his shots even his putts. He was able to slice and fade the ball at exhibitions; however, he always used the shot that he was able to repeat at tournaments.

171

"BLESS MY SOUL, ZORG, HE THINKS YOU'RE SOME KIND OF GOD"

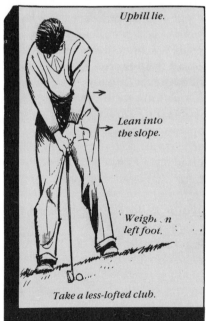

Uphill lie.

Lean into the slope.

Weight on left foot.

Take a less-lofted club.

Hanging lie.

Steep back swing.

use a more-lofted club.

Weight on left foot.

Open stance clubface open on impact.

Follow through down the slope.

One cannot stress enough the importance of developing a routine on the golf course, by practising setting-up to the ball in exactly the same way every time. In fact it could be said that when you play a round all you have to think of is the set-up and everything else will fall into place. The second phase is to develop a swing that repeats itself and there is every chance then that the shots will also be consistent. All the top players use a routine, and in this way, it is much easier for them to repeat the shot and to concentrate.

To conclude, this is what Peter Thompson says: **"Muscular strength is not particularly advantageous in golf. Control and direction pays off better.** Plan your round before you tee off. Plan each hole and stick to that plan. Golf is at least 50% a mental game and, if you recognise that the mind prompts us physically, you can almost say golf is an entirely mental effort."

How to deal with yourself on the course

Golf is the type of game which calls for many skills, but I believe that perhaps more than others, there are two inter-related skills which must be emphasised in any discussion on the achievement of your best. The first important skill is in relation to one's physical make-up and one's ability to strike the ball effectively. The second skill is within the realm of the psychological and is related to one's ability at evaluating, planning and thinking through the different facets of play. The first demands knowledge, practice, method, dedication. The second is more dependent upon one's temperament, one's mental-thought pattern. I believe that it is one's self-discovery and in the evaluation of one's limitations and capabilities, wherein lies the secret of success. Every player is as different psychologcially as he is physically and his approach to the game should be concerned with the building of a style which best suits his physique and temperament.

There are two different types of personality trait categories which I would like to deal with in relation to golf.

(a) Those who are of a **logical bent** of mind and who use an analytical approach to the game.

(b) Those who are really the opposite and who work more by **instinct.**

There are different personality attributes in each one of us, no two persons are alike. Consequently, we must adopt a system or approach to the game which best suits our physical and psychological make-up. You must never follow blindly a style or method which may not be suitable for you.

If we take a look at the golfing greats, Ben Hogan and Jack Nicklaus,

173

LEAVING YOUR MARK ON THE COURSE.

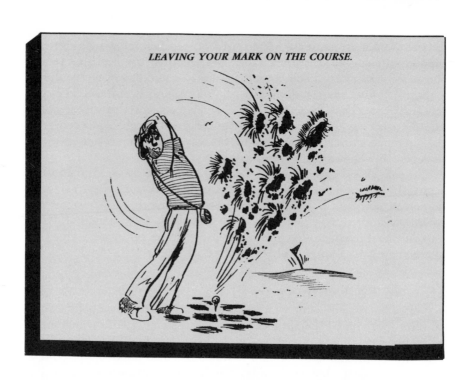

Approaching the last!

I shudda shot 63!

The world's against me!

Rub of the green.

we will find that, while they are different physically, they are quite alike mentally. Psychologically, both men are serious people, and both use an analytical approach to the game. Hogan was known by the Scots as "Wee Ice Mon". What is important, however, is that both of these players played their game in a most logical manner, mechanised, automated you might say. Their mental preparation was highly organised. Jack Nicklaus once stated that he never hit a shot, even in practice, without having a very short in-focus picture of it in his head, such was his programmed approach. They both were able to dismantle the swing and the way in which they played. They were able to concentrate intensely over a long period of time, isolating themselves completely from the crowd. In order to give you some idea of this automated approach to golf, Hogan used yardages in the 1950s. However, it was Nicklaus who developed the idea of mapping golf courses. In the 1961 U.S. Amateur Open at Pebble Beach, Dean Beman, P.G.A. Tour Commissioner, introduced Jack Nicklaus to measuring approach shot yardages. Though both of these great golfers rate as number one and two all-time greats and an "aura" surrounds them, their play tended to be slow and somewhat boring.

Arnold Palmer and Severiano Ballesteros, on the other hand, tend more towards the instinctive. They have the theory, but play more by "feel". They have what might be regarded as a "cavalier" approach to their play – shoot first and deal with it later. Palmer, when asked why he took twelve at a par five when leading a tournament replied: **"I missed a putt for an eleven!"** Their play tends to be exciting because they are likely to do the unexpected. Needless to say, both of these players have a good rapport with the crowd.

It is important then to figure out for yourself a system which best suits your temperament and personality. When Arnold Palmer tried to change his style and model himself on Ben Hogan, he suffered a devastating slump in his fortunes and didn't recover until he had returned to his old system. I always remember giving a lesson to one lady and advising her on a grip change – whereupon she replied: "Ah, but Jack Nicklaus grips it this way." **Obviously, the similarity between the lady and Jack Nicklaus was nil. Over-identification with a technique or style,** which is being used by some of the golfing greats, **can be foolhardy** in that there may be no similarity whatsoever in either physique or temperament. As I have previously stated, Ben Hogan thought out in a positive way, his every shot, while Palmer exemplifies the player whose thought pattern was primarily instinctive. My advice to you **is to discover for yourself what system suits you best.**

175

Positive thinking in relation to performance

It is important that you should try and cultivate a positive thought pattern in your approach to the game. What we do with our game and the problems which we encounter in our play are very much dependent upon our mental climate and attitude, especially when we realise that many of the obstacles in our game are mental in character. **William James, the American psychologist, pointed out that the greatest factor in any undertaking is one's belief about it.** If you have a sustained approach it will set in motion a thought pattern which will unquestionably assist you in the attainment of that standard. **The mental picture must be one of expectation, not one of doubt.**

Avoid negatives or any form of negative thinking in your mental outlook. **Negative mental attitudes serve to inhibit you, to throw you off your timing as they only cause a freezing of the muscles,** thereby preventing an easy flow of power to your play. The secret is to blot out all the dangers so that you might only see a picture of yourself picking the ball out of the hole. Harry Bradshaw, when asked once at a clinic what was the secret of his great putting, replied: "I only see the hole"; and he concluded: "There is no such thing as a line." How often can one become overwhelmed with self-doubt when approaching a tricky putt. **The answer, then, is to blow out of your mind all that might go wrong for you, and try and associate any difficult shot with a mental image of your succeeding.**

It is an attitude of mind which I feel is imperative to have in your golfing psychology. In summary, let me apply the psychology of positive thinking to your game in the most practical way.

First of all, you should always remember that **repetition** is the key to good golf and this usually:

(a) Begins with **a repetitive thought pattern.**

(b) Secondly, it is **important to picture mentally your shot before swinging the club.** The better you can picture the shot in your mind, the greater the chance of accomplishing your targets. Your attitude must be one of expectation, not one of doubt. If putting, picture yourself mentally picking the ball out of the hole.

(c) **Every golfer builds for himself a series of key swing thoughts:** left arm straight; turn shoulders 90°; Joe Carr is reputed to have written on his glove: "Turn, you fool," right elbow in; start down with lower body; stay behind ball; keep eye on ball; etc. The most advisable approach should be to **choose one key swing thought,** concentrating positively each day. It is impossible to contend with more than one key idea at any one time.

(d) It is important to think as much about tactics as about swing.

176

How often do you see a golfer making a perfect swing but never taking account of alignment or the correct club to use?

(e) In relation to your adaptation of a style or technique, I believe that it must be in keeping with what best suits your physique and temperament. We have been examining the two contrasting styles of Ballesteros and Nicklaus as examples of play by ''feel'' or ''instinct'' and play in an analytical sense.

(f) **Relaxation between each shot can help to ameliorate or alter** particular problems which can arise between shots. It is of advantage if you can direct your mind away from the pressure of the moment. Tension can pose difficulties for the golfer. I would like to share with you a little ploy, which you may find helpful. **Before you strike the ball, remember to tighten every muscle as hard as you can, gripping the club with all your might, then relax the system again.** This is a useful formula in helping to dispel pent-up tension in the system. You are now ready to play.

(g) Will power and determination are fundamental ingredients in effecting positive progress in your performance. Arnold Palmer, more than any other of the golfing greats, had these most important qualities in abundance. Palmer's positiveness, his determination, his will to win made him great among champions. Perhaps it is this quality of will power which marks the clear demarcation line between the great and the ordinary. The following lines from Palmer's book, *Going for Broke*, best sums up what I mean, in reference to will power and positive thought patterns:

If you think you are beaten you are,
If you think you dare not, you don't,
If you would like to win but think you can't,
It is almost certain you won't.
Life's battles don't always go
To the stronger or faster man,
But sooner or later the man who wins
Is the man who thinks he can.

The last word I will leave **with the American psychologist, Emerson,** as a fitting and appropriate ending to this chapter on how to achieve your best:

They conquer who believe they can.

SPECIAL LESSON 13

THE VAST MAJORITY OF BAD SHOTS ARE STRUCK FROM THE OUTSIDE WITH THE HEEL OF THE CLUBFACE!

IF YOU COULD IMPROVE YOUR STRIKING BY A FRACTION OF AN INCH, YOU COULD BECOME A SCRATCH PLAYER

CONSIDER THE FACE OF THE CLUB

HOWEVER THE MAJORITY OF HIGH HANDICAPPERS RETURN THE FACE TO THIS

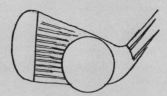

AND SOMETIMES OFF THE ACTUAL SOCKET

The front of the face is only 2" long. The difference between bad and good golf is miniscule.

THE TOP CLASS PLAYER STARTS HERE

AND RETURNS THE FACE TO THIS AT IMPACT

BALL IS FARTHER AWAY FROM SHAFT (SOCKET OF CLUB)

IMPORTANT POINT: All bad golf is played near shaft of club head as the bad golfer is unable to keep the face inside the ball – He unvariably hits across

TRY THE TWO BALL TEST. IF YOU STRIKE NEAR TO SHAFT, YOU WILL HIT OUTSIDE THE BALL.

All top class players have personal swings, but they are all inside ball at impact. Eamonn Darcy has a very unconventional swing looping out on his back swing but he is, as he says himself, "very conventional" – before and through impact.

CHAPTER 18

Corrective golf

Part 1: How to improve through practise

The golden rule here is: "never practise a mistake". It often happens that potentially good players come to me for tuition with a "grooved" fault in their swing. They are difficult to help because the swing follows the same pattern and repeats the mistake. At the driving range it is very common to see players slogging away hoping to make progress with no real hope of succeeding. They are wasting time, energy and money.

They are hoping to hit the ball better and are concentrating on the swing. Imaginary changes are made in their swing. The problem is (1) the swing is over in less than three seconds; (2) the potentially good player cannot see his swing, therefore he cannot see his faults. If he thinks he is actually correcting them he can have no idea if he is in fact doing so. Because the swing is over in a flash, it has already been determined by the set-up.

I have used the video system for many years now. I started out with the Polaroid black and white type. It had no sound recorder and the film had to be processed. I had a very good friend, a golf fanatic, whom I thought should see his own swing on film. He was forever on the practise ground. I shot the film, developed it, and kept it in my shop for a few days before showing it to him. He was a disciple of Ben Hogan, who had a flat, rounded type of swing. What he did not realise was that he had a terrible "pick-up" on his back swing which resulted in a collapsed position at the top of the back swing. Hence my reluctance to show it to him. He had been at sea for many years as a radio officer and was always swinging a club in his spare time out on the deck of the ship. One day (many years prior to this) as he was swinging, the captain, who was sitting in a deck chair on the bridge, shouted down at him: "You are lifting it!" When we eventually sat down to look at it together, he was amazed. He never realised what he really meant until he saw it for himself on film. He has now given his left side more prominence in his set-up and developed a left side take-away and his game has improved remarkably. He is no longer practising mistakes.

I remember another friend of mine coming to me for a lesson. He was a very keen golfer who practised intensely. He had, he reminded me, seven kinds of swings, and he wanted to compare them in order to decide which one he was going to use. He had a slip of paper naming each one and I recorded them individually. When we sat down to look at the film, we found out that there was little or no difference in any of his swings. His swing repeated itself consistently. However, there was a real problem with the swing itself, a problem he never envisaged because he had never previously seen his swing. This problem repeated itself consistently. Some thirty years previous to this, he had taken lessons from a professional and had been told of his problem and shown how to correct it. Not believing the story, he continued on his way, playing golf despite the flaw only because of his determination to succeed. He too has since corrected the fault and is enjoying the game again.

If you are serious about improving, have your swing checked and then take follow-up action. If you ever get a chance of seeing your swing you should not hesitate to do so as it will be of considerable help in the long term. It is amazing to note the reaction of people watching their swing on video. They notice the ''bald patch'', the weight problem, their voice is different and, lastly, they talk about the swing. It is worth remembering that the wealthy recluse, Howard Hughes, became a scratch player through watching a video of his swing alone.

You must be sensible in your approach to practise. Firstly, you must have a good set-up and this can be achieved easier than you think. Since this is a stationary exercise you could practise it in your own livingroom. With a club at hand, you should practise the set-up when the advertisements are on. There is no excuse for not having a good set-up. Try to model yourself on someone of a similar build to yourself.

The second stage is developing swing shape. You have to have a decent shape on your swing. An intelligent approach is essential. If you are in the early stages of learning the game, avoid practising with a low numbered club, as they are very difficult to master. Look on it as a progression. It is like climbing a stairs, you have to take one step at a time in order to reach the top. If you try to reach the top in one big jump you may miss the top step and land on your butt again. It is very common for potentially good players to try to master the driver first. This is a disastrous approach.

The seven iron is a sensible starter-club, because it is in between, not too difficult and not too easy. It is easy to groove a swing with it.Once it falls into a pattern, you will be able to use it with the more difficult clubs.

If you go to the other extreme and practise with the high irons, you will encourage yourself to scoop the ball which would have an adverse effect on the long game. The longest hitter on the U.S. circuit, Dan

Pohl, has a suspect short game. When he tries to improve it, his long game suffers.

Conclusion

The only way to make progress on your own on the practise ground **is to understand "ball flight" and to respond correctly to it. You must be able to understand what is happening in the air and relate it back to what has happened on the ground. You must be able to use the ball as you would a video recording.**

Use the ball as a video

The earliest balls were known as "featheries". The leather that was used was mainly bullhide, which was softened and cut into strips and sewn together. The feathers (enough to fill a top hat) were boiled and stuffed through a hole which was left. The ball was then shaped and painted. Because a person could only make about four a day they were very expensive, four shillings and six pence each.

Thomas Matheson (1743) wrote a poem about a ball maker Bobson:

> *Who with matchless art,*
> *Shapes the firm hide, connecting every part,*
> *Then in a socket sets the well-stitched hide,*
> *And through the eyelets drives the downy tide;*
> *Crowds urging crowds to forceful brogue impels,*
> *The feathers harden, and the leather swells,*
> *He grins and sweats, yet grins and urges more,*
> *Till scarce, the turgid globe contains its store.*
> *Such is famed Bobson, who in Andrea thrives.*

In 1848 the gutta-percha appeared and this discovery brought the game within reach of the ordinary people. However, in those early stages there were problems. It tended to duck suddenly down to earth for no apparent reason. However, it was found to fly much farther when it became damaged through use and had indentations on its surface. Thus, they decided to make indentations on the surfaces of these balls when manufacturing them. These indentations in flight gripped the compressed air which was previously resisting the ball's flight and drove it back behind the ball, prolonging its passage through the air. It was a much more durable ball than the featherie, easier to make, cheaper, it flew farther and rolled truer on the greens. It is ironic, however, that in the "old featherie" the seams (caused by the stitching) acted in a similar fashion to the indentations on the gutta-percha.

In the 1902 British Open at Hoylake, Alec Herd was persuaded at the last minute to use a "rubber core wound ball". This ball was invented by Cobuna Haskell from Cleveland, U.S.A., who had been unhappy with the gutta-percha ball and experimented using rubber strips wound round the rubber core. It is history now that Alec Herd won that Open and so dramatic were the results with the Haskell ball that the courses themselves had to be lengthened to accommodate it. The ball that you use today is basically the same as the one used by Alec Herd in that Open.

LUCKY FELLOW!

Part 2: Use real evidence

● How to read ball flight.

● The bad shots in golf

The vagabond ball; the ball has no brains; no feelings or emotions and is totally immune to the needs of the player. One could be out with his boss, his bank manager, or indeed some clients whom he wishes to impress and hopes to have some dialogue with on the way around – yet the damn ball couldn't care less! He may be able to, as one writer put it, get over the terrible inertia of the ball, but it is likely to take off in any direction to an extent that the next time he will meet his playing partners will be on the following tee from which once again he will proceed to take the scenic route.

So before starting out you might as well know all about the vagabond ball – the bad shots in the game, how to avoid them and hopefully to correct them. This section then is not on how the game should be played, but rather to straighten you out. What this means is that you do not have to go through the whole book in order to find a cure for your ills. Contrary to what many golfers believe, there are not a thousand, but **only nine bad shots in golf,** and, of these nine, many are closely related.

When the player comes to me for a lesson, I always like to ask the question why has he come for tuition? What is the problem? Or what is his bad shot? It sometimes happens that the player is able to accurately define the bad shot, but alas, more often than not, one hears the comment "I am terribly inconsistent" and this is very frustrating because it means very little from the teaching point of view. However,

MARRIAGE ENCOUNTER IN MIXED FOURSOMES

185

what it really means is that among the odd good shots the player is hitting, he is hitting a **number of these bad shots.** What the player must realise is that these **apparently different shots may be closely related.** So the first two points to be made are: (a) you must be able to accurately describe and define the shot you are hitting and (b) if you are an inconsistent golfer, you must be able to look at the relationship between these bad shots. *(See diagrams 121, 122).* To take the first point, it sometimes happens that a player accurately describes the shot he is hitting and then calls it by the wrong name. Now if he is looking for the correction of that shot he will be looking for the correction in the wrong area. For example, a player will often say he is "hooking" the ball – when in actual fact the shot he has hit has started **left** and continued in a leftwards direction. This is not a "hook" it is a "pulled" shot. *(See diagram 123).*

The hook shot is one that starts **right of the target** and veers towards the left in the latter stages of its flight. *(See diagram 124).* The point to be made here is that while the "pull" comes from an **out to in swing,** the "hook" comes from an **in to out swing.** They are two completely different swings. So that is the first point. Be able to accurately **describe** and then to **define.**

The second point to be made is that a player can stand up on a tee and he can hit a tee-shot left of target. He can stand up on the following tee and hit one that goes fifty to sixty yards right of target. He will automatically assume that he has made two completely different swings, when in actual fact he more than likely may not have. The swing that caused the ball to fly left of the target was an **out to in** swing, with the clubface square to the direction of his swing. *(See diagram 125).* On the other hand, the shot that ended up fifty yards right of the target was caused by the same **out to in** swing, but this time the clubface was pointing right of the direction of where he was swinging and caused this slice. *(See diagram 126).* So the shots had a completely different result; but the swing was the same **out to in** swing; the variable was the clubface. In one instance *(See diagram 127)* it was facing in the same direction as he was swinging and in the other instance it was open to the swing line. *(See diagram 128).* So these shots are closely related. The correction for both is to be found in the same area (hitting from the outside). It often happens, in fact, that the player can make **exactly** the same swing and the clubface can be in **exactly** the same position and the shots can be completely different, by virtue of the fact that he was using different clubs. Sometimes the player will "hook" his high irons and "slice" his woods, or alternatively, to a finer point of view, **will hit the driver with a "slice" and hit the three wood**

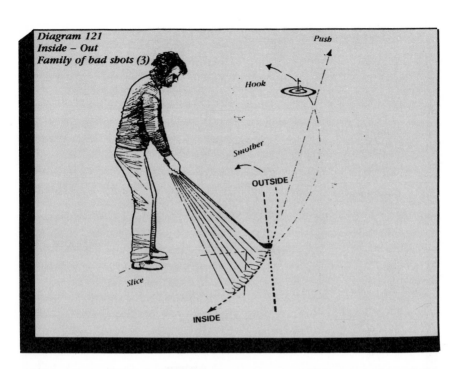

Diagram 121
Inside – Out
Family of bad shots (3)

Push

Hook

Smother

OUTSIDE

Slice

INSIDE

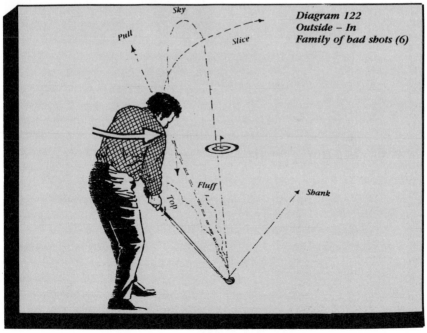

Sky

Pull

Slice

Diagram 122
Outside – In
Family of bad shots (6)

Fluff

Top

Shank

Please note the difference between the pull and the hook. The ball ends up left for both shots, but th swings used are completely different.

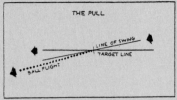

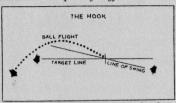

Diagram 123 The pull shot. Out to in swing.

Diagram 124 The genuine hook shot. In to out swing.

Diagram 125 Clubface square to swing.

Diagram 126 Clubface open to swing.

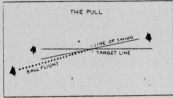

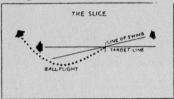

Out to in swing.

Out to in Swing.

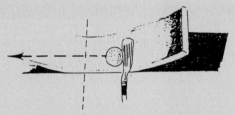

Diagram 127 clubface square to swing.

Diagram 128 Clubface open to swing.

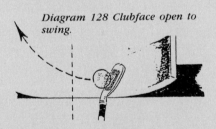

straight. The cause of this is the loft angle factor on the face of the clubs. The driver with the straight face, when open to the swing line, causes side spin and slice as the face hits the middle of the ball whereas the lofted club will send in the direction of the swing line because the bottom of the face makes contact with the ball irrespective of the open face. *(See diagram 129)*. You are now getting two completely different shots from exactly the same swing and from exactly the same face angle. The variable here is the loft factor on the face of the club. If you want to find out about your clubface, what it is doing at impact, i.e. whether it is open or closed, the driver is a very good club to indicate it for you and if you want to find out what your swinging line is, or what direction it is – is it **out to in** or **in to out** – you get a nine iron, or a wedge (lofted face) and the ball will tend to go where it is hit.

You should be able to accurately describe and then to define the bad shot and, if you happen to be an inconsistent golfer, you must be able to group the good shots and the bad ones into a particular family.

When you hit a golf ball, the **direction it takes off** is the result of the **force of the swing** your swing line. If the force of the swing is left of the target – that is the direction the ball will take off, or if it is towards the target, or right of the target, that will determine the early directional path of the ball. As the ball reaches the latter stages of its flight, the direction it veers in is **governed by the angle of the club-face.** In other words, the spin is governed by the angle of the clubface at impact. For example, if the ball starts to veer wickedly to the right *(See diagram 130)* in the latter stage of the flight, the clubface was pointing right of the target at impact – even though the force was left and, alternatively, if a ball goes leftwards through the latter stages of its flight, the angle of the clubface was left of where the force was applied. *(See diagram 130a)*. So the **start of the flight of the ball,** or the start of the journey that the ball takes will tell **you your swing line.** And the **end of the flight** of the ball will tell you about your **clubface,** what it is doing at impact. If you hit a ball with a flat-faced club that flies straight left, or for that matter straight right, or straight towards the target, this will tell you that the **force of your swing and the clubface angle are together.** *(See diagram 131)*. In other words, the force of the swing was to the left and the club was just pointing towards the left, or if you hit it a "push" shot to the right, the force of the swing was to the right and so was the clubface. *(See diagram 132)*. So if you are hitting the ball in a direction where it is going straight in that direction, you will know that even though your swing line may not be on target, you will know that your swing line and your clubface are together.

189

.Diagram 129 Two completely different shots from same swing and club-face angle.

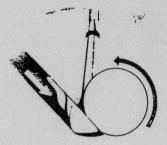

Lofted face prevents sidespin.

Flat face encourages sidespin.

Diagram 130A
Clubface closed to force.
Ball swerves to left at end.

Diagram 130
Clubface open to force.
Ball swerves to right at end.

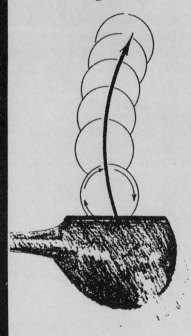

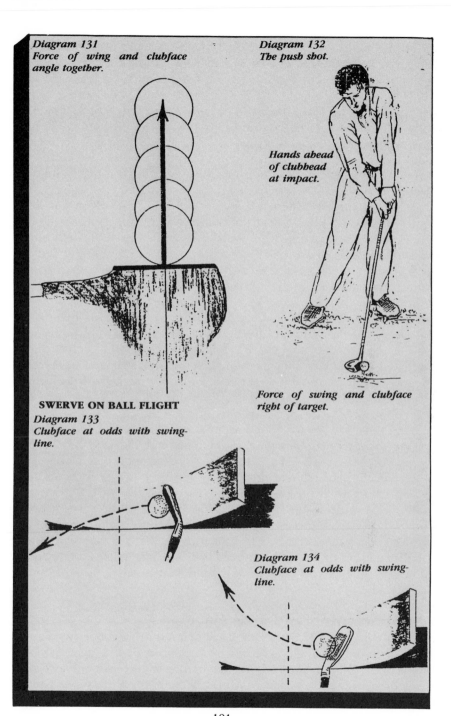

Diagram 131
Force of wing and clubface angle together.

Diagram 132
The push shot.

Hands ahead of clubhead at impact.

Force of swing and clubface right of target.

SWERVE ON BALL FLIGHT

Diagram 133
Clubface at odds with swing-line.

Diagram 134
Clubface at odds with swing-line.

While if you get a lot of **swerve** on the ball, especially towards the latter stages of its flight, you will know that your **clubface is misbehaving,** or your clubface and your swing line are at odds. *(See diagrams 133, 134).*

Finally, the **golf ball itself** can be hit in **three different places:** You can hit it on the **top,** in the **middle,** or towards the **bottom** of the ball. *(See diagrams 135, 136).* If you hit the ball on top, you will get the top shot, where you drive the ball down into the ground or towards the ground. If you hit the ball in the middle, you will get a reasonable trajectory on the ball. *(See diagram 137).* Now, if you hit the bottom of the ball, what happens is the tendency to create a lot of back-spin and the ball tends to ''sky'' as a result of this excessive back-spin. So the bad shots generally will come from either hitting the **top** of the ball, or hitting the **bottom** of the ball.

You should have concluded at this stage that there are three important factors that relate to a golf shot:

● One is the direction of the swing: In other words the force of the swing, whether it is on target, left of target or right of target.
● The second is the angle of the clubface: Is it on target, left or right?
● The third factor is the part of the ball the head strikes: Does it come down steep on the top of the ball, or does it come in from behind the ball and is it a shallow attack on the ball?

And these are the three important points. If you can get correct or on target the force of the swing, the clubface and the angle that it comes in at, you have a good shot. If one of these factors is out, it will cause a certain misbehaviour in the shot. If you have two or more of these – you are in an awful lot of trouble! To repeat: the direction the ball **takes off** is the result of your **swing line.** The direction it **spins towards** at the latter stages of the flight is the result of the **angle of the clubface** and the **height** or lack of it is a result of the **steepness** or **shallowness** of the swing. In other words, the angle the clubface comes down on the ball and the part of the ball that is struck (upper, middle or bottom).

A forewarning and a message!
Before naming the bad shots, I want you to be aware of the fact that swerve on the ball-flight is caused by the clubface being open or closed to the force of the swing and that this in turn is the result of faulty grip. It is therefore the grip that controls the clubface. **Ninety per cent of the high handicap shots start out left of the target** as a result of the

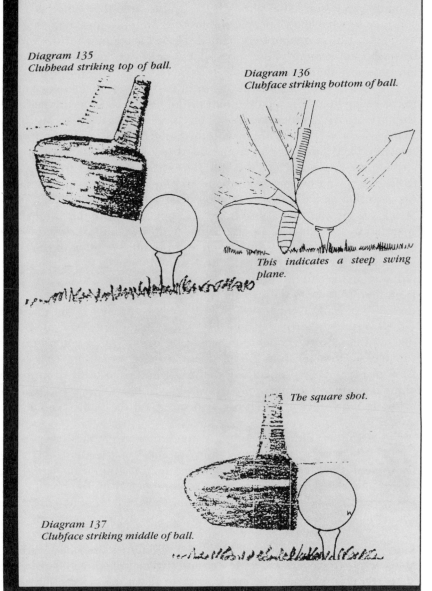

Diagram 135
Clubhead striking top of ball.

Diagram 136
Clubface striking bottom of ball.

This indicates a steep swing plane.

The square shot.

Diagram 137
Clubface striking middle of ball.

force being applied **from the outside.** If you, as an aspiring golfer, can somehow manage to start the **ball's journey out right of where you intend it to finish,** you will have broken a very big barrier indeed.

I am now going to name the bad shots in golf.

There is the "slice"; the "pull"; the "sky"; the "fluff"; the "shank"; the "top"; the "hook"; the "push" and the "smother". So contrary to what many people think there are only nine bad shots in the game. I have deliberately named the bad shots in a certain order, because I am keeping those shots which are closely related together. I am grouping them into families.

The "slice" comes from an **out to in** swing, with the clubface open to the swing line. The "pull" comes from an **out to in** swing with the clubface square to the swing line. The "sky" comes from an **out to in** swing with a very steep angle with the clubface striking the bottom of the ball. The "fluff" comes from an **out to in** swing with the clubface striking the ground before the ball. The "shank" comes from an **out to in** swing – an exaggerated **out to in** swing where it is the shank of the club that actually strikes the ball. The "top" is from a very steep attack on the top of the ball from the outside. Now the "hook" is sparkled by a shallow **in to out** swing, with the clubface closed to the swing line. The "push" comes from an **in to out** swing, with the clubface square to the swing line. The "smother" is from an **in to out** swing, with the clubface closed down to the swing line. So you will note from that, that six of the bad shots are hit from **outside to inside** and three are possible from **inside to outside,** two are not really that bad – the "push" in particular and the "hook" – the only bad one being the smother. So the conclusion would be that 75% of golfers unfortunately hit the ball from the outside and those remaining 25% hit it from inside out, or inside along the target line. If you hit from inside along the target line, the approach would also be shallow. You will get a lower, more **forward driving trajectory** on the ball. (*See diagrams 138, 139).*

But if you are hitting outside the line, you can get the "slice", the "pull", the "sky", the "fluff", the "shank" or the "top". Hitting from the outside means across the target line, it also means left of the target, the ball starts left, the angle of approach from the outside will always be steep. There will be a tendency to have a lot of height on the shot as a result of hitting the bottom of the ball from a steep angle and, as I've said, six of the possible nine shots are possible. On the other hand, hitting from inside means along the target line, approaching **shallow** the trajectory will be **lower** and **three** of the possible **nine** bad shots. So if you want to be a golfer, or to reach your potential, there is no doubt about it that irrespective of how you take the club back or what your personal idiosyncrasies are, you must be able to hit the **ball from inside out.** Some pros take the club back on the outside. Some pros take it back sharply on the inside. Some pros take it back straight from the ball and this happens even amongst the top-class tournament players, but these top-class players are all the same in the hitting area – this is really where it matters. The question you have to ask yourself is – are you among the 75% or the 25% elite who hit from the inside out to the target. Imagine there is a slot or an area you must get the club into in order to hit from the inside.

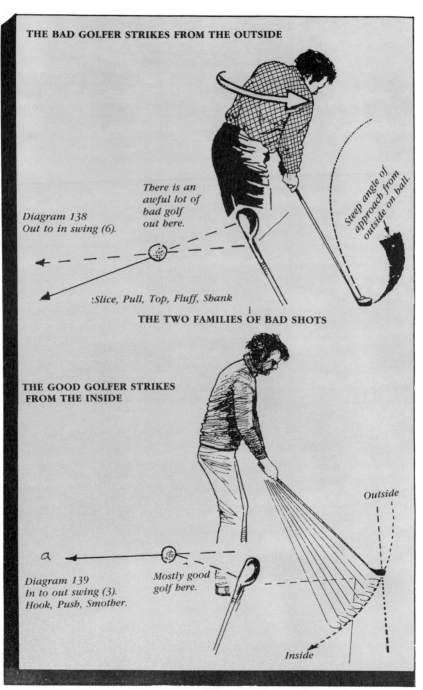

THE BAD GOLFER STRIKES FROM THE OUTSIDE

*Diagram 138
Out to in swing (6).*

*There is an
awful lot of
bad golf
out here.*

*Steep angle of
approach from
outside on ball.*

:Slice, Pull, Top, Fluff, Shank

THE TWO FAMILIES OF BAD SHOTS

**THE GOOD GOLFER STRIKES
FROM THE INSIDE**

Outside

*Mostly good
golf here.*

*Diagram 139
In to out swing (3).
Hook, Push, Smother.*

Inside

196

SPECIAL LESSON 14

Why is it so difficult to hit from the inside? Why is the slice with the drive the most common shot in golf?

There are three very good reasons why it is so.

(a) You are told you must turn your shoulders going back while on your forward swing you are **warned you must not turn into the shots.** The tendency will always be there to turn going back and going forward.

(b) The clubhead is approximately five feet off the ground at the top of your back swing. The ball is only two inches off the ground. You must be able to swing that clubhead from five feet to two inches (that is the ball) in one-fifth of a second without having the driver head actually descending as it strikes. **The problem is the direct route from the top is straight down.** Only the top-class player is able to detour his/her down swing and bottom the club early in order to present a shallow angle form the inside for approach to the ball.

(c) From the top of your back swing the clubhead has to travel approximately **ten feet,** while your hands travel approximately **three feet** in order for them to reach level with the ball. The tendency will always be **for the hands to arrive early and leave a late open clubface from the outside – slice.**

(d) Three good reasons why you must start down inside: Set-up with a strong left side, swing back on the inside, and most of all start your down swing with your legs. Do not move outside with your right shoulder. If you start down with your bottom half this move automatically pulls your right shoulder down inside; creates a much shallower angle of approach; and provides a realitic chance of your clubhead actually being able to catch up with your hands by virtue of you having created for yourself time and space on your down swing. Imagine that there is a very large pane of glass just outside the ball and if you swing **down on the outside** you will **smash** into it.

(a) ● *You are asked to turn your shoulders going back – the natural impulse is to turn them back into the shot.*

Repeating back swing (turning into the shot).

(b) ● *The clubhead is approx. five feet off the ground and the ball is only two inches. The direct route is unfortunately straight down.*

(c) ● *The clubhead has to travel approx. ten feet and your hands only approx. three feet to impact. The tendency will always be for the hands to arrive early and the clubhead late and an inevitable slice.*

SPECIAL LESSON

The top of the back swing.
You must start down with your legs.
If you do this move will:
(1) pull your right shoulder down inside;
(2) create a shallow angle of approach; and
(3) this will provide you with a realistic chance of the clubhead actually catching up with your hands at imapct and securing a square hit.

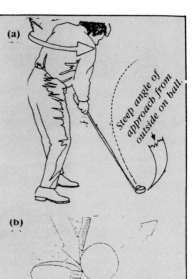

(a)

Steep angle of approach from outside on ball.

(b)

(c)

¹Distance × 3

Distance

Right elbow back to hip.

(4) **Always keep your down swing arc inside the back swing one.**

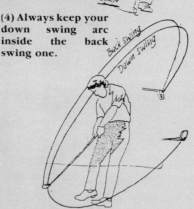

Back swing

Down swing

THE SLICE

(See diagram 140).

You hit a shot that starts left of target. However, as the ball reaches the latter stages of its flight it veers quickly towards the right. The natural reaction is simple. You look at the result – **the ball is in the right hand rough; the ball is over the fence on the right and you do the commonsense thing; you aim away from trouble to the left.** Unfortunately, the more you aim left and the more left you hit the ball, it tends to end more to the right. What have you not accounted for? **The second element in flight is namely spin. The ball ends up right because it was spinning in a clockwise direction and because of the introduction of dimples, which cause the modern ball to hang longer in the air, spin has become the dominant factor.** The ball starts left and finishes right. Even though you aim left and you hit it left, it was spinning towards the right. You could say that you got one out of two right; you swing towards the left, but **you could not get the clubface pointing in the same direction,** that is, left at impact, and because the clubface was moving so fast at impact, you could not see the result, which is an open clubface resulting in the ball finishing on the right.

So, what you have discovered from watching the ball in flight is: (1) the direction of your swing was left, or out-to-in, but (2) the clubface was pointing right at impact. This was the crucial factor. You know quite a lot about your swing now. To correct the shot, you have to have the clubface facing towards the target at impact.

How to cure a slice

A slice shot is one where the ball when attacked takes off left of the target and then in the latter stages of its flight veers wickedly to the right. It will also be a higher than normal shot, lacking distance.

Preparation

What causes a slice shot?
Body aligned for outside swing *(See diagram 141)*

A sliced shot is caused by an out-to-in swing where the clubface is open to the swing line. In other words the face of the club is open to where you are swinging. It is **a bit like pouring water into a bucket with a hole in it.** The force of the swing is to the left but the face is pointing right. The door is open.

READING THE FLIGHT OF THE SLICE SHOT

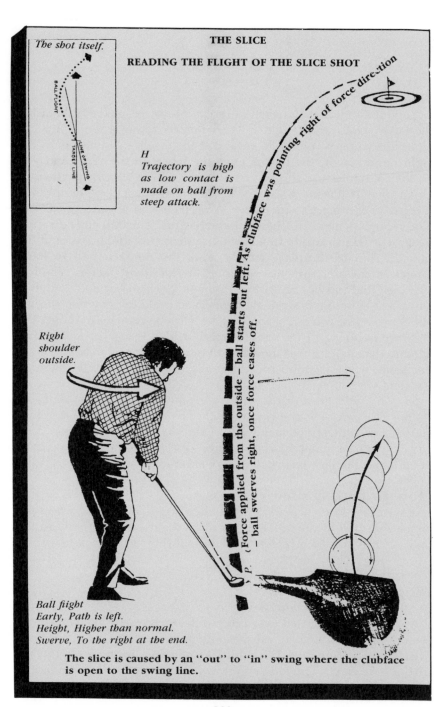

The shot itself.

BALL FLIGHT

LINE OF SWING

TARGET LINE

H
Trajectory is high as low contact is made on ball from steep attack.

As clubface was pointing right of force direction

Right shoulder outside.

(Force applied from the outside – ball starts out left. As clubface was pointing right, once force eases off. – ball swerves right, once force eases off.

P.

Ball flight
Early, Path is left.
Height, Higher than normal.
Swerve, To the right at the end.

The slice is caused by an "out" to "in" swing where the clubface is open to the swing line.

Diagram 141

CAUSES OF THE SLICE

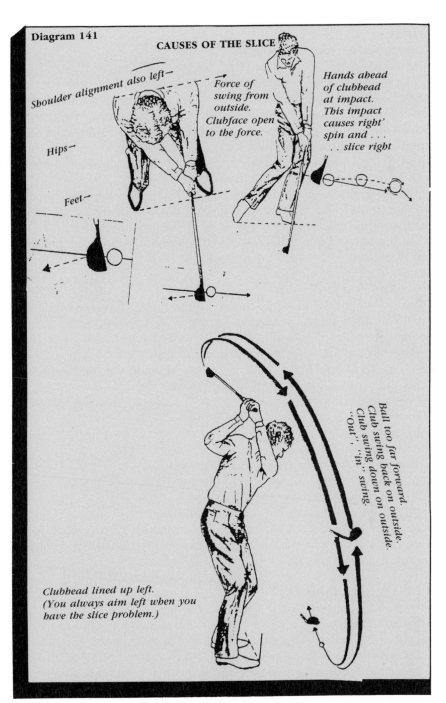

Shoulder alignment also left

Force of swing from outside. Clubface open to the force.

Hands ahead of clubhead at impact. This impact causes right' spin and . . .

. . slice right

Hips

Feet

Ball too far forward.
Club swing back on outside.
Club swing down on outside.
'Out', 'in' swing.

Clubhead lined up left.
(You always aim left when you have the slice problem.)

Address
How do we correct it?
Attack the grip. *(See diagrams 142, 143).*

The main problem is the open face. As it is our hands that control the face we must realise that there is **something wrong with way we are holding the club or putting our hands on the club.** We have to change the way we grip. We have to move our left hand in a clockwise direction so that three knuckles are visible without moving your head. This will feel very uncomfortable and your left hand will want to move back to its natural position the first chance it gets.

The first chance it gets is when you place the clubhead on the ground. It will also tend to sit closed on the take-away as left hand turns around the clubface will tend to "hook" going back.

On top is will be in a slightly closed position and produce a closed one at impact.

No easy way
Let me emphasise here if you have the problem there are no short-cuts. **You must attack your grip** even if it feels terrible at first. The feeling you will get is as if the club will fly out of your hands – a feeling of powerlessness in your left hand and strain in your left arm. If you say "I couldn't hit a ball with that", then you are in the right position.

Secondly you have to stand in such a way that will discourage an out-to-in and encourage an in to out one. *Stand inside* or in an in to out position.

Let's do it.

Aim clubface at target.

Ensure left hand is in correct position.

Align body – feet, hips and shoulders to right of target.

Now you have set the angles.

By aiming the clubhead at the target and your body slightly right of where your clubhead is lined up, you are setting up a swing when your clubhead will be at impact facing left of the direction where you are swinging.

The swing itself
Set-up with the left, hit it with the right
Swing along line of body, feet, hips and shoulders. On top of the back swing position the shaft at the target or right of it.

As you hit the ball use your right hand in such a way that it turns over your left and so turns clubface from an open position to closed one through impact. *(See diagram 144).*

202

Diagram 142

A weak grip moves back in swing and in doing so opens the fact of the club at impact. Essential move to cure slice.

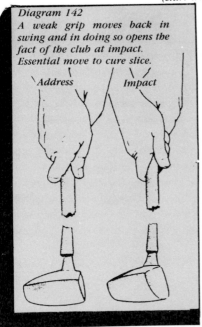

Address   *Impact*

A strong grip will close the face at impact.

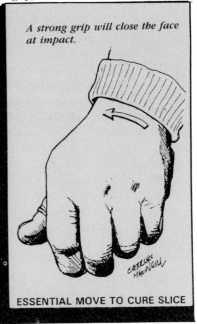

ESSENTIAL MOVE TO CURE SLICE

Preventing slice.

Diagram 144
Rotate right hand through the hitting area. To prevent slice.

Don't move your body into shot.

If you do not have a major problem with the slice you may have to make only minor adjustments. You may not have to interfere with your grip. The reason for the clubface being open may simply be "late" hitting. The body moves through first, leaving the clubhead behind. The door is open. Think of it like this. If you are driving your car and try to pass out another car in front of you. He suddenly speeds up, you will not be able to overtake. But if he were to suddenly stop, your car would immediately fly by. In the golf swing your arms, hands and the clubhead are all travelling towards the ball. The clubhead is way behind. If your top half speeds on the clubhead has no chance of ever catching up. But if your left arm puts up the **stop** sign (by applying a weight at the top of the grip) and you lever the clubhead end forward, you are in business. You must be able to apply a force directly against all the forward thrust of your swing, and have one force working against the other causing leverage at the bottom end of the golf club.

Simple cure

(1) Aim clubhead at target.

(2) Align body more to right.

(3) Release clubhead early. Think of letting the clubhead go, not holding on to it.

The slice may come from playing tight courses when you end up steering the ball or from too much theorising when you are not swinging the clubhead or concentrating on the left side to an extent that you are forgetting that you have a right side.

If you are out playing a round of golf and suffer a "spate" of slicing, and do not have time to make the change, what can you do? You might be in the middle of a tight fourball and under pressure from your partner who is complaining of the "hump on his back" from carrying you. You have to have a little chat with yourself and say "I know the reason why I am slicing the ball. It is because the face of the club is open at impact." The point is, when you are swinging through the ball as it happens so quickly you cannot see where the clubface – it is pointing.

So what you say to yourself is: "Well, I know what this is. How can I prevent it?"

There is one. When you are standing to the ball instead of aiming the clubhead at the target, simply (realising the problem is the open face at impact) "toe it in". Pre-turn it into a closed position. This will seem quite wrong but the effect it will have is that, because you have it in a closed position no matter how much you manage to open it dur-

Hood clubface at address to prevent slice.

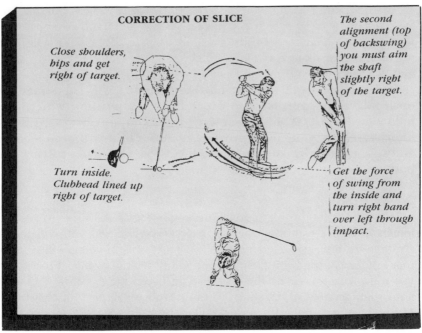

CORRECTION OF SLICE

Close shoulders, hips and get right of target.

The second alignment (top of backswing) you must aim the shaft slightly right of the target.

Turn inside. Clubhead lined up right of target.

Get the force of swing from the inside and turn right hand over left through impact.

ing your swing, it will come back more or less square to the ball – it certainly will not come back open. (By toeing the clubface you are actually strengthening your grip!) *(See diagram 145)*.

A final word of advice. If you have the "slice" problem, have a look at the clubs you are using. We must go back to the clubhead again – if you are slicing it is because the face is open – pointing right at impact. What you have to try is avoid a driver where the face is open. Try to get one where the face is "toed in" or one with "loft" on the face, or even a two wood. The reason for this is if you have a little loft on the driver or if you get a two wood (22° loft approx.) there is less chance of slicing.

With these low numbered flat-faced clubs the clubface meets the back of the ball when striking it, it is very much easier to impart side-spin to it. On a nine iron or wedge the face is angled back and because of the "nature" of the face you tend to hit the bottom of the ball. The clubface first makes contact with the bottom of the ball and you start to impart back-spin which means the ball is spinning straight back when you hit it.

If you bring this down to a finer point, you have smaller chance of slicing with a two wood or a lofted driver. The face of the club you should be looking for is one that is "toed in", one that will discourage a slice and encourage a draw or even a "hook".

Another point is that if you have thick grips they will tend to fall into the palm of the hand so that you have a "weak" left hand grip position. If you can manage to get thin grips *(See diagram 146)* , these will tend to fall into your fingers and so produce a stronger left hand grip – they will help encourage draw and prevent slice. *(See diagram 138)*.

Irons: If the head lies flat on the ground it will encourage an open face at impact. (It also depends on the position which you hold your hands.) If you have forged irons you can always get them knocked-up by your local pro and then the heel will ground first and so slow it down and the toe will close in as you are hitting the ball.

A synopsis

If you have the problem you must really attack the grip. Move the left hand into a position where it feels powerless and you will feel a strain in the left arm, a feeling that you can't turn. If you get these feelings you are in the right position and ready to cure a slice. Most of all you must learn to release the clubhead past your hands before you turn your shoulders out of the shot. You must release against the resistance of a solid upper left side, not a collapsed spinning one. *(See diagram 147)*.

206

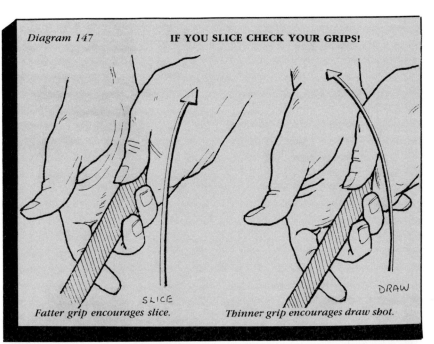

Diagram 147

IF YOU SLICE CHECK YOUR GRIPS!

SLICE

DRAW

Fatter grip encourages slice.   *Thinner grip encourages draw shot.*

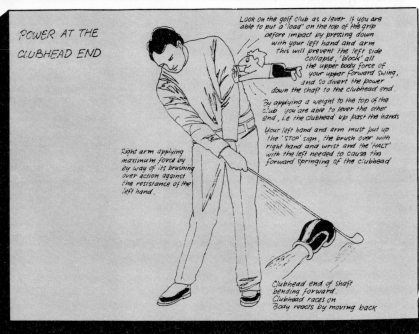

POWER AT THE CLUBHEAD END

Look on the golf club as a lever. If you are able to put a 'load' on the top of the grip before impact by pressing down with your left hand and arm this will prevent the left side collapse, 'block' all the upper body force of your upper forward swing, and so divert the power down the shaft to the clubhead end.

By applying a weight to the top of the club you are able to lever the other end, i.e. the clubhead up past the hands

Your left hand and arm must put up the 'STOP' sign, the brush over with right hand and wrist and the 'HALT' with the left needed to cause the forward springing of the clubhead

Right arm applying maximum force by by way of its brushing over action against the resistance of the left hand.

Clubhead end of shaft bending forward. Clubhead races on Body reacts by moving back

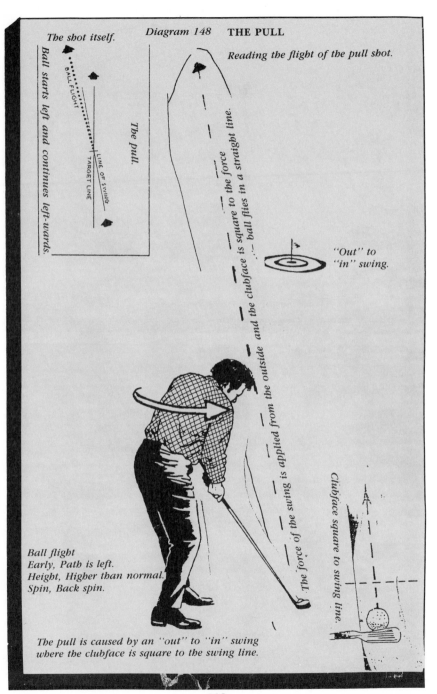

Diagram 148   **THE PULL**

The shot itself.

Reading the flight of the pull shot.

Ball starts left and continues left-wards.

BALL FLIGHT

The pull.

LINE OF SWING
TARGET LINE

...ball flies in a straight line.

...the clubface is square to the force

The force of the swing is applied from the outside and

"Out" to "in" swing.

Ball flight
Early, Path is left.
Height, Higher than normal.
Spin, Back spin.

Clubface square to swing line.

*The pull is caused by an "out" to "in" swing
where the clubface is square to the swing line.*

208

THE PULL SHOT

(See diagram 148).

The second shot is the **pull**. (The pull and the slice are closely related, as they are both produced from an **out to in** swing and the same corrections that were viable for the slice will be for the pull.) The pull is different by virtue of the fact that it is a shot that goes in a straight line to the left of the target. It is the exact reverse of the push. As the ball flies in a straight line with no swerve on it, the clubface and the swing line are united – they are both going left of the target. So we do not need to worry about the clubface. We are left with the direction of the force: which is left of the target and the angle the clubface comes at the ball is steep. There will be a tendency to get height on the shots. The **pull** shot is one where you could then say that the ball definitely has no brains – it is going where it is hit! And while it is not a bad shot in itself, it is a bad indication of the shape of your swing! Because if you are pulling the ball, there is always a danger of getting on to any of the other bad shots that result from hitting the ball from the outside – even the dreaded "shank".

What causes the pulled shot? *(See diagram 149).* One cause is bad preparation. **Clubface lined left of the target and body lined up left of the target.** The ball position will be generally too far forward in the stance. Study the diagram on ball positions. Now the first move on the back swing will tend to be outside and on the top of the back swing the shaft of the club will be pointing left of target. On the first move on the down swing, the club will be taken down on the outside and therefore approached from the outside and across with the clubface square to the force. So everything is geared for an **out to in** swing. We have to re-organise. By lining up the clubhead if anything slightly right of the target and similarly ensuring that the ball position is back in the stance, will ensure that the feet, the hips and the shoulders are pointing slightly to the right of the target. *(See diagram 150).* Now everything is geared up right of target. It is very important then to get the idea of the second alignment, that is the top of the back swing, to get the shaft of the club slightly across the line, as shown in diagram, or pointing slightly right of the target. The next important move is the start of the down swing, to ensure that you hit the ball from inside out, or away from yourself. It sometimes happens that a golfer can pull the ball from a relatively good position at the top of the back swing, by virtue of the fact that he **is using his top half** *(See diagram 151)* **too much,** and **his bottom half is not working.** So it is essential that the club is not thrown from the top. It is essential that the hips lead the down swing

CAUSES OF THE PULL

Your shoulders are open at address if you suffer from the pull.

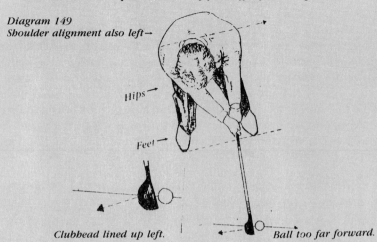

Diagram 149
Shoulder alignment also left→

Hips→

Feet→

Clubhead lined up left.

Ball too far forward.

Club swing back on outside.
Shaft laid off or pointing left on
top.

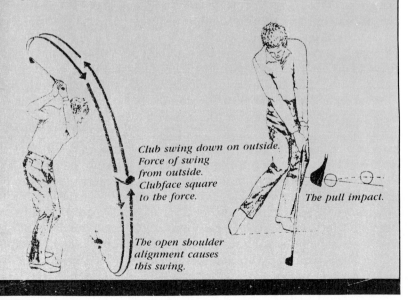

Club swing down on outside.
Force of swing
from outside.
Clubface square
to the force.

The pull impact.

The open shoulder
alignment causes
this swing.

CORRECTION FOR THE PULL
Close up your shoulders.

Diagram 150
Shoulder alignment
right of target.

The alignment – you must position
shaft slightly across the line at the
top.

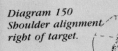

Hips

Feet

Shaft aimed slightly high of target
at the top.

Ball position moved back.

Clubhead line dup right of target.

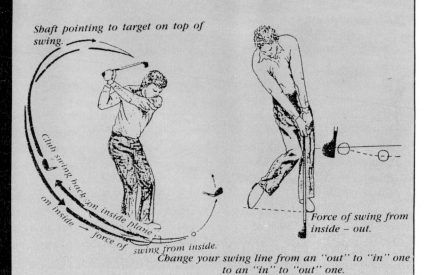

Shaft pointing to target on top of
swing.

Club swing back on inside plane — force of swing from inside.

Force of swing from
inside – out.

Change your swing line from an "out" to "in" one
to an "in" to "out" one.

and the hands follow – **not** the other way around. *(See diagram 152).*

Sometimes this happens if the legs are in bad shape or tired or if you just forget to use your legs through the hitting area. A **pull shot** is caused also by a **tilty back swing.** Where the preparation is wrong, body tends to be too far away from the ball *(See diagram 153)*. It is in a stooped position, club is taken back with a tilting motion of the shoulder *(See diagram 154)* – the left shoulder going down, the right shoulder moving up and then, on the down swing, hitting from outside. Now this will result in a pull, but occasionally will result in a very bad **slice** or for that matter any of the other bad shots that are caused by it. A pull shot can often occur from very **bad alignment,** this time very much to the right of the target. Sometimes golfers have the idea that they must line up their shoulders on target. What happens is that, if the golfer lines up his shoulders on target, he tends to aim the clubface well to the right of the target and everything is geared towards the right of the target. Now he may make a beautiful practise swing when there's nothing at stake and swing out to the right of the target, but when the ball goes down, what happens is that the player tries to **correct the misalignment** in the swing and tries to somehow **redirect the ball back towards the target.** Remembering that he is lined up well to the right of the target, or that the target is left of where he is aligned, the tendency will be to swing around himself in the hitting area and this will cause a pulled shot. In other words, the player lines up **miles to the right of the target and corrects the alignment by** pulling across his body through the hitting area. Most of the golf courses have boundaries and follow the St. Andrews mould, with the boundary on the right-hand side and even though the player is lined up on the boundary he is instinctively swinging back around to the target or away from the boundary, back around to the fairway. If you have this problem there is a very interesting way of practising. If you go out on the practise ground and line the clubhead up left of the target, ever so slightly, body left of the target, feet, hips and shoulders, left of the target, now, keep in mind at the same time where the target is and that the next move is to actually swing out to the target: do not swing where you are aiming, but swing out to the right. This will help you to get a feeling of what it is to swing away from yourself, or to swing on an **in to out** plane. It only makes sense that when you go out on the golf course, you line up the clubhead on target, body well to the left of the target. Now you've loads of room, loads of fairway out there to swing at. So you swing back on the inside and hit the ball from inside out, always endeavouring to get the club shaft across the line of the top of the back swing and to start the down swing with your legs, your bottom half, through the hitting area.

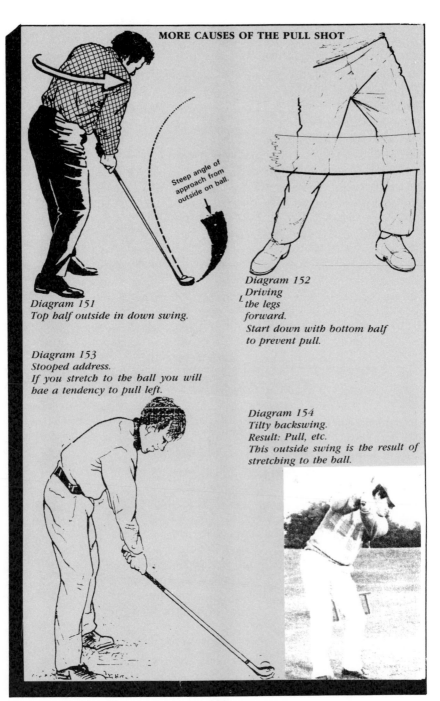

MORE CAUSES OF THE PULL SHOT

Steep angle of approach from outside on ball.

Diagram 151
Top half outside in down swing.

Diagram 152
Driving
the legs
forward.
Start down with bottom half
to prevent pull.

Diagram 153
Stooped address.
If you stretch to the ball you will
hae a tendency to pull left.

Diagram 154
Tilty backswing.
Result: Pull, etc.
This outside swing is the result of
stretching to the ball.

So I'm just going to finish with a few checks for the **pull.** You have to check the alignment:

- Misaligned left of target – encouraging a leftward swing (ball position too far forward).
- Misaligned right of the target – player swings around to the left in order to correct.
- Check the ball position.
- Check the start of the back swing – are you turning your shoulders correctly on a flat plane. At the top of the back swing the shaft must be across the line and the start of the down swing must be with your legs and of course start the down swing on the **inside.**
- Try to feel that you are leading with the back of your left hand and arm **out** towards the target.

"AH NOW, FAIR PLAY TO McCARTHY FOR MAKING THE EFFORT"

READING THE FLIGHT OF THE SKY SHOT

The cause of the sky shot is a steep outside swing with the clubhead contracting the ball very low.

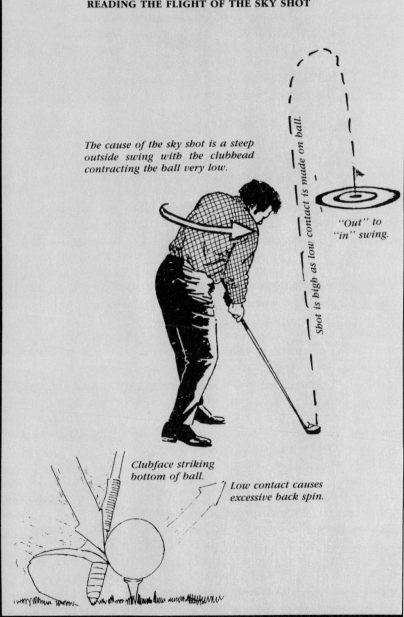

Shot is high as low contact is made on ball.

"Out" to "in" swing.

Clubface striking bottom of ball.

Low contact causes excessive back spin.

THE SKY

Cause – Letter "V" type swing.
Correction – Develop a wide base to your swing.

P.S.: This lesson will help you master the long game. It is a very important lesson. Read it if you have a bad long game. *(See diagram 155).*

The name "sky" tells us that the ball doesn't travel very far forward, but travels up towards the sky. It is sometimes regarded as the three hundred yards shot – a hundred and fifty yards up in the air and a hundred and fifty yards down again! It seems an awful waste of effort to hit that ball so hard and to see it travel upwards and then to pop down on to the ground approximately one hundred and fifty yards from the tee. You have to ask yourself straight away what is the cause of a skyed shot? A skyed shot is the result of **low contact with the ball. What this means is that the clubhead does not hit the top of the ball, nor does it hit the middle, it hits the bottom, travelling downwards and this creates excessive back-spin.** The ball, therefore, climbs up into the air. The next question you have to ask yourself is why does this happen? Why is it that the bottom of the ball is contacted, rather than the middle of the ball? There is more than one reason for this, however, but in general terms, one would have to say that if you have a problem with skying, your swing is **too steep** – it resembles the rugby ball. *(See diagram 156).* There is no width in it – what goes up must come down. In other words, if you pick the club up quickly on your back swing *(See diagram 157)* you will not have any width on the down swing, you will come down with a chopping action on top of the ball. *(See diagram 158).* Generally speaking, off the tee you will be inclined to take a divot and certainly you will always be looking for your tee. You have to ask yourself a question – why is it that you are inclined to have this steep swing and the resulting choppy action, causing low contact with the ball and an excessive back-spin? The reason that you have this steep swing is that the **right side is too strong** in your set up. *(See diagram 159).* This means that your strong hand, your right hand and your right arm are in a nearly straight position, with the right elbow too far out from the body. What happens then is very obvious on the swing. The **right side takes the club back and** *(See diagram 160)* **it lifts it up very quickly on the back swing.** On the top of the back swing the shaft of the club is laid off and there is little or no turn. The weight *(See diagram 161)* is much too much on the left leg and a down blow is struck on the ball. *(See diagram 162).*

How do we correct the **skied** shot? The first principle is to remember

216

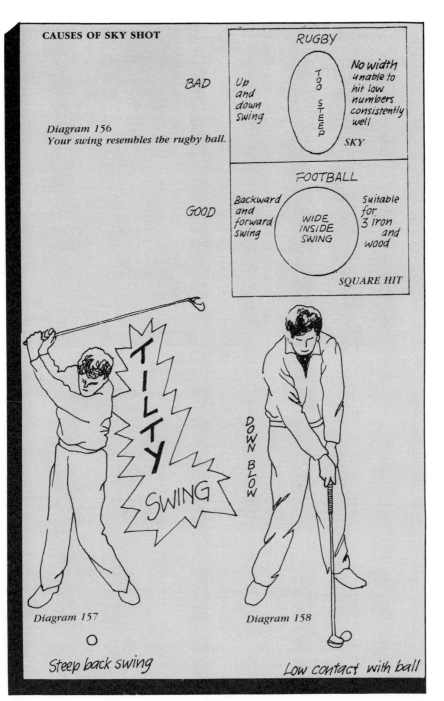

CAUSES OF SKY SHOT

BAD

Diagram 156
Your swing resembles the rugby ball.

RUGBY

Up and down swing

TOO STEEP

No width unable to hit low numbers consistently well

SKY

GOOD

FOOTBALL

Backward and forward swing

WIDE INSIDE SWING

Suitable for 3 iron and wood

SQUARE HIT

TILTY SWING

DOWN BLOW

Diagram 157

Diagram 158

Steep back swing

Low contact with ball

Diagram 159
Right side too strong.

Diagram 160
Pick up with right side.

Diagram 161
Steep top of swing.
Weight on left foot.

Diagram 162
Down blow to bottom half of ball.

what are you trying to do. You're trying to move a round object in a forward direction, with a flat-faced club – remember the words **forward direction** – it doesn't really make sense then to have a chopping action, does it? So what you have to do is set up for a swing that is not up and down, but **back and forward.** Remember, the pendulum of a clock, swinging back and forward, back and forward . . . Imagine if that pendulum on the clock was to swing upwards – it would automatically come down at a steep angle towards the ground. So what you have to do is set your weaker left side in a strong position. You start the grip in the fingers (not the palm) of your left hand *(See diagram 163)*. Your left arm is in line with the shaft. Your left hand is where the V is formed by the base of the index finger and the thumb that this V is pointing towards the **right** shoulder. The right hand is barely sitting on the club, with the elbow relaxed and tucked into the side *(See diagram 164)*. On the back swing keeping the **right hand and arm very quiet** and driving the left shoulder and arm and especially the **clubhead back along the ground** *(See diagram 165)* create the width on the way back so that you will take advantage of it on the way down and through. The approach is made from a shallow angle on the back of the ball *(See diagrams 166, 167)* leaving the tee in the ground. A simple way of clarifying all this is to **listen to the clubhead going back.** You must hear the clubhead rubbing off the grass on the back swing, and not only that but you must endeavour to hit the ball and leave the tee in the ground, or hit the ball as the clubhead is travelling away from and not into the ground. *(See diagram 168)*.

What we are talking about is the grass test. The grass is brushed down on the back swing by the clubhead and the width is created on the way back and availed of on the way down. Hand and hand with the steep back swing is a tilty shoulder movement. What this means is that the player tends to tilt his shoulders on the back swing. The left shoulder tends to go down. The right shoulder tends to move upwards. There is no coiling action. Generally this comes about from a player standing too far away from the ball, with the knees straight and the back bent forward. Weight is on the toes and the back on the outside and the right shoulder moving upwards – no coiling action. There is an over-swing tendency and, on the down swing, the clubhead is taken outside and across with a steep swing. . . . If you have a sky problem, in order to help you to create the width and the shallow angle of approaching the ball, you've got to stand into the ball . . . Crowd the ball out and keep the weight back on your heels with your knees flexed and **back in a straight position.**

219

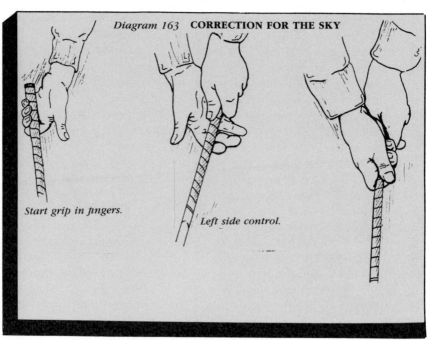

Diagram 163 **CORRECTION FOR THE SKY**

Start grip in fingers.

Left side control.

*Diagram 164
Inside set-up*

Right elbow relaxed inwards

*Set for flatter swing
– low approach.*

Diagram 165
If you push clubhead back along ground . . .

Diagram 166
. . . it will automatically approach from low angle to back of ball.

Diagram 167
Sweep the ball forward leaving tee in ground.

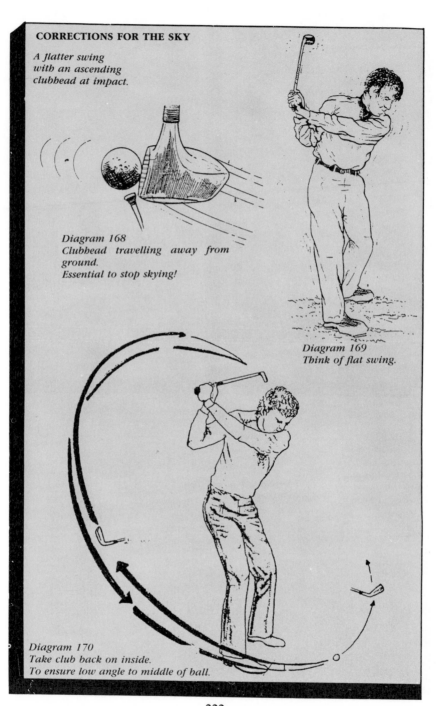

CORRECTIONS FOR THE SKY

A flatter swing with an ascending clubhead at impact.

Diagram 168
Clubhead travelling away from ground.
Essential to stop skying!

Diagram 169
Think of flat swing.

Diagram 170
Take club back on inside.
To ensure low angle to middle of ball.

Diagram 171
How to practice flat turn.
Hands opposite chin.

Diagram 172
Turn shoulders at. . .
. . . same level, to prevent tilty
back swing.

A flat swing for flat-faced clubs to ensure low approach on the ball

Get a mental picture of a **flat** swing . . . *(See diagram 169)*, a **flat** turn – where your two shoulders are turning at the same level, where you are turning around behind the ball and at the top of the back swing, where your back is facing the target. In other words, you've turned around on the back swing and automatically by **this flatter swing plane** you will hit more from **inside** and towards the back of the ball. *(See diagram 170)*. A very good way of practising this – we have done it earlier in practising to turn the shoulders – is, having placed your hands on the grip of the club in the normal position *(See diagram 171)*, to move your hands and your arms upwards to a position so that they are opposite your chin and then to turn your shoulders **on the same plane** and position the club. *(See diagram 172)*.

I am going to finish with the summaries for corrections:

- Check your preparation – is your right side too strong?
- Check the take-away.
- Is your back swing steep?
- Are your shoulders turning on a flat (correct) or tilty (incorrect) plane?
- Are you standing too far away from the ball?
- And, of course, hitting – do you knock the tee out of the ground or take an excessive divot?

P.S. In general these corrections apply in relation to your **long game.**

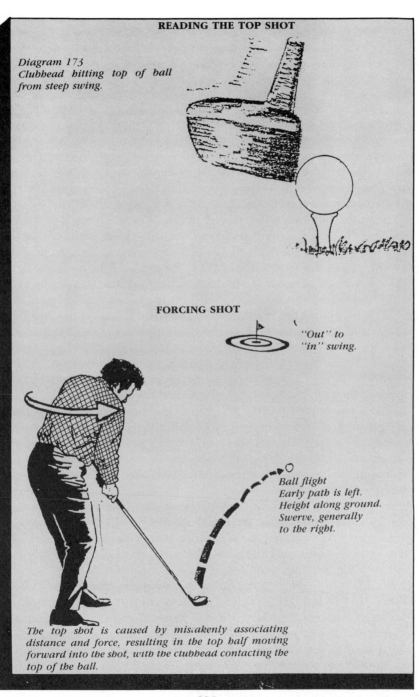

Diagram 173
Clubhead hitting top of ball
from steep swing.

FORCING SHOT

"Out" to
"in" swing.

Ball flight
Early path is left.
Height along ground.
Swerve, generally
to the right.

*The top shot is caused by mistakenly associating
distance and force, resulting in the top half moving
forward into the shot, with the clubhead contacting the
top of the ball.*

THE TOP

(See diagram 173).

If it is possible to hit the bottom of the ball and create the **sky** it is also possible to hit the top of the ball and to **top** it. The top shot is rarely the sin of the golfer with much experience. It is the common fault, however, of a duffer and the veritable bane of the beginner. The problem with the **top** shot is that much of the cause is tension and this is associated with the novice. He is anxious about the result of the shot and tends to grip the club very very tight with **the mistaken idea that the ball has to be forced** – that a lot of force has got to be applied in the swing. He moves the body into *(See diagram 174)* the shot to crush the ball into the ground. If you look at the diagram, this is one of the best known ways to top a shot. The player has failed to keep his head fixed as he swings the club down to the ball. His head has moved to his left and up as well and with the head have gone the shoulders and the upper part of the body. You can see the arc of the swing has been completely destroyed. Now this is referred to as head up by most helpful golfers, but in actual fact the reason the head moves up is because the body has moved forward and into the shot so it is not that the head has moved but the top half of the body has moved forward and upward. The correction for this is for the player to grip the club gently, like a tube of toothpaste. Relax the hands and then realise that you do not hit the ball with your body, with your feet, with your hips, with your shoulders or your head. **It is actually the head of the club that hits the ball!**

So rather than moving yourself *(See diagram 175)* into it, you have got to move the clubhead *(See diagram 176)* into it, and this will move the ball for you. **If you want to move the ball, you move the clubhead into it and it will move the ball for you.** So to keep the body back and out of the shot practise giving the ball a little flick with the clubhead. A little swish with your wrists would delegate the work away from yourself and down on to the clubhead.

The second major cause of moving forward and into the shot is that on the back swing you may have moved back. In other words, in your swing you do not have any decent shoulder turn, but what you have is a **lateral sway away from the ball.** If you sway back from the ball, where the weight has moved **outside** the right foot, what you have suc-

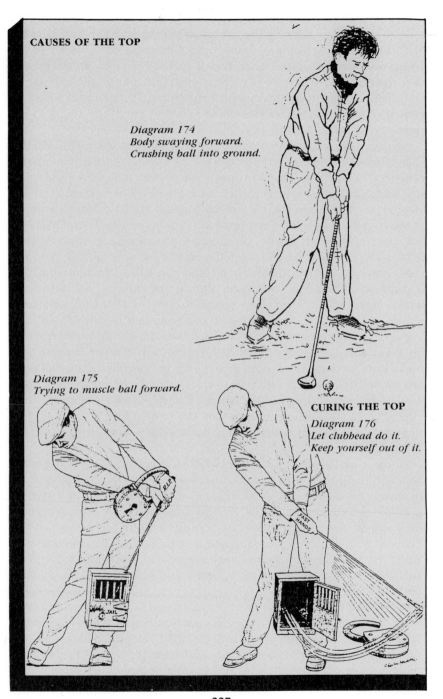

CAUSES OF THE TOP

Diagram 174
Body swaying forward.
Crushing ball into ground.

Diagram 175
Trying to muscle ball forward.

CURING THE TOP

Diagram 176
Let clubhead do it.
Keep yourself out of it.

ceeded in doing is moving the arc of the swing and, when you come back down because you have moved back from the ball, the arc of the swing will have bottomed out before it reached the ball and you come over the top of it. When the player sways to the right on the back swing and does not return on the down swing quite to the point at which he started to sway, he moves the whole axis and arc of the swing to the right.

Simple, isn't it! If your body is moving all over the place and this is causing your **head to move backwards and forwards,** there is one easy way to check it. Once you have taken your stance and addressed the ball then have a friend in fact an enemy will be just as good *(See diagram 177)* stand on the far side of the ball with his feet just out of range of the clubhead and facing you. Then, have your friend place his left hand lightly, but firmly, on your head, and take a swing. If your head pulls away, or turns under the hand, you will immediately feel the resistance of your friend's hand and you will know that you have a problem of moving your head during the swing. Jack Nicklaus, whose swing in his early days tended to have a lot of leg and body action as his hands were relatively small, tended to rely on his very strong legs to propel the ball forward. He had a lot of movement with his head and Jack Grout used to literally grab him by the hair and make him hit shots. Very soon young Jack got this idea that head must not move laterally, but that **it must stay in a fixed position around which the swing was made.** Arnold Palmer, whose swing was very violent, a hitter's action, emphasises the head position as being very important. The golfer, who tends to be more of a swinger type, will not have this problem.

Another cause of the **top** shot is **faulty posture,** just lke the **skied** shot and the **pulled** shot and all the other bad shots. If you look at the diagram *(See diagram 178)* you will see that the knees are in a straight position and the top half is in a stooped position. The body **weight is forward** in the stance. In other words, a crouched set up. What happens here is that if you lean and reach for the ball, you **are very likely to straighten up on the back swing** and to stay up on the down swing, so the arc of the swing is raised and you hit the ball on top – that's if at all!

Now from this faulty posture position it is also *(See diagram 179)* very likely that you will have **a very tilty action,** where your left shoulder goes down on your back swing and the right knee straightens, no coiling action whatsoever taking place, and an over swing. On the top of the back swing the weight is on the left foot opposite the ball and what happens on the down swing is very obvious – the weight shifts back to

228

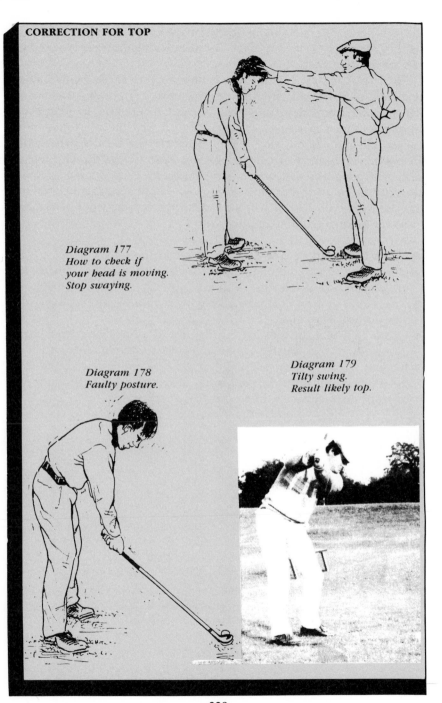

*Diagram 177
How to check if
your head is moving.
Stop swaying.*

*Diagram 178
Faulty posture.*

*Diagram 179
Tilty swing.
Result likely top.*

the right foot. There is the tendency for the arc of the swing to bottom out before it has reached the ball and the clubhead comes over the top and causes this shot!

Finally, let me say that a topped shot can very occasionally happen to a good player and it often comes from excessive body action in the down swing, related to a **push** shot and the failure to release the clubhead. You just come over the top of it and the correction is, of course, to get the hands working to release the clubhead a little earlier. In the final summary of corrections you have to line up with the left side in a good position and the right shoulder lower than your left shoulder, in an **in to out** preparation, where the tendency will be that the clubhead will approach from behind the ball and not above it.

So the corrections for topping are:

● Check that you are not gripping the club too tightly.
● Check that you are not moving your body into the shot, forward and up, as a result of tension.
● Check that you do not have a swaying action in your swing – that you do not sway away from the ball.
● Check that you are not raising the arc of your swing from faulty posture and that you do not have a reverse weight shift.
● Finally, if you're a top-class player who occasionally suffered from the top, you must know it is from a failure to release the clubhead, or from an excessively **in to out** body-type swing.

THE
FLUFF
SHOT

"Out" to
"in" swing.

Steep angle of
approach from
outside on ball.

*Ground
is contacted
before ball..*

*The fluff is caused by an over swing
and a resulting early casting across on
the down swing.*

Diagram 180

THE FLUFFED SHOT

(See diagram 180).

This type of shot generally associates with an awful lot of effort being put into the swing. The player tends to get very tired after hitting a number of balls. Once again, this is the failure to realise that it is the clubhead that does the work – not you. **There is also the mistaken idea that the longer the back swing, the farther the ball will travel.** Of course it is the exact opposite, as the **long back swing tends to break down into a collapsed position at the top** and there is no coiling action and no wound-up power. If you look at the drawing *(See diagram 181)* and if you want to hit the ground behind the ball, this is an excellent position to be in. There is so much weight on the left leg and the next thing is on the down – you will straighten that left leg, throw the weight back on to the right and then when you chop down **at the ball you'll hit the ground before the ball.** *(See diagram 182).* See second drawing. Now, what is the cause of this terrible body type swing? Well, basically **the right hand and arm are in much too strong a position, causing an over swing.** And on the down swing, a casting action is on the outside. Where the clubhead is thrown and on the top of the back swing the weight was on the left foot and on the down swing the weight moves back to the right foot very very quickly and the ground is hit before the ball. Now what you have to do is give your right side a holiday! It has been working much too hard and your left side has been idling. So you set up with your left side – your weaker side – in a strong position at address and barely have your right hand on the club and have your right elbow tucked in, in a relaxed position.

Now the first move on the back swing must be to turn. **Just to turn your shoulders on a flat plane using a short back swing.** You may have a guilt complex as a result of this. This is not so. Get your left side in a strong position and practise by straightening the fingers on the right hand. Just simply turn your shoulders on the same plane. *(See diagrams 183, 184).*

Turn your shoulder on the first half of your back swing
(See diagram 185).

A great help here is to have your right shoulder in vision of the corner of your eye and on the **first move** on the back swing the right shoulder should disappear around behind you. A much flatter swing. If you feel your swing is very flat, this is what we are looking for. The tendency with the **fluff** shot will always be for the player to duck the right shoulder down into the shot. The reason that the player ducks or

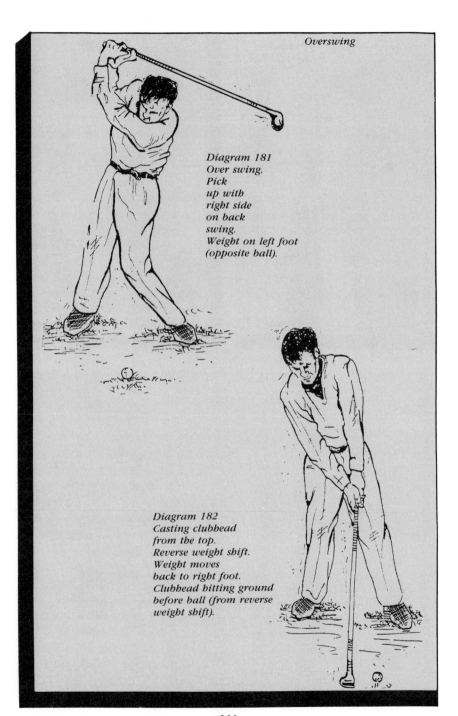

*Diagram 181
Over swing.
Pick
up with
right side
on back
swing.
Weight on left foot
(opposite ball).*

*Diagram 182
Casting clubhead
from the top.
Reverse weight shift.
Weight moves
back to right foot.
Clubhead hitting ground
before ball (from reverse
weight shift).*

Diagram 183
Give right a holiday.
Open fingers on right hand.

Diagram 184
Just turn using left side.
Short back swing sufficient.

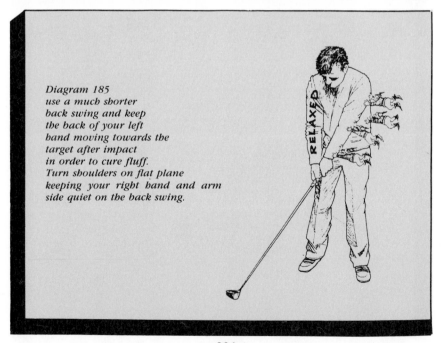

Diagram 185
use a much shorter
back swing and keep
the back of your left
hand moving towards the
target after impact
in order to cure fluff.
Turn shoulders on flat plane
keeping your right hand and arm
side quiet on the back swing.

drops his right side into the shot is because the whole swing is wrong. If it was right, he wouldn't duck: for there is nothing in the correct swing that impels the golfer to duck into the shot. So by getting the shoulders to turn on a flatter plane, with **a much shorter controlled back swing,** you correct the "dip" on the back swing and therefore there will be no need for a **compensatory "dip"** on the forward swing. In other words, if your left shoulder goes down in a dipping action on the back swing, on the down swing, your right shoulder will have to compensate by dipping into the shot. While on the other hand, if your shoulder is turned on a flat plane around behind the ball, then you have created the angle, that the clubhead will automatically come in from behind the ball and drive it forward. It sometimes happens that a good player gets into this position by an exaggerated set-up, encouraging an **in to out** swing. What happens is that the right shoulder is set under the left and the right elbow is tucked in very close to the body (an excessive inside set-up). Unfortunately the swing is so much from the inside that the player manages to hit the ground before the ball from this shallow approach.

The summary for corrections for the **fluff** shot:

- You have got to check the preparation – that your right side is not in too strong a position.
- And very important check the back swing.
- Make sure that you are **turning** your shoulders and not tilting them.
- At the top of the back swing, check that the weight is not on the left foot.
- Of course you have to check if you have an **over swing,** which is really the crucial factor in the fluff shot as the tendency from the over swing will be to cast the club on the outside and hit the ground before the ball.
- After impact check if your left arm is collapsed or extended.

THE SOCKET

Cause – Hitting ball with socket of club.
Correction – Hit ball with toe of club.
(See diagram 186).

The socket in the world of ordinary life may not mean very much but in the golf world it is a word not to be mentioned in company (do not let any golfer know you are reading this chapter). It is like one of those tropical (or topical) diseases which, if you were unluckl enough to come into contact with, could be **lethal.** The problem is that this disease is not spread through bodily contact but can be by a mere exchange of ideas so much that, if the image of one were to come into your mind, it may happen to you. This is why one of the dirtiest "bustles" in the game is to mention the word to your opponent especially if he happened to be one up on the 18th hole and was facing a delicate chip over a bunker. A remark like "I didn't have a socket for a week" in earshot of your opponent could have very serious repercursions on the 19th. You could easily be left out in the rounds when it came to drinks. The immediate effect of mentioning the socket results in anxiety and when golfers attempt to prevent its occurrence the grip **tightens** so much that he may not let go. The result is the body moves through first **leaving the clubhead behind and wide open** and sure enough he has one. The problem then is that he is really afraid of having another and his **grip becomes even tighter** and he may eventually have to "pocket" the ball.

If you happen to bring up the point in company in the clubhouse you may wonder why suddenly you are sitting there talking to yourself.

What is a socket shot? A socket shot is one where the ball comes off the socket of the club, and shoots off directly to the right.

Where is the socket part of the club?

It's the part of the club between the shaft and the head. (Wooden clubs do not have a socket.) As you can see from the diagram it has a completely different nature to the face of the club. If you hit a genuine socket, the ball does not actually come into contact with the face of the club!

How could you socket the ball?

We know what it is. If you start in the normal position at address and at impact your clubhead has come back to this position (socket country) you know something has happened during your swing. In other words you started with the ball in the middle of the face and it **is in the socket part of the club when you hit the ball.**

236

RETIRE TO THE 19th.

In the genuine socket the face itself does not actually come into contact with the ball.
Diagram 186
Reading the
socket.

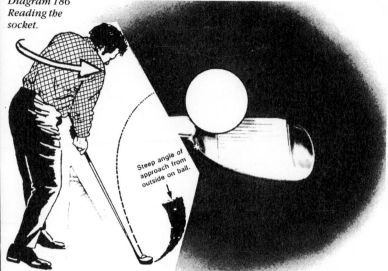

Steep angle of approach from outside on ball.

. . . as it is the socket of the club that strikes the ball. "Out" to "in" swing.

Diagram 187
Rolling face open causes a socket.

Diagram 188
Coming down on outside
also causes a socket.

What does this tell you?

Very simply your clubhead is coming down on a line that is outside a line straight back from the ball.

The question is how did you get out there?

There is unfortunately more than one way of doing it. There are two swings that can cause it. The first and the most obvious is outside and across. In other words the swing line was always "outside". The other is where the club is swung on an exaggerated inside path by rolling the wrists and so opening the clubface. *(See diagram 187)*.

On the forward swing the clubhead is looped outside and face left open through the shot. The arc the clubhead makes could best be described as the figure 8. *(See diagram 188)*.

In the former "outside across" the first move in the down swing is always with the right shoulder and the whole body moves through the hitting area ahead of the clubhead. The down swing is much too "steep". A pull shot tells you that you are hitting the ball near the socket part of the club. Golfers, who socket, have already been "pullers" of the ball. This stands to reason as the socket nearly always occurs with the high irons and as these clubs inflict more backspin than side spin, thus, if you are swinging from "outside" to "across" the ball will go straight left. **You can check what part of the face is making contact with the ball by marking the back of the ball with chalk and then see where the marks are on the clubface after you struck the ball.**

How do you correct it?

You have to swing in such a way that your clubhead approaches the ball not from outside a line straight back from the ball, but **inside the line that is straight back from the ball.**

This may mean simple or dramatic action!

If you want to hit the ball from the inside it means aiming the clubhead at the target and moving the left hand stronger on the grip or turned to the right. On the take-away moving the clubhead straight back from the ball (without rolling the wrists or opening the face of the club). **Above all it means coming at the ball for inside and releasing the clubhead at the target or moving right hand into the shot** — so preventing the body moving outside through the "hitting area".

There are drills that may help you. One is to put a piece of wood down on the ground and placing a ball inside it. Practise taking the club straight back parallel to the piece of wood and hitting the ball without striking the wood. *(See diagrams 189, 190)*.

Diagram 189
To prevent you swinging the clubhead down on the outside, place a deterrent outside the ball on the ground.

Diagram 190
Hit from inside to prevent socket.

Diagram 191
Take inside ball to practice hitting from inside.

Diagram 192
If you hit the two you are hitting from the outside.

A second way is to put two balls down and (see diagram) practise taking the "inside" one. This is an educational way. **You will move the two balls together if you approach the inside ball from the outside.** *(See diagrams 191, 192).*

A third way is to separate the hands on the grip. This is especially helpful in the milder attacks where the main problem is that the body has moved through leaving the clubhead very open and the ball "shoots" right. The drill is aim the clubhead at the target, move clubhead back in a straight line and you will notice the right hand will automatically come into the shot. (If the problem is severe leave a big gap between hands.)

There is another helpful tip if you feel you need an added insurance to ensure that your clubhead does not hit the ball with the shank of the club. Simply place the ball out near the toe of the club. Finally if you are in a stooped position at address where weight is on your toes the tendency will be to have a tilted swing with the tendency to hit the ball from the outside. Move weight back onto heels, stand more erect nearer the ball with knees and hips slightly flexed and the back in straight position and keep weight back during swing. Do not move on to your toes as this will move everything outside.

The shank is without doubt the most unusual and mysterious in the game as far as the potentially good player is concerned and, as is the unknown, that terrifies. **Golfers who suffer from it have no feel for the clubhead.** The socket is the most terrifying shot in the game.

However, let me end on an optimistic note by saying that everybody is affected at some time by this shot, but once the causes are understood, there is no earthly reason for you to have a problem with it.

Hook, Push and Smother

(See diagram 193).

We are now going to deal with the other family of bad shots. The reason these are in a different family is that they come about from a different type of swing. They come from an **in to out** swing, or a swing that is from the **inside.**

241

SPECIAL LESSON 15

(A) What is the difference between a Pull and a Hook? (B) What is the significance?

A pulled shot starts left of target and continues leftwards.

In order for the ball to start left the power of the swing, or force must have been applied from the outside

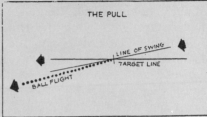

THE PULL

LINE OF SWING
TARGET LINE
BALL FLIGHT

The Pull Shot
Out to in swing.

bad way

The point is, once your swing is outside, you are likely not only to pull, but might consider the slice, shank, fluff, top, sky among your repertoire. It is not only a bad shot, it is also a bad indication of the state of your swing. The fact is that if you are swinging the clubhead down on the outside to the ball, it will also be descending from a steep angle and across the target line in a leftwards direction — certain trouble ahead

Right shoulder outside on downswing.

The genuine hook on the other hand is a completely different type of shot, even though the ball finishes left of the target.

Steep angle of approach from outside on ball.

WHY
IS
THIS SO
?

&→

242

The ball travelled a completely different route
It started right of the target first and turned from right to left.
The point is the power of the swing was from inside, and a lot of good golf follows. The top class player strikes the ball from the inside—

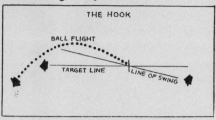

THE HOOK

BALL FLIGHT

TARGET LINE

LINE OF SWING

The genuine hook shot
In to out swing.

fights a hook—but that's the limit of his bad play. You must realize, if the clubhead arrives from inside the ball, it will have travelled paralell to the ground in a forward direction, and this ensures a square hit to the back of the back of the ball.

It is not only a good shot, but is also a very good indication of the state of your game.

Right elbow back to right pocket

To conclude, the shots may seem similar (both left of target) but there is an enormous difference between the signifance of the two. The pull shot is a very bad shot for you!

Real evidence of a pull swing
• Divot left
• Marks on sole plate leftward
• Missing greens to the left with your 8, 9, W, S.W.

HITTING FROM INSIDE LIKE ALL THE GREATS!

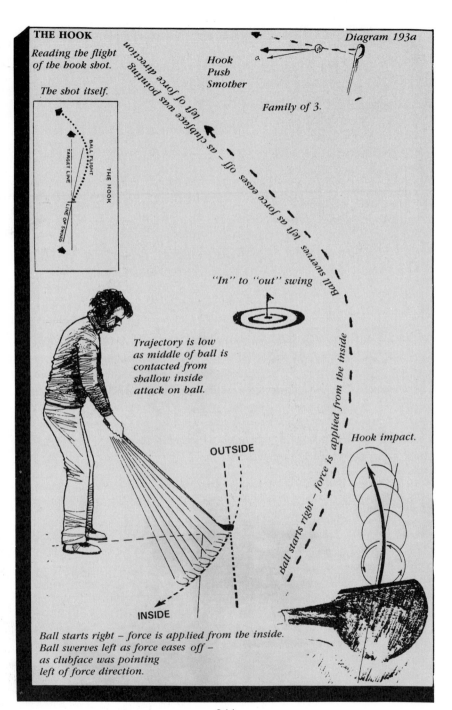

THE HOOK

Reading the flight of the book shot.

The shot itself.

THE HOOK

BALL FLIGHT

TARGET LINE

LINE OF SWING

Hook
Push
Smother

Family of 3.

Diagram 193a

Ball swerves left as force eases off – as clubface was pointing left of force direction

"In" to "out" swing

Trajectory is low as middle of ball is contacted from shallow inside attack on ball.

OUTSIDE

INSIDE

ball starts right – force is applied from the inside

Hook impact.

Ball starts right – force is applied from the inside.
Ball swerves left as force eases off –
as clubface was pointing
left of force direction.

244

THE HOOK

(See diagram 193a).

Even the great Ben Hogan had this problem at one time during his career. What is the cause of a **hook** shot? Basically it is a **closed club-face**. The clubface is pointing left at impact. It is also linked with an **in to out** swing – a swing that is towards the right of the target. Because the force of the swing is right of the target, the ball will start right of the target and, because the clubface is pointing left of where the force of the swing is, it will tend to veer towards the left at the end of the flight or as it reaches the latter stages of its flight. Three factors affect the golf shot:

The direction of the swing.

The angle of the clubface.

The part of the ball that was struck by the head.

As in this case, the angle that the clubhead comes down on the ball is a shallow one. We have to deal with the other two factors. We have to deal with the direction of the swing line and **more importantly the angle of the clubhead.** If we can correct the clubface angle, we have corrected the hook! Now, as it is your hands that control the clubface, the cure is to be found **in the faulty grip.** What has happened is that you have what is known as a **hooker's grip** *(See diagram 194)*. What this means is that the hands are turned too far to the right of the grip, with **too many knuckles visible on the left hand** and the right hand underneath the shaft. As your hands and arms have a natural position relative to the rest of your body, if they are turned out of or positioned out of their natural position, they will tend to revert back to their natural position once any motion takes place. Now, do a little experiment!

Position your hands on the grip, but move your hands in a clockwise position or to the right. Place the club on the ground and you will see automatically what has happened is that the club tends to sit open. Next turn, without moving your hands off the grip. Turn your hands to the **left** and you will see that the clubface is very much closed. Now this is what happens during the swing. If you position your hands on the grip, where your left hand shows too many knuckles and your right hand is underneath on the take-away, the clubface will tend to be

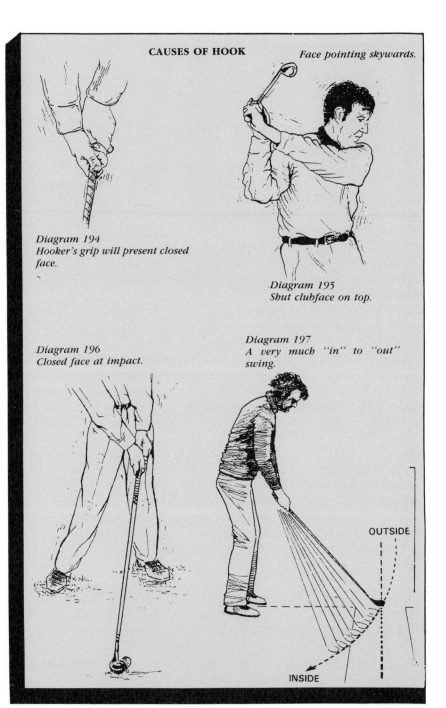

CAUSES OF HOOK

Face pointing skywards.

*Diagram 194
Hooker's grip will present closed
face.*

*Diagram 195
Shut clubface on top.*

*Diagram 196
Closed face at impact.*

*Diagram 197
A very much "in" to "out"
swing.*

OUTSIDE

INSIDE

246

hooded. *(See diagram 195)*. On the top of the back swing, the clubface will be shut and this in turn will produce a shut clubface at impact. *(See diagram 196)*.

Unfortunately, a person who has the hook problem will tend to shy away from the left-hand side of the course and, in his preparation for the shot, will tend to line up right of the target. This, in turn, will encourage a hooker's grip, with the shoulders closed and a very much **inside/out** swing, which will also encourage the **hook** shot. So let's correct it:

First, you've got to line up the clubhead on target, or even slightly left of the target.

Secondly, position the right hand on the grip in such a way that the V formed by the thumb and the base of the index finger points back up to the chin *(See diagram 197)* or move the position of the left hand on the grip so that it is more in **the palm of the left hand** and not down on the fingers, with **no knuckles visible on the left hand.** You then must position your **right hand** on the club where it is on **top of the left hand** pointing towards your chin, or where your right hand covers the left hand. This grip position will feel totally uncomfortable. However, it will guarantee you one thing – the clubface will not be shut on the take-away and will be square on the top of the back swing or even slightly open and, of course, produce an open clubface in the hitting area. *(See diagrams 198, 199)*.

You must adopt a weak grip where no knuckles are visible on the left hand, and move your right hand well over on top. You must then line up the clubhead slightly left of target and your feet, hips and shoulders similarly in order to encourage an upright swing plane. On your back swing encourage a more upright swing plane and endeavour to strike the ball with the clubface slightly open to the force of the swing. *(See diagrams 200, 201, 202)*. The weak grip also gives you the freedom of being able to release the clubhead for the first time in your life. With the hooker grip, the tendency always is to hang on to the clubhead, because, if the clubhead is released, the tendency would be for the hook shot to become a bit on the chronic side. But now, with the weak grip, you can release the clubhead as much as you like and you will not produce a **hook.** Golfers with the hooker's grip have a tendency to shy away from two clubs: one is the driver and the second is the wedge. And the reason for this is that, with the hooker's, grip the tendency will be that the closed clubface will kill off the loft on the driver. You will be unable to get a driver airborne and end up with a terrible duck-hook, if you manage to get the driver into the air! So the tendency will be to use a three wood, even if the face is closed, because

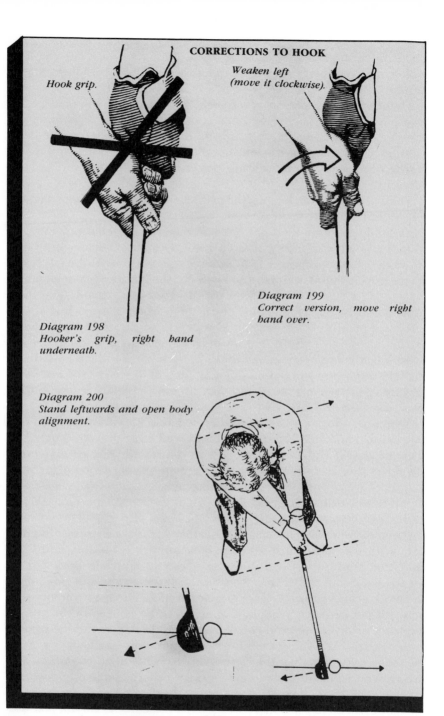

CORRECTIONS TO HOOK

Hook grip.

*Weaken left
(move it clockwise).*

*Diagram 199
Correct version, move right
hand over.*

*Diagram 198
Hooker's grip, right hand
underneath.*

*Diagram 200
Stand leftwards and open body
alignment.*

CORRECTION OF HOOK

Diagram 201
Swing more upright.

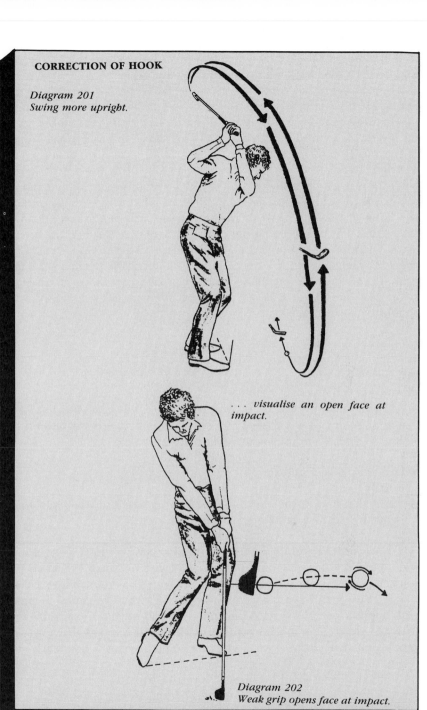

. . . visualise an open face at impact.

Diagram 202
Weak grip opens face at impact.

of the angle on the face, the face will meet the bottom half of the ball and create more back-spin and prevent the side-spin.

There is one other cause for the hook shot. In a swing where there is too much wrist action, the tendency will be for an over-swing and, on the down swing, hitting the ball early, or casting the club slightly on the down swing and causing the hook shot. In other words, there **is too much right hand in the hitting area,** too much rotation with the right hand, the right hand is turning over to the hitting area. The correction is to weaken the right hand by relaxing the right hand on the grip and getting more left side through the hitting area by **getting the back of the left hand to move out towards the target,** through the hitting area and holding the clubface on target, through the hitting area, **without allowing the right hand to turn it over.** One of the ways of practising left-side domination is to adopt the Bernhard Langer grip, by placing the left hand below the right on the grip. Practise swing like that and it will give a feeling for what left side domination should be in the swing.

- Check your grip.
- Have you got a hooker's grip?
- Check your alignment.
- Are you anticipating a hook?
- Are you lined up right of the target in such a way that your feet, hips and shoulders are lined up for a very much **inside** swing and, of course, the strong and inevitable hook.
- Check the position of the clubhead at the top of the back swing.
- Is it in a closed position?
  Finally
- check that you do not have an over-swing and that the right hand is not turning over through the hitting area.

To conclude, if you look after your grip, you will have gone a long way to correcting the hook, but you must always remember when you weaken your grip the tendency will be for your hook to turn into a slice.

P.S. You may have got rid of one problem but you may be stuck with another one – a slice to the right. So you have to make sure that with the weak grip you release the clubhead at the ball, because you should not hook from a weak grip position, no matter how early you release the clubhead. The point is, with the hooker's grip, if you release the clubhead, you would probably end up with a duck-hook. So when you weaken your **left** hand on the grip (that is return your **left** hand into a position where there is no knuckle visible on it), you have to make sure that you really give the ball a whack with your **right** hand.

To conclude, two causes of the hook shot, a genuine hook shot, when the ball starts out **right** of the target and veers towards the **left** in the latter stages of its flight are: (1) faulty grip – this is far and away the main cause of a hook shot, and (2) it can occur from a neutral grip position. In other words, where your grip is not a hooker's grip, but from an over-swing with a neutral grip will cause a hook, or, hitting early, or too much right hand in the hitting.

The Helpful Pro.

The Vanishing Pro.

THE PUSH SHOT

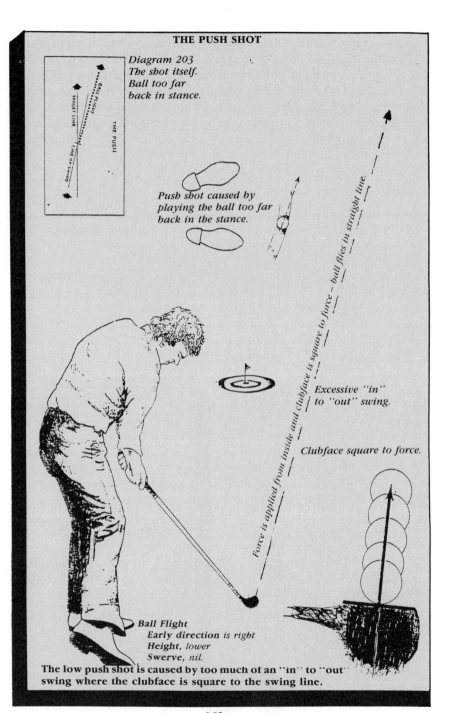

Diagram 203
The shot itself.
Ball too far
back in stance.

BALL FLIGHT

TARGET LINE

LINE OF SWING

THE PUSH

Push shot caused by
playing the ball too far
back in the stance.

Force is applied from inside and clubface is square to force — ball flies in straight line.

Excessive "in"
to "out" swing.

Clubface square to force.

Ball Flight
  Early direction *is right*
  Height, *lower*
  Swerve, *nil.*

The low push shot is caused by too much of an "in" to "out"
swing where the clubface is square to the swing line.

252

PUSH SHOT

(See diagram 203).

The **push** shot is one where the ball flies straight, right of the target. It comes from an **in to out** swing, where the clubface is square to the direction of the swing. The **push** shot can come about from too much left side control. The hands are ahead slightly of the clubhead in the hitting area and, while the swing is well from the **inside**, the clubhead has not caught up with the hand at impact and so causes the **push** shot. And this can be brought about by the body being ahead of the ball in the hitting area. It can also come about from a very flat back swing. Or alternatively, it could be very simply playing the ball too far back in the stance.

To deal with these causes now

Playing the ball too far back in the stance – this places the body naturally ahead of the ball at impact. The effect is the same as playing the ball from the correct position, but swaying to the left on the down swing. In each instance, the body gets ahead of the ball and the clubhead reaches the ball before the face can get square to the directional line. In each case, the face, with an **inside out** swing, is square to the direction the clubhead is following, but still a little bit open to the intended line. If you look at the diagram, you will see that in the hitting area, the clubhead describes a semi-circle and if the ball is towards the beginning of that semi-circle, the ball is still travelling **outward.** The other cause of the push shot is **moving into the hitting area with the body.** If the body moves into the hitting area, the hands will automatically be ahead of the clubhead at impact and the **push** shot is inevitable. So, once again, it is going back to realising that it is not you who moves the ball, but the clubhead. Having taken up your position you should adopt a strong grip in order to encourage a draw, and to take the club back on the inside and be certain to rotate right hand through the hitting area – close the door to prevent the push shot. Another cause of a push shot that is related to a hook shot is a **very flat-type swing.** In other words, too much of an **inside out** swing and sometimes it can happen because the clubhead is taken back much too sharply on the inside.

So the corrections for a **pushed** shot are:

- Check the ball position – is it too far back in stance?
- Check the sway moving back from the ball on the back swing and moving into the ball in the hitting area.
- Check a flat back swing.
- Check are you releasing the clubhead. *(See diagram 203a).*

DO NOT BECOME PERSONALLY INVOLVED IN THE STRIKE!

If you are pushing the ball, you are blocking the shot. You are not releasing the clubhead. The secret to the game is that you have to try not to hit the ball yourself and allow the clubhead to hit it for you.

To be able to move the clubhead without actually moving yur hands laterally allow the clubhead to hit it for you.

Diagram 203a
To be able to move the clubhead without actually moving your hands laterally. Allow the clubhead to hit it for you.

SMOTHER SHOT

(See diagram 204).

The cause of a smother shot is a hooded clubface. That is that the clubface is hooded at the moment it strikes the ball. The loft that the manufacturer built into the clubface not only is eliminated, but actually reversed by the turning over of the clubhead. It is quite difficult to get the ball into the air. Golfers who have this problem have two causes for it. *(See diagrams 205, 206, 207).*

One cause for it is generally a hooker's grip. The symptom of the problem is that they tend to shy away from a driver. Remember that a driver has only eleven degrees loft on the face, so the tendency will be with the hooker's grip and the closed face on impact to kill off the loft on the drive and produce a duck-hook. However, with the three wood, the tendency will be to hit the ball reasonably well, to turn the three wood into about a one and a half – to get tremendous distance with the three wood and also with the eight iron to be able to turn it into about a five iron with the grip and the hooded clubface. The correction is to attack the grip.

You have to place the hands on the grip especially the left hand where it is in the palm, and the V formed by the thumb and the base of the index finger pointing towards your chin and your right hand on top of the left hand, or the right hand V (formed by the index finger and the thumb of the right hand) pointing towards your chin also. This will feel very uncomfortable! On the take-away the tendency will be to have the clubface, if anything, slightly open and on the top likewise and produce a slightly open clubface at impact. The player should immediatley notice a lot more height on the flight of the shots and even an odd slice creeping in. It will be desperately uncomfortable, but the

*Diagram 204
Reading the smother.*

The cause of the smother is that the loft the manufacturer's built into the clubface not only is eliminated but actually reversed by the turning over of the clubface.

CAUSES OF THE SMOTHER

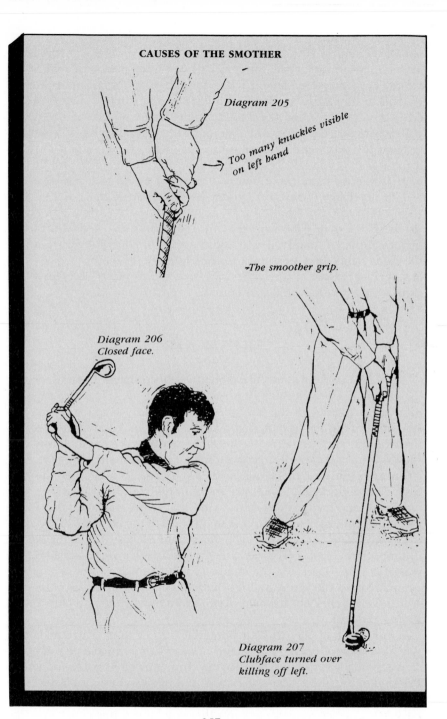

Diagram 205

→ *Too many knuckles visible on left hand*

→*The smoother grip.*

*Diagram 206
Closed face.*

*Diagram 207
Clubface turned over
killing off left.*

fact of the matter is that if you have a **smother** problem, or the **hook** problem, you must attack the grip and you must persevere with it, no matter how uncomfortable it feels. You have to get out on a practise ground and practise to play and not be trying to play to practise. In other words, not trying these alternations in the middle of a round of golf, where you have only one shot and a lot depending on it. You have to have the single-mindedness to practise with the alteration to make it natural that you will be able to know what the reaction will be and have it part of your game **before** you stand up on the first tee.

The summary of the corrections for the **smother** are:

● Check the grip – be sure that no more than the knuckles of two fingers of the left hand show at address and, of course, be certain that the right hand **does not** point to the right shoulder.
● Check at the top of the back swing that the clubface isn't closed. (If clubface points skywards it is closed).

FRESH AIR

The one shot I have not mentioned is the complete **fresh air** where the clubhead doesn't actually meet the ball at all. This shot happens to novices. It reminds me of a story – a beginner playing a course and standing on the first tee, taking a swipe at the ball and missing it and then having another go, with the same result and stepping away and standing up again and having another go and missing it again . . .! Turning round to his playing partner – having looked down the fairway – he remarked: "This is a really tough course, isn't it!"

If you are having problems with the **fresh air** shot it will be inevitably because you are trying to hit the ball too far to force the shot. What you have to do is relax your hands on the grip, settle for a short distance and get the ball away. In other words, let the clubhead do the work for you. Just move the clubhead into the ball as if in a chipping action around the green and let the ball go away from the clubhead. Now, every golfer has his own personal way of swinging a club and of hitting the ball.

If you want to play to your potential (rather than your handicap), you have to be prepared to practise. This does not mean endlessly pursuing futile ideas that might help you. It means having a sound knowledge of the game – the causes and the effects. Being able to know yourself – your swing – and when you creep into your bad faults; to be able to correct yourself; to know that you have slipped back into that fault again. The secret of success means knowing yourself. There's no point in knowing yourself, if you cannot correct yourself. It is also very true to say that you should play when you are playing and practise to play. If the correction does not work straight away, you must be prepared to work at it. I often think that there is a tendency among many, a certain curiosity, and a mentality for the pupil to believe deep down that he or she somehow knows more than the teacher. What happens is that the pupil will not submit himself or herself to the lesson.

He arranges for one lesson, never practising afterwards, dashes from the car on the following Sunday morning in the direction of the clubhouse enquiring to the waiting golfers: "Are you fixed up." He explains on the first tee that he may not be up to much that day, as he is trying out something new. Now he knows he is on a winner because if he plays badly, he can always say: "That bloody pro destroyed me!" Not only has he got the inside story on the pro's teaching ability but also a cast iron excuse for his bad play. Let's be straight about one thing. All you can ever hope to achieve on one lesson is a quick cure. Can you imagine learning to play a piano in just one lesson, trying to self-teach yourself the piano? Can you imagine the noise 125,000 non-practising self-taught cocky pianists would make.

Every now and then I come across a pupil who wants to learn, who will say without reservation: "I know what you mean – this is what you want me to do." This type of pupil improves rapidly because he/she is not trying to assimilate something new at the same time as being a doubting Thomas. They also realise that you cannot practise while playing where you have only one shot and a lot depending on it.

If you are an inconsistent golfer, one day you are brilliant, the next horrible, you should be looking for the group of shots that are closely related, the family of bad shots. **The slice, the pull, the top, the shank and the fluff could be, at some stage or other, part of your game.**

If this is the case, what you have to do is **change your swing line,** change the approach. Start to hit the ball from the **inside out** and this will guarantee a shallow approach on the ball and you will be able to master the low numbers – the long game. Whenever the player brings the clubhead down to the ball at a sharp angle instead of sweeping it along nearly parallel to the ground, he is heading for the "danger zone". In the correct swing the clubhead moves close to the ground, for some little distance before it hits the ball and after it hits the ball. With a swing like that, there's little danger of hitting behind the ball **(fluff)** or under it **(sky)** and there's not much chance of hitting the **top** of it. It is also true to say that the angle of approach will be shallow and from the inside. *(See diagram 207a)*.

259

This section then is not on how the game should be played, but rather to straighten you out. What I hope I have achieved is to enable you to identify your bad shot, or shots and to go to the correction directly. What it should mean is that you do not have to read the whole book to find your faults and the corrections for your faults.

Summary

As a summary of corrective golf I have devised a formula to help you (a) identify your bad shot, or shots and (b) hopefully to take correct action. I call it the PHS formula, that is P for path – flight path or direction; H for height of shot; S is the particular spin that is imparted on the ball. In simple terms the **force** of the swing governs the **early directional path.** Take the example of the ball starting left of target (irrespective of where it finishes). In order for it to start left, the force must have been applied from the outside. H or **height** depends upon **the part of the ball** that was struck. If the shot is high, you must assume that the clubhead struck the bottom of the ball from a steep angle causing a lot of back-spin. If the ball swerves in the air, it will not take place until the end of the flight, as the "force", which is driving the ball forward, begins to ease off. **Side-spin** to the left or right is caused by the **clubface** being open or closed to the force.

Let us now use the PHS formula

You are continually striking the ball, that is, taking off left of the target. You must assume the force of your swing was outside. The ball starts out left but swerves wickedly to the right at the end. Why? It was always spinning in that direction as a result of the **face being open to the force.** You are swinging from the **outside** and the clubface is **open.** The shots are also high. This tells you that you are making low contact with the ball, creating too much back-spin.

Therefore from the PHS point of view you are swinging from the outside, striking the bottom of the ball and the face is open to its force. To correct this you must set-up to swing from the **inside** with the face **square** to the force from a **shallow** angle towards the **middle** of the ball.

The hook shot. P – ball is starting right, force is from inside; H – trajectory is low, upper middle contact with ball; and S – is swerving to left at end of flight. You are swinging too flat, from too much inside, hitting the ball too high up, and the **clubface is closed to the swing direction.**

The **sky,** high and left. P – force is from outside; H – it is very high, contact with very bottom of the ball from a very steep swing; S – spin

260

is back-spin. The main feature is the height. You must correct both P and H. Hit from inside with a shallow **approach** (not a steep one) **to upper middle of ball.** If you understand the relevance of the early directional path, the height or lack of it, and finally the spin on the ball then you have a very good chance of being able to improve your play, or be able to take corrective action during a round of golf.

To play to your potential start the ball on target, have a reasonable trajectory and have back-spin on it. In order to do this as it is the grip that controls the clubface and shoulder alignment your swing line, you must be able to perfect the best grip for your game and secondly line-up on target. You must be able to **GATAI. G** is grip. Perfect your grip, look after your clubface. **A** is alignment, aim clubhead towards the target. **T** is turn, start your back swing by turning (first move on back swing). **A** is aim, align shaft across line at top of your back swing. **I** is always hit shot from the inside out. See the ultimate shot (special lesson).

If you want to play you must be able to observe the **early ball direction** and deduce your **swing line from it.** Observe the **height** on the flight and deduce if shot **swing plane** is steep or shallow and finally by observing the **spin** of the ball, if the **clubface** was open, square or closed to the swing line. If you want to play you must know your PHS and be able to GATAI!

Never say what have I done wrong in the swing – say what does the ball tell me!

Here are some immediate observations you could make:

The slice – no right hand at impact – use it.

The sky – steep swing – use a low inside swing.

The hook – strong left hand grip – weaken it.

Generally inconsistent – too much right hand – **build up a strong left side through impact.**

The most common fault in golf is the failure of the golfer to use the power he/she creates in swing effort. **At the top of your back swing your swing power is high and resistance is low (right knee). At impact (as the ball is low) you should resist high (press back with left hand) and release swing power forward low – through the bottom end of the club.** The golf club works like a gun, you load it at the grip end before impact and it should explode at the clubhead end. The swing power you create must manifest itself at the working end of your golf club when striking the ball. You must be able to **use the head!**

PEOPLE WHO PLAY GOLF

SPECIAL LESSON 16

FLAN'S LAW

The angle at which you approach the ball must not be greater than the loft on the face of the club. For example, if a driver has a face loft of 11° and if you are to use it to its maximum effect the angle the clubhead approaches the ball should not be greater than 11° off the ground. *(See Diagram 11)*.

To explain it more simply, if you have 55° loft on a sand wedge, you will get away with the clubhead approaching from less than the same angle off the ground as there will be enough loft on the face to move the ball forward. For example, your angle of approach could be 45°.

THE HEADS

The driver has a flat face.   *The wedge (no. 10) has a lofted face.*

RESPECT THE LOFT ON THE LOW NUMBERED CLUBS!

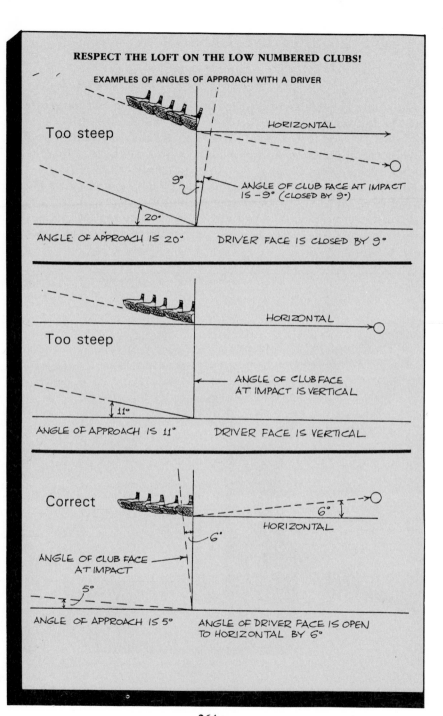

EXAMPLES OF ANGLES OF APPROACH WITH A DRIVER

Too steep

HORIZONTAL

9°

ANGLE OF CLUB FACE AT IMPACT IS −9° (CLOSED BY 9°)

20°

ANGLE OF APPROACH IS 20°   DRIVER FACE IS CLOSED BY 9°

Too steep

HORIZONTAL

ANGLE OF CLUB FACE AT IMPACT IS VERTICAL

11°

ANGLE OF APPROACH IS 11°   DRIVER FACE IS VERTICAL

Correct

6°

HORIZONTAL

6°

ANGLE OF CLUB FACE AT IMPACT

5°

ANGLE OF APPROACH IS 5°   ANGLE OF DRIVER FACE IS OPEN TO HORIZONTAL BY 6°

264

CHAPTER 19

Use real not imaginary evidence

This is the secret to your improvement

The first part of organising is taking a look at the implements we use, understanding their limitations and realising the importance of accommodating them is in setting up to hit a shot.

It is also true to say that once we play we can learn an awful lot from the **marks we leave on the clubs or indeed on the course.** Look on it like a detective would be looking on the marks a criminal would leave after the scene of a crime in order to find out what type of person the criminal was and who he was. You should look on the marks you leave as a way of telling you what type of golfer you are, what technique you are using, or what your basic "swing shape" is. I hope you don't play like a criminal!

I remember an old teaching professional who would always "hold" the pupil in chat before going out to the teaching bay. It wasn't just a sociable chat, he was using it to find out by "casually" looking at the "markings" on the clubs what kind of a swing the pupil was using. He would look at the **markings on the sole plate of the woods and by the lines he would know if he were an "out to in" or an "in to out" swinger.** He could "double" check this by looking at the irons, and from the markings on the face what part of it was "meeting" the ball. He would also admire the woods and check the paint to see if he was using a steep swing and chipping the paint on the top of the head.

From this information he would have a very good idea of what type of a pupil he had to deal with. If there happened to be a tag on his bag with his club name on it, and if he knew the particular course in which he was a member, he might remark: "Are you having trouble with the 7th, 13th, 16th on your course?" knowing these holes might be the ones that would cause him most trouble according to the markings on the clubs. Now he would have got all his information quietly and quickly and the pupil would be totally unaware of this. The pupil would be very impressed by the fact that the professional would know what he was doing wrong long before he ever hit a shot. If the teacher told him to stand on his head in order to hit the ball, he would! As he now had him in the palm of his hand.

Mister Divot

The most obvious silent educator is Mr. Divot. Take for example a **divot which indicates a swing path that is towards the left or "out to in"**. As we know from this, the ball is going to at least start left and will stay left or veer to the right depending on what club you were using and which direction the clubface was pointing at impact. *(See diagram 208)*.

How would you correct it?

Simply align the clubhead more to the right. Ensure that your left-hand grip is turned to the right (stronger grip). Align your feet, hips and shoulders to right. Swing along the line of the body **and make sure that you release the clubhead and do not let the body go with it.**

On the other hand if the divot is "going the other way" or is straight towards the target you are in much better shape. If the ball is still not hitting the target it is because, even though you are swinging in the direction of the target, your clubface is not pointing at the target at impact. It is "open" or "closed". You have to check your grip and organise it in such a way that will help return the face square to where you want the ball to go.

Leave the digging for the garden

If you have the a problem of taking a very "heavy" divot, it will always be from "lunge" through the hit. It is also encouraged by a **very "tight" grip** and a failure to "release" the clubhead. I remember one pupil who had this particular problem and I corrected it. He told me afterwards that lining him up "right" and swinging on an "inside" plane worked, but what really helped him was that he used to actually try to see the clubhead coming in to meet the ball. In other words **he would "hold himself there"** until after he had hit the ball.

There is another way of looking at it. Imagine a piece of elastic. Now stretch it and let it go. It will smack off your other hand. Now stretch it again and this time let your right hand go with it as you let it go. The speed it smacks off your other hand is very much less because your hand was moving with the release. It is the same with the clubhead, **if your upper half moves into the shot, i.e. shoulders, your clubhead speed is greatly reduced and a digging action takes place** – "leave the digging for the garden". **Practise "picking" the ball clean, "swishing" the ball off the top of the grass using just "wrist" and clubhead to do it – keep body out of it, or keep it back through the hit.**

266

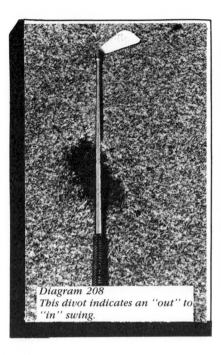

Diagram 208
This divot indicates an "out" to "in" swing.

Diagram 209
Leaving the tee in the ground indicates an up swing.

Diagram 210
With the straight face club you should always strike as the head is moving away from (and not down towards) the ground.

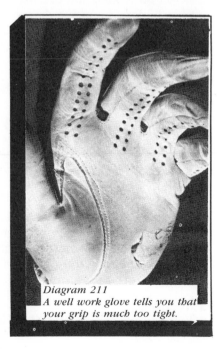

Diagram 211
A well work glove tells you that your grip is much too tight.

The tee

If you are given an advantage in life you should always take it.

The second "indicator" believe it or not is the tee. If you are continually looking for your tee after your drive there is something wrong. Your game is not only costing you too much money, but it also indicates a faulty swing. I remember a member who would always pick up a tee after one of his playing partners would have driven and hold it up. If it was for example a red one – which his playing partner was looking for – he would say "Did anybody loose a blue tee?" holding up the red one. He is probably a tee millionaire now.

If you are continually breaking the tee, even knocking it out of the ground or driving it into the turf, **your swing is too steep and coming "down" on the ball.** You are swinging towards the ground as you hit the ball. This is disatrous for low numbered clubs! *(See diagram 209).*

Adopt the motto that "you cannot tee the ball too high". **Tee the ball up high** and taking a few "half swings", **practise swinging the club over the ball,** without making contact with it. Then hit the ball "off the tee" and leave the tee there *(see diagram).* **Hit the ball with the clubhead travelling upwards, or away from,** not down into the **ground.** It is helpful if you get to practise by placing the ball well above your feet on a bank and practise hitting it or simply "imagine" a tee two feet high and imagine the swing you would have to make in order to hit the ball off that tee. Also take note of tour pros on television driving off. Watch the tee, and observe that 90% of the time the tee is still in the ground after they make the strike. They are driving the ball on their upswing. *(See diagram 210).*

The clubhead

The clubhead, as I have already mentioned, will reveal a lot. **Pick it up and take a close look at the sole plate. If the lines are going in a leftward direction, you know what your swing line is and how to correct it.**

The glove

The markings on the glove will tell you if you are having much "movement" on the grip while you are swinging. If you look at the diagram you will note that the grip is too much in the palm. Move into the fingers to encourage a good left side and also from the finger grip a "wrist cock" and release the clubhead. *(See diagram 211).*

The grip

You cannot grip too lightly. Hold it like a tube of toothpaste. *(See diagram 212).*

268

Diagram 211
This well worn grip indicates you are swinging much too hard at the ball.

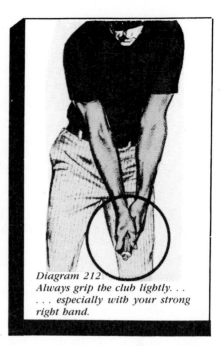

Diagram 212
*Always grip the club lightly. . .
. . . especially with your strong right hand.*

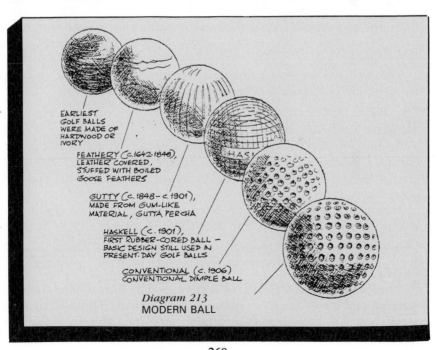

EARLIEST
GOLF BALLS
WERE MADE OF
HARDWOOD OR
IVORY

FEATHERY (c. 1642-1848),
LEATHER COVERED,
STUFFED WITH BOILED
GOOSE FEATHERS

GUTTY (c. 1848 - c. 1901),
MADE FROM GUM-LIKE
MATERIAL, GUTTA PERCHA

HASKELL (c. 1901),
FIRST RUBBER-CORED BALL —
BASIC DESIGN STILL USED IN
PRESENT-DAY GOLF BALLS

CONVENTIONAL (c. 1906)
CONVENTIONAL DIMPLE BALL

Diagram 213
MODERN BALL

You can also look at the grip on the shaft of the clubs. The markings on the grip will also reveal if the club is moving too much in your swing. If you are wearing your grips a lot, you are gripping the club too tightly, swinging too much with your hands and much too fast. Your game would improve a lot, if you had respected your grips. It is important not to "strangle" the club with your hands. No matter how lightly you hold the club it will always "firm" up when the ball goes down and you make a swing at it. **On the other hand if you grip very tightly at address it will ease on the take-away. It will always be a fast right side take-away which immediately loosens at the top,** and you will lose control through the hitting area.

The cure is to grip very loosely like as if the club was going to "fly" out of your hands, and practise hitting half the distance with a full swing. Feel your arms are swinging not just your hands.

In other words move your whole left side back while you keep your stronger right side quiet on the backswing.

Finally you should use your feet as educators when you have to play a shot from the sand. By "shuffling" your feet you will be able to gauge for yourself the density of the sand. Remember, **the ball will come out much faster from hard sand and the opposite from soft sand.** If you feel that the sand is soft, you must play a much firmer shot trying to be past the pin. If the sand is hard, play an easier shot.

The ball

The high compression golf ball is in contact and with the clubface for 4/10,000 of a second. *(See diagram 213).*

Baloney about balls

Despite the advertising claims, **there's not much difference in the distance you will get from balls of comparable quality.** Tests conducted by the U.S.G.A. resulted in an agreement that no brand is appreciably superior to its several nearest competitors.

I remember a group of people being shown round a golf equipment manufacturing factory. At this time there was great rivalry between two brands of balls, and to the surprise of the golfers attending, the two balls were manufactured at the same factory but were printed and packed separately.

The distance a ball will carry is governed by how much it is compressed and its ability to snap back when struck. This will depend upon how hard the ball is and how hard it is struck.*(See diagram 214).*

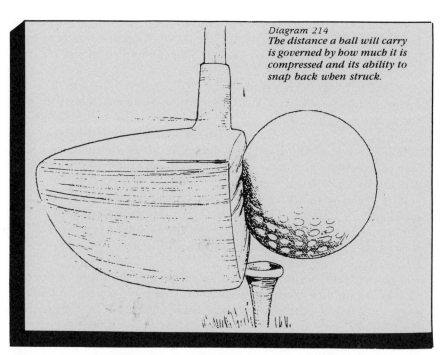

Diagram 214
The distance a ball will carry is governed by how much it is compressed and its ability to snap back when struck.

Diagram 215
"I think you would make a great committee man."

Modern balls range from 100 compression to 60. 100 suitable to hard hitters while average should use 80-90. Compression goes up in cold conditions and decreases in heat. This is why you should play with a softer ball in the winter.

A ball may not weigh more than 1.62 ounces or be less than 1.68 inches in diameter (for G.U.I. competitions). The earliest balls were stuffed with feathers called a gutta percha, later they had rubber liquid or steel centre wound with stretched rubber bands and balata.

Solid balls are cut-proof. Aerodynamics of 336 dimples and back-spin of from 2000 to 8000 r.p.m. keep the ball airborne twice as far as a ball with smooth surface.

The speed with which ball leaves face of driver when struck by good golfers is about 170 m.p.h. The high compression ball is in contact with the clubface for four ten thousandths of a second. The softer ball stays on the clubface longer and, therefore, it can be controlled better. *(See diagram 215)*.

The best real evidence you will ever have is the flight of the ball. If you are able to read ball flight you will have a very big advantage over your opponent. (Explained in detail in "Corrective Golf".)

Cheating

If you answer yes to most of these questions you are in the cheat's class no matter what your heading is.

- On the tee do you tee up in front of the markers even just a little?
- Do you on the green put your marker in front of the ball and then play your ball in front of the marker?
- Do you when you are identifying the ball press your heel down behind the ball in order to improve the lie?
- Do you decide to wash your ball when it's your turn to drive?
- Do you talk, laugh, walk about or rattle your clubs when another is addressing the ball?
- Do you walk ahead of others in your group and risk being hit?
- Do you stand too close to someone about to play a shot?
- Do you play out of turn?
- Do you forget to count strokes when you have a fresh air?
- Do you pull up weeds or grass when in the rough or break off branches that obstruct your swing?
- Do you leave footprints in the sand in a bunker?
- Do you touch the sand with the club when adressing the ball?
- Do you change to a new ball on the putting green?

272

- Do you walk on another golfer's line of putt?
- Do you stand in the line of putt so that you are in sight of the person putting?
- Do you fail to repair plug marks?
- Do you leave your ball in the cup after holding out when another still has to putt?
- Are you not ready to putt when it's your turn?
- After putting out, do you stay in the green counting your strokes on marking your score? *(See diagram 216).*

If the majority are yesses . . . there's always . . . a prayer!

Blessed be the poor golfer: for his kingdom is a better club!
Blessed be the humble golfer: for his is a better score!
Blessed is the thirsty golfer: for his is the 19th hole!
Blessed is the peacemaker: for his fairway has no divots!
Blessed is he who mourns: for his kingdom will be mulligan!
Blessed be these champions of us all: **and have mercy, Lord, on us duffers still looking for the ball!**

*"Mulligan" is thought to have originated from a club manager who was always rushing from club to the tee which his partner had already driven, and because he always considered it unfair he would demand that his first shot did not really count – if he hit a bad one off the first tee.

FIGHTING THEIR BATTLE OVER AGAIN

CHAPTER 20

The draw

Maximum distance shot

All you have to do is read this chapter if you want to increase your distance, because I am going to tell you about the golf shot, and show you how to play it!

How to play the golf shot – or "the draw for distance shot".

First of all let us look at why the "fade" shot was advocated.

The safe "fade" has been advocated for many years now. The problem with the "fade" is that it has been advocated by players who have either been "drawers" of the ball or even had a problem with a hook. An example would be Ben Hogan. He had an overswing and the problem was that that every once in a while, he would play a terrible hook which would destroy his score. He did not become a great golfer until he sacrificed some of his distance. He developed a more left-sided back swing, and the safe "fade" shot. Jack Nicklaus was another who played it.

Why it does not suit you. *(See diagram 217)*.

The problem with all this is that the people who advocated it are those who have been getting a lot of distance, but have not been able to control it. They were used to playing tournament golf on tight courses with narrow fairways and punishing rough where the errant shot was penalised. If they were to win, they generally used a "safe driver" that will not get their maximum distance but would keep the ball in play.

The golfers at the club do not have to play under the same extreme conditions. More than likely they have never gone through the "draw" or "hook" stage, **and in the main their problem isn't to control distance – it is to find it.** In other words the golfer has to be able to hit the ball a distance first before he looks for control.

If you want your maximum distance you have to play the draw. The reason for this is that with the "fade" shot the angle of approach on the ball is "steep" and the spin is slightly left to right spin because the clubface is open. As a result of the steeper attack with the clubface open you are going to get a higher than normal flight on the ball. **The power is directed more downwards, therefore you are going to lose some of the forward thrust.** On the other hand with the "draw" you are going to approach from a much shallower angle – from more

274

Diagram 216
Try to be careful of your playing partner's line!

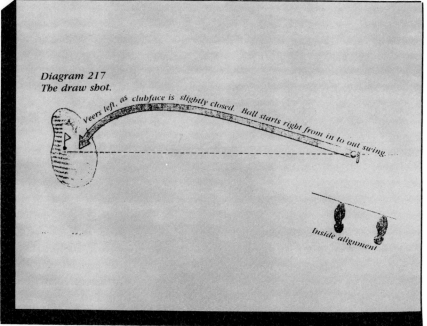

Diagram 217
The draw shot.

Veers left, as clubface is slightly closed. Ball starts right from in to out swing.

Inside alignment

behind the ball – and to clubhead is going to move into the back of the ball giving you a lower trajectory with the clubface slightly closed to the direction of the swing. **This type of shot is a "much more driven forward" one** and one when the ball hits it will "take off again because there will be top-spin on it". **It is the shot that will get you your maximum distance.**

To summarise, if you are looking for distance and a shot that repeats, play the "draw" shot.

How do you organise this shot?

Like everything else, if you want to get a draw you organise beforehand. **The swing line must be "in" to "out" and the clubface must be slightly closed to it.**

Preparation. As it is your **hands** that control the **clubface** and your **alignment** your **swing line,** firstly you must have your hands on the grip in such a way that the clubface will be slighty closed on impact and stand in a way that will encourage an in-to-out swing-line.

Let's do it!

Aim. Aim clubhead at the target.

Address. Make sure your left hand is on the grip in such a way that the V formed by thumb and index finger points at right shoulder or **turn it in a slightly clockwise direction** (three knuckle grip). This will feel slightly uncomfortable and in turning back to its natural position will close the face for you.

Align your body slightly right of the target in such a way that a line across your feet, hips and shoulders point right of the target.

You have set yourself up in such a way that your clubface is lined up slightly left of where your body is lined and should result in a swing where the clubface is slightly closed left to your swing line when you are hitting the ball.

As I have said before the way you swing is determined by the way you organise yourself before your swing.

Swing along line of body (inside). Be sure to position the shaft on top in such a way that it is also pointing slightly right of target and then the angles are set in such a way that you will approach the ball from the **"inside"** and hit the ball away from yourself with the clubface slightly closed. Of course it is important to realise that when you are coming into the ball, **to use your right hand, to release the clubhead, throw the clubhead at the ball – keep you body back and let the clubhead go. It is like a piece of elastic pulled and let go.**

Think of it in this way. Close "up shop" with your left arm,

276

shoulder and hand through impact and release the clubhead past your left arm, shoulder and hand. Swing against your right knee on your back swing and release the clubhead against your top half through impact. *(See diagram 218)*.

Your left hand goes in an anti-clockwise direction through impact, as you press back with your left hand, put a weight on the top of the grip in order to lever the other end, i.e. the clubhead, forward.

"JUNIOR GOLF"

THE CASE OF THE
VANISHING TREE!!

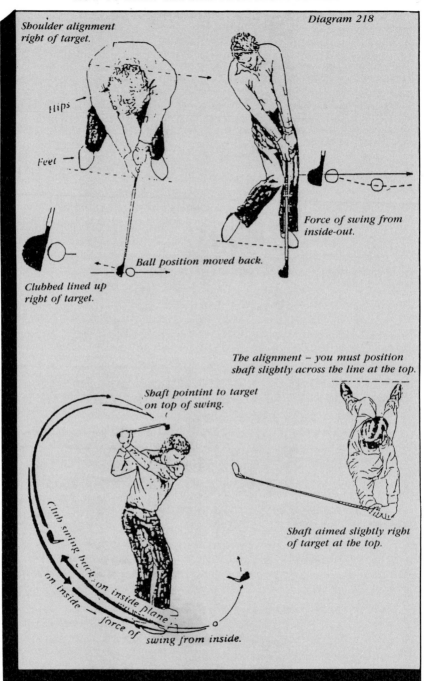

Diagram 218

Shoulder alignment right of target.

Hips

Feet

Force of swing from inside-out.

Clubbed lined up right of target.

Ball position moved back.

The alignment – you must position shaft slightly across the line at the top.

Shaft pointint to target on top of swing.

Club swing back on inside plane

on inside — force of swing from inside.

Shaft aimed slightly right of target at the top.

CHAPTER 21

History of the game

The name golf is sometimes thought to derive from the German word Kolbe (club) and may be a Celtic version of it.

The first known instance of a game resembling golf was a game called pagawica, which was played by Roman soldiers using a curved club and a leather ball stuffed with feathers. The Romans, who came to conquer Britain, occupied parts of Scotland and England from about 55 BC to AD 409. However, it must be emphasised that there is no direct evidence to suggest that pagawica was in any way related to golf. A similar game to golf, called cambuca, was played in England with a wooden ball but there is no certainty as to the kind of club that was used to hit the ball. It probably was similar to the kind of club used in pagawica. There was an illustration of a game of golf, showing a figure striking the ball, on a stained glass window in Gloucester Cathedral, as far back as the year 1310. According to historical anti-quity on this particular depiction, it is accepted that the figure shown is a golfer in action. In France around the same period, there is evidence of a similar game which was called chole, being played. It, too, consisted to hitting the ball with a club towards some fixed point.

Many people believe that golf originated in Scotland and, of course, there are many claims by Scottish writers to this effect. That well-known literary figure, Robert Browning, in his *History of Scotland*, makes a strong case in defence of his claim. However, it is now widely recognised that it was the Dutch who invented the modern game and called it for the first time Kolf. The origin of golf as we know it today can be traced back to a little village in Holland called **Leonan.** There is evidence which suggests that the game was played there as far back as 1296. Those same records show proof of the establishment of as many as thirty or more centres where Kolf was played. In wintertime, the game was played on ice. In numerous Dutch paintings from the period as shown, people are depicted playing golf in open spaces. Apparently, the game was quite popular between the period 1300-1700, but in the early part of the eighteenth century the game died out. It wasn't until 1890 that the game was revived after centuries of neglect in Holland. This revival was due, interestingly, to a group of Scottish golfers who opened a club and course at The Hague. Golf had returned once more to its true roots.

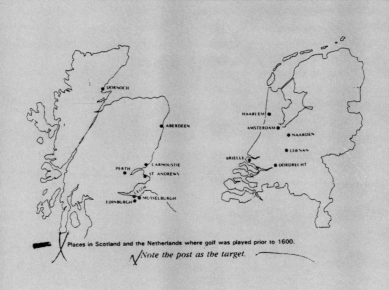

Places in Scotland and the Netherlands where golf was played prior to 1600.
Note the post as the target.

Diagram 219
   Places in Scotland and the Netherlands where golf was played prior to 1600.
   Early Dutch golfers – note the post as the target.

With regard to the history of the game in Scotland, it is of significance that golf was to appear on the east coat and can be directly attributable to the close trading links between both countries. When the seas receded around the coastline on the east of Scotland, there were wild undulating pastures unsuitable for agricultural purposes, but ideal for golf course lay-out. In these early stages the golfer had to share the "commons" with fishermen drying nets, women drying clothes, footballers at play, the army on manoeuvres and many other competing interests.

The rich and poor mingled on what came to be known as the seaside "commons". This particular mingling of the classes was to be particularly significant in that the aristocratic golfer was prepared to fight and pay for the legal battles which were fought in order to preserve the land for everyone's use.

The slow progress in the development of the game in Scotland could be related to the type of ball being used. It was a leather ball stuffed with feathers – "the feathery". This was the kind of ball along with specially-made wooden clubs which were used by the King and his nobles. The majority of people used a more simple kind of wooden stick and a ball made of wood. The high cost of the "feathery" certainly hindered the early growth of the game in terms of popularity.

When discussing the early history of golf, it is important to mention the role of the Masonic Order in establishing the game on a firm footing. There is evidence of a strong masonic membership in the early beginnings of the Royal and Ancient Golf Club of St. Andrews, Royal Golfing Society of Edinburgh, Royal Blackheaths. There are three other significant factors worth noting. Scottish golfing holidays became popular, especially with the patronage of the game by such famous people as Earl Haig and Asquith, who went on a golfing holiday to Scotland on a regular basis. The game was helped further by the advent of the "new technology" of that particular age, the invention of grass-cutting mowers. Before this development the game was played in winter-time when the grass was short. Only then was it possible to move away from seaside to inland links. Another interesting factor was the development of railways. Golf became popular, especially in towns which had a railway link with hinterland regions.

Why did St. Andrews become the home of golf?

I would advance two reasons which, in my view, were central to St. Andrews becoming the most important golf centre in Scotland in these early years.

The first must be the powerful and influential group of Freemasons who were enthusiastic followers of the game and certainly were the guiding lights in the early fortunes of St. Andrews. Secondly, the year 1522 is very significant in the annals of this world-famous club, for in that year John Hamilton, Archbishop of St. Andrews, confirmed the right of the community to play golf over the links, only when he was granted a licence to breed rabbits within the precincts of the northern parts of the course. It is interesting to note that from 1522 the people of this famous golfing centre had free golf on all courses in the town up until about 1846.

The big breakthrough – "the ball that made it"

The big breakthrough in the development of the game took place in 1848 with the **discovery of gutta-percha.** It is a milky juice which is obtained chiefly from the Palaquium gutta trees of the Malay Peninsula and, as a substance, was used as insulation for electric wire and submarine cables. It was also used for castings, surgical bandages and even at one time for temporary tooth fillings. It was used for a time, replacing "the feathery", as a new type of golf ball. At the time, the new ball was cheap, durable and its discovery was responsible for bringing the game within the reach of those who could not afford "the feathery". The **discovery of gutta-percha** was at an opportune time indeed, around the year 1848. In the preceding years a sudden diminution in the popularity of the game had occurred. Golf had reached its lowest ebb from about 1820-1850. The game had died in Holland; in Britain it was preserved by the enthusiasm and support of the Masonic Order and the wealthy merchant classes, but certainly it had become more elitist and more the preserve of the rich, prior to the introduction of the gutta-percha. It must also be remembered that when gutta-percha was introduced to the game, golf clubs had to be developed and changed.

1850-1910

During the years after the introduction of this new, less-expensive, long-lasting golf ball, the game was to flourish and become popular through all five continents. Apart from the ball there were other secondary, outside factors which had positive consequences for the game. Close trading links were established between Britain and those new colonial outposts; the merchant adventurers were also to play a significant part in fostering the game in these far-flung corners of the world. A further discovery with regard to improving the ball took place around 1901 with the invention of yet another new ball called the Haskell (the first generation of modern balls), because of its discovery by a Cleveland golfer called Coburn Haskell.

Historical landmarks

As you can see, we have been witnessing some significant developments especially during the nineteenth century. In order to put into perspective historically what actually occurred, let us look at the following synopsis of special events and dates recorded.

1567 Mary Queen of Scots is reputed to have played a game of golf at Seton House in Scotland, shortly after the death of her husband, Lord Darnley.

1641 The news of the uprising in Ireland was conveyed by King Charles while he played a game of golf at Leith. The king was being beaten in the game and, as he rushed off on hearing the news, it was remarked that he wished to save his "half-crown rather than his crown".

1658 First reference to the playing of golf in England, it having spread down the east coastline of Scotland, golf recorded for this particular year was played outside London.

1744 The first rules of the game were drafted at Leith. There were thirteen rules drawn up in all.

1780 Royal Aberdeen Golf Club was founded.

1829 The game had reached India with the formation of the Royal Calcutta Club. This was a date of significance in that it was the first club which was established outside of Britain.

1856 The first club on the continent of Europe was established in France, in the Basque region.

1867 The first ladies club was founded at St. Andrews.

1871 Dunedin, New Zealand, established its first golf club.

1874 Royal Montreal founded.

1881 Royal Belfast founded.

1883 Curragh golf club founded.

1885 Royal Cape of South Africa founded.

1888 The first golf club established in America at Yonkers, New York, by two Scotsmen, John Reid and Robert Lockhart.

1890 The first golf club founded in Belgium. This same year witnessed the return of golf to its original home, in Holland, where it had undergone centuries of decline and decay. It merely underlines the enormous contribution of the Scots to the game, for yet again it was a group of Scottish golfers who opened a club and course at the Hague.

1891 Long Island, New York, founded.
Lahinch, Co. Clare, founded.

1897 Bray golf club founded.

1898 Copenhagen established its first club.

1901   Japan established first club.
1904   Gothenburg, Sweden, established first club.
1908   Buenos Aires, Argentina, established first club.
1963   The year 1963 is significant in that the game had now reached all five continents, culminating in the establishment of the Asian Golfing Association.

From our synopsis of special events in the development of the game worldwide, let us focus more particularly on the game in Sweden, Japan, Spain and America. In Sweden the game has grown in popularity in recent years with a dramatic increase in the number of courses built, making Sweden one of the strongest nations in Europe. The game in that northern country received a powerful boost from the outstanding athlete Sven Tumba, who became a superstar and folk hero as an ice-hockey player. On turning to golf, he focused the consciousness of the people towards this new, developing game. It was principally due to his enormous influence that golfing fever became an epidemic, capturing the imagination of millions of Swedes. Today, Sweden stands on the threshold of manifesting itself as a great golfing nation.

The story of Japanese golf is, in many ways, more remarkable. The game is still very much at an embryonic stage of development and one might say as a national pastime has only taken off in the last thirty years. In a country small in size, over-populated, highly-industrialised, mountainous, naturally whatever land that is available is taken up for agriculture. Consequently, with so little land available for golf course lay-out, land on the tops of mountains and other rocky and remote areas were blasted and many multi-storeyed driving ranges were built near cities of Japan. The most well-known driving range is Shiba Park in the centre of Tokyo, a three-storey complex. These really are a substitution for courses and can be better understood when one realises the national importance of every inch of land for cultivation.

In Spain, the craze for golf came about with the developing tourist industry. As tourist facilities were developed for the thousands flocking to the golden beaches of the Iberian Peninsula, golf courses were as essential a facility as the swimming pool. Holiday tourists were in need of caddies whenever they played a game of golf and it was in this way that Spain's greatest ambassadors of the game took the golfing world by storm. It was through this system that the Miguel brothers, Manuel Pinero and the great Severiano Ballesteros came to the fore. The rest is history.

The man responsible for planting the first seed of golf on the newly-emerging continent of North America was Alexandra Dennistoun. He was born in Edinburgh in the early years of the 1820s and emigrated to Canada about 1874. He was the founder of Royal Montreal. The establishment of other golfing societies in Canada came about because of the presence of Scottish regiments who were on overseas service in that part of the Commonwealth in the latter years of the nineteenth century. Then in 1888 another Scot, a native of Dunfermline, a certain John Reid, founded St. Andrews Golf Club at Yonkers. Willie Dunne, yet another famous son of bonnie Scotland, built the first course in Long Island. America had been captured. The game was now about to expand and in the short space of no more than fifteen years more than one thousand clubs were established all over the States. One might wonder how the game came to develop to the degree that it now has in the U.S. There are three important factors which should be considered.

First of all the 1890s was a time of massive economic and material development and nationally this had an important bearing. Secondly, with the advent of television, the new sport was given intensive coverage, just like in Japan, at a time when one of the great charismatic figures of American golf burst forth on the golfing scene, Arnold Palmer. He more than anyone else turned golf into a national pastime and television sport. And this brings us to the third factor and the reason why golf became such a success. Arnold Palmer and his close friend, President Eishenhower, more than any other people, helped immeasurably the advancement of the game. Palmer has charisma. He was aggressive, likeable, a risk-taker, adventurous, brilliant as a champion. He personified more than any other sporting hero of all time all that was good in the American personality. He became the hero from humble beginnings. He more than any other person was golf's greatest asset. He, Dwight D. Eisenhower, a national hero from his second world war exploits, became one of the great afficionados of the game. He was shown regularly on television having a game of golf.

No chapter on the history of golf would be complete without reference to the contribution made by the all-time greats. Harry Vardon, the self-taught champion, created his own individual and unique style and technique. His was a major input in elevating the game to a high degree of skill and challenge. Walter Hagen, the flamboyant champion of the cavalier type, gave to the sport style, character and sophistication. He will be remembered for his single-handed battle to emancipate his fellow professionals from a lowly status. As one writer so accurately put it: "He brought the professional from the locker-room to the tea-room." It must be remembered that this was a time when the golfing professional was prevented from socialising in the clubhouse. Hagen would arrive in his chauffeur-driven limousine

285

and would order champagne and oysters, having his party in the car park, when refused entry to a clubhouse. Hagen was influenced by the attitude and ethos of the Michigan golf club where he was the professional. The Fords, the Chryslers were members there, all of them coming from lowly and humble origins. They believed that their fellowman should be judged not by his background, but by his ability, his success. "It is not where you come from but where you are going to that best characterised this new entrepreneurial spirit of these self-made millionaires." The great Gene Sarazen once stated: "Whenever a tournament pro holds a large winner's cheque between his fingers, he should give silent thanks to Hagen." Hagen won ten major championships, Sarazen seven.

Bobby Jones, another champion among champions, gave to golf something new. Having degrees in law and engineering, Jones more than any of the stars of his time, best captured in an articulate sense, the demands and challenges of the game. In a seven-year span, he recorded thirteen national titles in the U.S. and Britain.

The names of Henry Cotton and Ben Hogan represented a new era in golf. The days of the wild and inimitable Hagen were over. In order to be champion, Cotton and Hogan believed that a new commitment, discipline and exhaustive preparation were essential. Hogan was the first to analyse the game in the most fundamental way possible, programming his game in a meticulous manner. In more recent times, Nicklaus, Thompson, Tom Watson, Ballesteros, Trevino and now Lyle, Woosnam, Norman, Aoki, Azinger and Langer have heralded a new breed of champion, diverse in personality, articulating their game in divergent respects which in many ways were but a progressing development on the styles and techniques of their illustrious predecessors.

If I were to pick out a personal star among stars I would choose the great Palmer. The career of many a superstar is like a short story, but that of Arnold Palmer has the amplitude of a great novel. Many of the great stars are masters within an accepted mould. Palmer was a breaker and maker of moulds. Moments of beauty in golf just like in any other sport are all the sweeter because they are so difficult, so hard to attain. The beloved Palmer contributed many, many such moments and his humanity struck a chord in the hearts of millions over the world that was to set him apart from all the rest. Palmer showed that **supreme form** depends as much on charisma and likeability as on titles and champonships won.

In this short historical tour around the world, it is indeed fascinating to note how in such a short period of time the game set root in so many diverse corners of the world, becoming truly international indeed. The only remaining part of the world where golf has yet failed to take root is within East European countries where the game is still looked upon as an elitist pastime, which, of course, is not in keeping with official ideology. Perhaps in the not too distant future it will become the one game most capable of establishing that international bond between peoples around the world, whether it be in Peking, Moscow, Dublin, Edinburgh, Tokyo, Stockholm, Copenhagen or Augusta, Georgia.

In summary, let me say that no matter what the rival claims may be with regard to the original home of this wonderful game, whether it was the Scots, the Romans or the French who were the innovators, it is to the eternal credit and honour of the Scots that the game was pre-served and developed. There is some truth in Ernest Rewen's belief that the Celts mistake dreams for reality. It might be nearer the truth to state that they sense a world beyond what is commonly known as the real world. Surely that must be the intuition at the heart of the Scotsman's passion for sport, their passion for golf; for above all it expresses the quest for glory in the challenge of field games. It was this enthusiasm, this quest for glory, perhaps the adventurism of their temperament which saw the Scots in the forefront of a great sporting crusade, pioneering the game in different corners of the world. Their love of golf is an eternal testimony to a great sporting people.

CHAPTER 22

Invest wisely in the game

Buying clubs is a major decision. Price or the prestige should not be deciding factors in the exercise. You should buy the clubs that will suit your game and help you to play better golf.

Generally speaking, heavier clubs will give you more distance, while the lighter club will be more accurate. Tour players, on the whole, favour very light clubs.

1. The grip

Let us deal with the grip first. If you have small hands, or for that matter, a problem with a slice, you should not buy clubs with thick grips, as they will tend to fall into the palm of the hand and cause you to slice the ball. A narrow grip remains in the fingers, helping you to manipulate the clubhead, get distance and draw the ball from right to left. Narrow grips tend to give a low trajectory to the ball. The thicker grip will give you a high trajectory.

2. The shaft

The last great Scottish contribution to the game of golf was the steel shaft, a fact that is not very well known. It was around the year 1894 that Thomas Horsburg, a blacksmith by trade and an ardent follower of the game, invented and patented the steel shaft. As it transpired, this new invention was not to win the approval of the Royal and Ancient. It was, in fact, thirty years later, under pressure from the American Golfing Association, that the steel shaft we have today was introduced. The greatest development in the clubmaking aspect of the game has been in relation to the shaft.

Modern clubs have light shafts and have the swing weight contained near the head of the club. The stiff shaft suits a fast swinger, who is also very strong and needs accuracy. If it's distance you are seeking, you should look for clubs with whippier or lighter (regular) shafts. Lengthening a shaft because of one's height should be considered carefully. It's my opinion that unless one is excessively tall, one should not alter the length of the club as it will also change the balance. It is certainly unsuited to the shorter irons – seven, eight, nine and wedge. However, a longer shaft will provide a wider arch and more distance with a driver. Bing Crosby, who once played off one handicap, had the shaft in his driver lengthened in order "to keep up with the big boys".

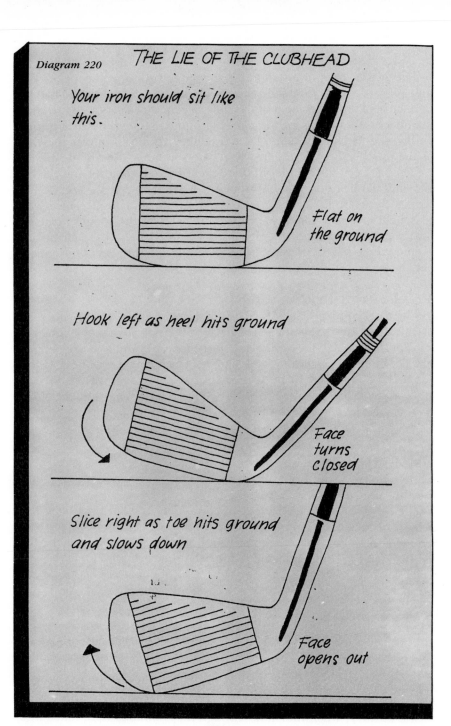

Diagram 220 — THE LIE OF THE CLUBHEAD

Your iron should sit like this.

Flat on the ground

Hook left as heel hits ground

Face turns closed

Slice right as toe hits ground and slows down

Face opens out

3. The face

The face is very important and can vary according to the make. The tour players favour the blade club, no gimmicks. They hit the ball off the centre of the sweep-spot of the club face most of the time. However, manufacturers aiming for the majority of the market by concentrating on the middle handicappers, have produced various innovations. One of these is the very common "heel and toe face". In simple terms, weight has been distributed in these areas in both the heel and the toe allowing the handicap player to have a wider sweep-spot. You do not have to be entirely accurate and you can hit the ball off centre with reasonable results. The low profile clubface had the weight centered near the sole as an aid to getting the ball airborne. It is worthwhile keeping these points in mind when assessing the clubface. One should not, however, go to either extreme.

4. The iron head

There is the forged head and a stainless steel investment cast one. Stainless steel investment cast heads are not generally favoured by the tour professionals. However, the forged head, which is a piece of shaped metal, has more "feel" to it, producing a "softer" shot. American clubs **tend to be forged,** but they are **susceptible to rust** and, as such, are unsuited to a wet climate. They are suitable, however, for a player who can afford to change his clubs often.

5. Loft and lie

Modern clubs generally have less loft, because of the change in swing patterns away from "flat" to upright. Many now believe that they are not sufficiently lofted.

The lie of the clubface is very important. If an iron face has a flat lie, i.e. it sits on the ground with the toe lower than the heel, you will tend to slice the ball. On the other hand, if it has "an upright lie", the face will tend to come in closed to the ball because the heel hits the turf first, slowing down and allowing the toe to dominate. This results in a "pull" or "draw" towards the left. *(See diagram).*

6. The woods

In the early stages, woods were the most commonly used clubs. It was usual to carry only one iron because a mishit shot with the iron had disastrous effects on the feathery ball of that era. Hence, the derivation of the name "mashie" for an iron club. The wooden heads were long and narrow, suitable for the feathery. However, in the eighteenth century, when the paths through the commons were made into roads, it was found that the wooden head needed protection against the hard surfaces of these roads. A brass plate was put on the sole of the wooden heads. It was found to be very effective and was later added to all the woods. Hence, the use of "brassie" for the wooden club.

7. The wooden head

The face of the wooden head varies according to the manufacturer. Some driver heads tend to be more, some less lofted, and have either and open or shut face. Some people know instinctively when they place the clubhead on the ground whether it suits them or not. If you have a problem with a slice, avoid an "open face" club (one pointing towards the right of target when it is sitting in its natural position). Tend towards a "hooded" or closed club face. If you drive best with a two or three wood, you should be looking for a more lofted driver.

In the woods there are laminated, persimmon, graphite and steel varieties. Laminated, compressed timber, while persimmon is a seasoned piece of timber, which has been shafted into a clubhead, like the forged head of an iron. Laminated is not as hard as persimmon, but it is more durable. The older persimmon was more consistent than the modern variety. The system of clubmaking allowed the timber to season in a loft, while being moved along according to the timber heads being taken out at the other end for clubmaking. It was a slow, laborious method and it worked very well. However, during the second world war this system broke down because timber was needed for other uses and the supply of seasoned heads dried up. Modern persimmon is not as consistent, though there is much more "feel" off it at impact. It will provide more distance as it is harder than the laminated. It is also much more expensive and is favoured by the touring professionals.

8. The metal head

A recent innovation is a metal head because it is very durable. The face of certain brands is lofted, sits in behind the ball well and is to be recommended for handicap players. The metal three and five woods are also very good out of rough.

9. The insert

There is the insert, i.e. that part of the face that makes contact with the ball. The screw-in insert is most suitable from a durability point of view as it will not damage easily.

10. The tee

The type of tee you use will affect the way you play. If you use a short tee and tee the ball low, you are encouraging a slice. A ball on a low tee indicates a more upright or more **out to in** swing, encouraging a "steep" attack on the ball. If you wish to play your best with the driver you should tee the ball high and encourage yourself to have a "shallow" or more from behind approach to the ball as this works best with all the flat-faced clubs, especially the driver. You will, with this high tee, have to take the ball and leave the tee as the top professionals do. It is a more rounded, forward moving swing and it encourages you to hit the ball on your upswing. To comprehend this fully, imagine a tee that is two feet high. This will result in a more upward hit, preventing the downward one, where the power of the swing is directed towards the ground and not forward, even though you wish the ball to go forward.

Whatever clubs you buy or acquire, you will probably change them before you settle for a particular set yourself. As a "starting" set, you should buy secondhand and there are many to be found in professional shops around the country.

In the final analysis, there are clubs that should be chosen individually – not as part of a set. These are the driver, sand-wedge and putter. They are like human relationships, very personal. Often times you should rely on instinct. You look at it, it sits well and you know it suits you. It is love at first sight. Happy shopping!

Set up to swing from the inside.

Practise by placing a piece of wood parallel to your feet and position a ball as shown in photo. *(See diagram)*. Your aim is to hit the ball without disturbing the timber. If you are able to achieve this much good golf will follow. A friend who was hitting the ball from way outside the line had a terrible time shanking and, through anxiety, he was unable to cease. However, as he knew the problem (hitting from way outside) he succeeded in playing immaculate golf until his playing partner noticed what he was doing. Having driven off the tee, he would casually position his caddy car nearly on top of the ball but just outside it. He knew that if he came down on the outside he would smack the wheel of the caddy and hence he always managed to avoid it and so hit from the inside avoiding the shank through fear!

Practise using a deterrent outside the ball as this is the most important aspect of golf – irrespective of all else hit **from the inside**.

RESULT HERE

4 The ball is driven FORWARD...	4 ...to its MAXIMUM DISTANCE...	4 ...with BACKSPIN
3 The force of your swing must be applied from BEHIND...	3 ...and you also need CLUBHEAD SPEED...	3 ...with a SQUARE CLUBFACE at impact
2 Your actual swing must be a WIDE SWING...	2 ...with a full RELEASE OF THE CLUBHEAD....	2 ...and a NEUTRAL GRIP at impact
1 Start by setting up with a GOOD LEFT SIDE....	1 ...and with OILY WRISTS....	1 ...and a NEUTRAL GRIP and PERFECT ALIGNMENT AT ADDRESS

You start here . . .

Please note the link from setting up to the result. A good left side (left arm in line with shaft) helps create a **wide** swing, encourages a shallow approach from **behind** the ball and enables the player to drive it **forward**. Oily (relaxed) wrists encourage a release of the club and so help create clubhead speed and therefore **distance.** Perfect alignment and a neutral grip at address help with same at impact therefore a square clubface and swingline and a back-spinng ball. The perfect shot is the result of a swing whereupon the clubhead approached the ball from a **shallow** angle, was **released** at the ball and was **square** to the target line at impact. All three **elements are required to produce it and all start in your set-up.** The state of your game also depends upon the balance of all three elements. You may be able to drive the ball forward but lack distance. You may well have distance but not accuracy. The nearer you reach all three elements the lower your handicap will become and the better your game.

293

SPECIAL LESSON 17

The ultimate shot

The three stages to learning the swing

In order for you to reach your poetntial, you must be able to consistently drive the ball **forward** to its **maximum distance** and of course in the **right direction.** It may take a number of years to reach this ultimate goal, or it may never occur. The main point for you to recognise here is the correct sequence to improving. Firstly, you need **width,** you need to develop a solid base to your swing, a consistent shape with your bigger muscles. Secondly, you must add **wrists** (clubhead speed) to this solid base. Thirdly, you look for **control.** My book is deliberately laid out in this fashion. Let us now look at the three stages of learning.

(a) The ball is driven **forward** to its **maximum** distance with **backspin** towards the target.

(b) What you need is **force** to be applied from **behind** the ball and of course **clubhead speed** with the **clubface square** to the target line.

(c) In order for you to achieve this you must have a **wide swing** and a free swing **(a swinging wrist-cock)** with a **neutral grip** at impact.

(d) First you must ensure at address that you have a **good left side** (left side dominant), a relaxed grip with **oily wrists** and **perfect alignment.**

The end or final goal distance and direction is achieved only through a relaxed **neutral grip, perfect alignment, a good left side,** which should result in a **wide swing** and **the full release of the clubhead towards the target.**

As you can see, the vast majority of good golf results from perfecting the set-up and alignment. As this is a stationary exercise it is a very much attainable goal for you.

Forward drive: First phase: The correct sequence **is to start by developing width,** learn a back and forward movement with your arms. Above all **visualise the clubhead coming in parallel to the ground from behind, sweeping the ball forward** cleanly off the ground. Extend your left arm back and extend it forward. Push your left shoulder back under your chin (short back swing) and drive your legs through the shot. The swing is back and forward, not up and down. Learn the middle part to your swing before impact. **Develop a wide base to your swing with a shallow approach to the back of the ball.** Use an eight iron as a trainer – "extension – extension".